Practice*Planners*®

Homework Planners feature dozens of behaviorally based, ready-to-use assignme. that are designed for use between sessions, as well as a disk (Microsoft Word) contain all of the assignments—allowing you to customize them to suit your unique client nee

- ❏ Brief Therapy Homework Planner...0-471-24611-5 / $49.
- ❏ Brief Couples Therapy Homework Planner...0-471-29511-6 / $49.
- ❏ Brief Child Therapy Homework Planner..0-471-32366-7 / $49.
- ❏ Child Therapy Activity and Homework Planner ....0-471-25684-6 / $49.
- ❏ Brief Adolescent Therapy Homework Planner ....0-471-34465-6 / $49.
- ❏ Addiction Treatment Homework Planner, Second Edition................................0-471-27459-3 / $49.
- ❏ Brief Employee Assistance Homework Planner..0-471-38088-1 / $49.
- ❏ Brief Family Therapy Homework Planner..0-471-38512-3 / $49.
- ❏ Grief Counseling Homework Planner..0-471-43318-7 / $49.
- ❏ Divorce Counseling Homework Planner ....0-471-43319-5 / $49.
- ❏ Group Therapy Homework Planner...0-471-41822-6 / $49.
- ❏ The School Counseling and School Social Work Homework Planner...........0-471-09114-6 / $49.
- ❏ Adolescent Psychotherapy Homework Planner II..0-471-27493-3 / $49.
- ❏ Adult Psychotherapy Homework Planner ....0-471-27395-3 / $49.
- ❏ The Parenting Skills Homework Planner ....0-471-48182-3 / $49.

Progress Notes Planners contain complete prewritten progress notes for each presenti▮ problem in the companion Treatment Planners.

- ❏ The Adult Psychotherapy Progress Notes Planner ....0-471-45978-X / $49.9
- ❏ The Adolescent Psychotherapy Progress Notes Planner.............................0-471-45979-8 / $49.9
- ❏ The Severe and Persistent Mental Illness Progress Notes Planner ....0-471-21986-X / $49.9
- ❏ The Child Psychotherapy Progress Notes Planner ....0-471-45980-1 / $49.9
- ❏ The Addiction Progress Notes Planner ....0-471-10330-6 / $49.9
- ❏ The Couples Psychotherapy Progress Notes Planner...................................0-471-27460-7 / $49.9
- ❏ The Family Therapy Progress Notes Planner..0-471-48443-1 / $49.9

Client Education Handout Planners contain elegantly designed handouts that can b▮ printed out from the enclosed CD-ROM and provide information on a wide range c▮ psychological and emotional disorders and life skills issues. Use as patient literature handouts at presentations, and aids for promoting your mental health practice.

- ❏ Adult Client Education Handout Planner..0-471-20232-0 / $49.9▮
- ❏ Child and Adolescent Client Education Handout Planner ....0-471-20233-9 / $49.9▮
- ❏ Couples and Family Client Education Handout Planner ....0-471-20234-7 / $49.95

Name_____

Affiliation_____

Address _____

City/State/Zip_____

Phone/Fax_____

▮ail_____

▮ck enclosed ❏ Visa ❏ MasterCard ❏ American Express

_____

▮ate _____

▮n for first book, $1 for each additional book. Please add your local sales tax to all orders.
▮ change without notice.

To order by phone in the US:
Call toll free 1-877-762-2974

Fax: 1-800-597-3299

Online: www.practiceplanners.wiley.com

Mail this order form to:
John Wiley & Sons, Attn: J. Knott,
111 River Street, Hoboken, NJ 07030

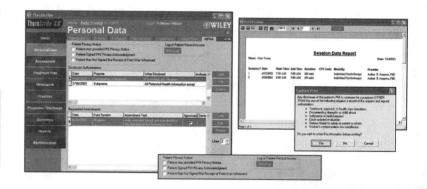

Need Help Getting Started?

Getting Started in Personal and Executive Coaching offers a go-to reference designed to help build, manage, and sustain a thriving coaching practice. Packed with hundreds of proven strategies and techniques, this nuts-and-bolts guide covers all aspects of the coaching business with step-by-step instructions and real-world illustrations that prepare you for every phase of starting your own coaching business.

This single, reliable book offers straightforward advice and tools for running a successful practice, including:

- Seven secrets of highly successful coaches
- Fifteen strategies for landing paying clients
- Ten marketing mistakes to avoid
- Sample business and marketing plans
- Worksheets for setting rates and managing revenue

Getting Started in Personal and Executive Coaching
Stephen G. Fairley and Chris E. Stout
ISBN 0-471-42624-5
Paper • $24.95 • 356pp • December 2003

Getting Started in Private Practice provides all the information you need to confidently start and grow your own mental health practice. This book breaks down the ingredients of practice into more manageable and achievable components and will teach you the skills you need to avoid making costly mistakes. Containing dozens of tools that you can use to achieve your goals, this book has specific information that can be applied to your business today, worksheets that will help you calculate the true costs of various expenditures and activities, checklists that might save you from disaster, and lists of resources to investigate. Includes:

- Forms and examples of various practice aspects
- Step-by-step advice on writing a business plan and marketing your business
- Suggestions and ideas intended to help you get your creative juices flowing
- Practical and simple formulas to help calculate rates, revenues, and Return on Investment
- Comprehensive information on licensing procedures and risk management

Getting Started in Private Practice
Chris E. Stout and Laurie Cope Grand
ISBN 0-471-42623-7
Paper • $24.95 • 304 pp. • October 2004

Now you know.

wiley.com

The Adolescent Psychotherapy
Treatment Planner

PRACTICE*PLANNERS*® SERIES

Treatment Planners

The Complete Adult Psychotherapy Treatment Planner, 3e
The Child Psychotherapy Treatment Planner, 3e
The Adolescent Psychotherapy Treatment Planner, 3e
The Continuum of Care Treatment Planner
The Couples Psychotherapy Treatment Planner
The Employee Assistance Treatment Planner
The Pastoral Counseling Treatment Planner
The Older Adult Psychotherapy Treatment Planner
The Behavioral Medicine Treatment Planner
The Group Therapy Treatment Planner
The Gay and Lesbian Psychotherapy Treatment Planner
The Family Therapy Treatment Planner
The Severe and Persistent Mental Illness Treatment Planner
The Mental Retardation and Developmental Disability Treatment Planner
The Social Work and Human Services Treatment Planner
The Crisis Counseling and Traumatic Events Treatment Planner
The Personality Disorders Treatment Planner
The Rehabilitation Psychology Treatment Planner
The Addiction Treatment Planner, 2e
The Special Education Treatment Planner
The Juvenile Justice and Residential Care Treatment Planner
The School Counseling and School Social Work Treatment Planner
The Sexual Abuse Victim and Sexual Offender Treatment Planner
The Probation and Parole Treatment Planner

Progress Notes Planners

The Child Psychotherapy Progress Notes Planner
The Adolescent Psychotherapy Progress Notes Planner
The Adult Psychotherapy Progress Notes Planner
The Addiction Progress Notes Planner
The Severe and Persistent Mental Illness Progress Notes Planner

Homework Planners

Brief Therapy Homework Planner
Brief Couples Therapy Homework Planner
Chemical Dependence Treatment Homework Planner
Brief Child Therapy Homework Planner
Brief Adolescent Therapy Homework Planner
Brief Employee Assistance Homework Planner
Brief Family Therapy Homework Planner
Grief Counseling Homework Planner
Group Therapy Homework Planner
Divorce Counseling Homework Planner
School Counseling and School Social Work Homework Planner
Child Therapy Activity and Homework Planner

Client Education Handout Planners

Adult Client Education Handout Planner
Child and Adolescent Client Education Handout Planner
Couples and Family Client Education Handout Planner

Documentation Sourcebooks

The Clinical Documentation Sourcebook
The Forensic Documentation Sourcebook
The Psychotherapy Documentation Primer
The Chemical Dependence Treatment Documentation Sourcebook
The Clinical Child Documentation Sourcebook
The Couple and Family Clinical Documentation Sourcebook
The Clinical Documentation Sourcebook, 2e
The Continuum of Care Clinical Documentation Sourcebook

Practice*Planners*®

Arthur E. Jongsma, Jr., Series Editor

The Adolescent Psychotherapy Treatment Planner

Third Edition

Arthur E. Jongsma, Jr.

L. Mark Peterson

William P. McInnis

JOHN WILEY & SONS, INC.

Published by John Wiley & Sons, Inc., Hoboken, New Jersey.
Published simultaneously in Canada.

Library of Congress Cataloging-in-Publication Data:

Jongsma, Arthur E., 1943–
    The adolescent psychotherapy treatment planner/Arthur E. Jongsma, Jr., L. Mark Peterson, William P. McInnis.—3rd ed.
       p. cm.—(Practice planners series)
    Includes bibliographical references and index.
    ISBN 0-471-27049-0
       1. Adolescent psychotherapy—Handbooks, manuals, etc.   I. Peterson, L. Mark.
    II. McInnis, William P.   III. Title.   IV. Practice planners.   V. Series.
    RJ503 .J665 2002
    616.89′14′0835—dc21

Printed in the United States of America

10 9 8 7 6 5 4 3 2

To our wives: Judy, Cherry, and Lynn. We reach our long-term goals only due to your faithful interventions of love and encouragement.

PRACTICE*PLANNERS*® SERIES PREFACE

The practice of psychotherapy has a dimension that did not exist 30, 20, or even 15 years ago—accountability. Treatment programs, public agencies, clinics, and even group and solo practitioners must now justify the treatment of patients to outside review entities that control the payment of fees. This development has resulted in an explosion of paperwork.

Clinicians must now document what has been done in treatment, what is planned for the future, and what the anticipated outcomes of the interventions are. The books and software in this Practice*Planners* series are designed to help practitioners fulfill these documentation requirements efficiently and professionally.

The Practice*Planners* series is growing rapidly. It now includes not only the original *Complete Adult Psychotherapy Treatment Planner,* third edition; *The Child Psychotherapy Treatment Planner,* third edition; and *The Adolescent Psychotherapy Treatment Planner,* third edition, but also Treatment Planners targeted to specialty areas of practice, including: addictions, juvenile justice/residential care, couples therapy, employee assistance, behavioral medicine, therapy with older adults, pastoral counseling, family therapy, group therapy, neuropsychology, therapy with gays and lesbians, special education, school counseling, and more.

A number of the Treatment Planner books now have companion Progress Notes Planners (e.g., Adult, Adolescent, Child, Addictions, Severe and Persistent Mental Illness). These planners provide a menu of progress statements that elaborate on the client's symptom presentation and the provider's therapeutic intervention. Each Progress Notes Planner statement is directly integrated with "Behavioral Definitions" and "Therapeutic Interventions" items from the companion Treatment Planner.

The list of therapeutic Homework Planners is also growing from the original Brief Therapy Homework for adults to Adolescent, Child, Couples, Group, Family, Chemical Dependence, Divorce, Grief, Employee Assistance, and School Counseling/School Social Work Homework Plan-

xiv   PRACTICEPLANNERS® SERIES PREFACE

ners. Each of these books can be used alone or in conjunction with their companion Treatment Planner. Homework assignments are designed around each presenting problem (e.g., Anxiety, Depression, Chemical Dependence, Anger Management, Panic, Eating Disorders) that is the focus of a chapter in its corresponding Treatment Planner).

Client Education Handout Planners, a new branch in the series, provides brochures and handouts to help educate and inform adult, child, adolescent, couples, and family clients on a myriad of mental health issues, as well as life skills techniques. Handouts are included on CD-ROMs and are ideal for use in waiting rooms, at presentations, or as newsletters.

In addition, the series also includes Thera*Scribe*®, the latest version of the popular treatment planning, clinical record-keeping software. Thera*Scribe* allows the user to import the data from any of the Treatment Planner, Progress Notes Planner, or Homework Planner books into the software's expandable database. Using this database the practioner can create a detailed, neatly organized, individualized, and customized treatment plan along with optional integrated progress notes and homework assignments.

Adjunctive books, such as *The Psychotherapy Documentation Primer,* and *Clinical, Forensic, Child, Couples and Family, Continuum of Care,* and *Chemical Dependence Documentation Sourcebook* contain forms and resources to aid the mental health practice management. The goal of the series is to provide practitioners with the resources they need in order to provide high-quality care in the era of accountability—or, to put it simply, we seek to help you spend more time on patients, and less time on paperwork.

ARTHUR E. JONGSMA, JR.
Grand Rapids, Michigan

ACKNOWLEDGMENTS

The authors recognize that any book manuscript that makes it to publication relies on the talents and services of many, many hard-working people. We would like to acknowledge Sue Rhoda for her assistance with typing under time deadlines. Jen Byrne continues to bring order out of chaos in typing and organizing the final manuscript. Peggy Alexander, Cristina Wojdylo, and Judi Knott at John Wiley & Sons have provided professional support services to keep the Practice Planner project moving forward. The staff at North Market Street Graphics has consistently provided extremely thorough and competent manuscript review, copyediting, and preparation for production.

We thank these people who work diligently behind the scenes whose names do not make it to the book cover, but are indispensable to us.

INTRODUCTION

Since the early 1960s, formalized treatment planning has gradually become a vital aspect of the health care delivery system, whether it is treatment related to physical health, mental health, child welfare, or substance abuse. What started in the medical sector in the 1960s spread into the mental health sector in the 1970s as clinics, psychiatric hospitals, agencies, and so on began to seek accreditation from bodies such as the Joint Commission on Accreditation of Healthcare Organizations (JCAHO) to qualify for third-party reimbursements. With the advent of managed care in the 1980s, treatment planning took on greater importance. Managed care systems required clinicians to move rapidly from problem assessment to the formulation and implementation of the treatment plan. The goal of most managed care companies is to expedite the treatment process by encouraging the client and treatment provider to focus on identifying and changing behavioral problems as quickly as possible. Treatment plans must be specific as to the presenting problems, behaviorally defined symptoms, treatment goals and objectives, and interventions. Treatment plans must be individualized to meet the client's needs and goals, and the observable objectives must allow for setting milestones that can be used to chart the client's progress. Pressure from third-party payers, accrediting agencies, and other outside parties has increased the need for clinicians to produce effective, high-quality treatment plans in a short time frame. However, many mental health providers have little experience in treatment plan development. Our purpose in writing this book is to clarify, simplify, and accelerate the treatment planning process.

PLANNER FOCUS

The *Adolescent Psychotherapy Treatment Planner* offers a menu of statements that can be included in outpatient and inpatient treatment plans for children 13 to 18 years old. The objectives and interventions

1

suggested are not focused on any one treatment modality. Instead, the items reflect an eclectic approach of family therapy, individual therapy, pharmacotherapy, insight orientation, cognitive and behavioral techniques, and others. The clinician may select items from the menu that best fit the therapeutic approach and the client's individual strengths and needs.

This third edition of the *Adolescent Psychotherapy Treatment Planner* contains several content changes compared to the second edition, including:

- Three new presenting problem chapters—Negative Peer Influences, Parenting, and School Violence.
- Refinements to previous treatment plan statements—Each item from the second edition was carefully reviewed to clarify the language, reduce redundancies, and sharpen the focus of interventions coordinated with objectives.
- An additional sample treatment plan revised into more specific and measurable terms illustrates how to modify a treatment plan to include more quantifiable language.
- An appendix with a chapter revised into measurable, quantifiable language.

The new Appendix A contains the Anger Management chapter, which has been revised into more measurable, quantifiable language than in previous editions. In today's clinical-economic marketplaces of both managed care/third-party payors and accrediting bodies—JCAHO, NCQA, and CARF—there is an increased emphasis on behaviorally observable and/or quantifiable aspects of treatment plans. Among the reasons for this is a general and national movement toward even shorter stays in inpatient facilities (public and private hospitals, and residential facilities) and briefer managed outpatient treatment, with the focus on very specific symptom resolution. If you are experiencing such pressure, you may need to alter our Treatment Planner observable behavioral criteria into language that is more measurable and quantifiable.

Clinicians may want to look for the opportunity to craft measurable/quantifiable aspects of the patient's behaviors into their treatment plans. This can be accomplished by introducing measurability at the symptomatic level (e.g., Behavioral Definitions) and/or at the treatment outcome level (e.g., Short-Term Objectives). Behavioral Definition terms such as *repeated, frequent, tendency, pattern, consistent, excessive, high level, persistent, displays, heightened, recurrent,* and the like, and even words like *verbalizes, displays, demonstrates, refuses, unable, avoids, seeks, difficulty, increasing,* or *declining* can all have frequencies or circumstances added to quantify the item. For example, the Definition item

"Verbalizes having suicidal ideation" can be made more quantifiably measurable by changing it to "Verbalizes having suicidal ideation once to twice daily for the last two weeks."

Clinicians may add aspects of severity to symptom Definition statements, in addition to frequency, to introduce greater measurability. For example, "Verbalizes having sad thoughts four to five times daily for the last two weeks, and on a scale from 1 to 10 (10 being the worst), were judged to be at an 8." Or, alternatively, the clinician may list quantified psychometric data as a criterion measure, such as scores from symptom screening instruments such as the BPRS, BDI, Ham-D, BSI, SCL-90-R, or GAF. This helps in decreasing subjectivity.

The Short-Term Objective language found in the Treatment Planner can also be modified to follow the more quantified approach; thus "Engage in physical and recreational activities that reflect increased energy and interest" becomes "Engage in physical and recreational activities that reflect increased energy and interest, at least five times per shift within one week's time (by 1/20/2004)." Also, "Verbally express an understanding of the relationship between depressed mood and repression of sadness and anger" becomes "Verbally express an understanding of the relationship between depressed mood and repression of sadness and anger (by 1/18/2004)."

HOW TO DEVELOP A TREATMENT PLAN

The process of developing a treatment plan involves a logical series of steps that build on each other, much like constructing a house. The foundation of any effective treatment plan is the data gathered in a thorough biopsychosocial assessment. As the client presents himself or herself for treatment, the clinician must sensitively listen to and understand what the client struggles with in terms of family-of-origin issues, current stressors, emotional status, social network, physical health, coping skills, interpersonal conflicts, self-esteem, and so on. Assessment data may be gathered from a social history, physical exam, clinical interview, psychological testing, or contact with a client's significant others. The integration of the data by the clinician or the multidisciplinary treatment team members is critical for understanding the client, as is an awareness of the basis of the client's struggle. We have identified six specific steps for developing an effective treatment plan based on the assessment data.

STEP ONE: PROBLEM SELECTION

Although the client may discuss a variety of issues during the assessment, the clinician must ferret out the most significant problems on which to focus the treatment process. Usually a *primary* problem will surface, and *secondary* problems may also be evident. Some *other* problems may have to be set aside as not urgent enough to require treatment at this time. An effective treatment plan can only deal with a few selected problems or treatment will lose its direction. This Planner offers 33 problems from which to select those that most accurately represent your client's presenting issues.

As the problems to be selected become clear to the clinician or the treatment team, it is important to include opinions from the client as to his or her prioritization of issues for which help is being sought. A client's motivation to participate in and cooperate with the treatment process depends to some extent on the degree to which treatment addresses his or her greatest needs.

STEP TWO: PROBLEM DEFINITION

Each individual client presents with unique nuances as to how a problem behaviorally reveals itself in his or her life. Therefore, each problem that is selected for treatment focus requires a specific definition about how it is evidenced in the particular client. The symptom pattern should be associated with diagnostic criteria and codes such as those found in the *Diagnostic and Statistical Manual (DSM-IV-TR)* or the *International Classification of Diseases*. The Planner, following the pattern established by *DSM-IV-TR*, offers such behaviorally specific definition statements to choose from or to serve as a model for your own personally crafted statements. You will find several behavior symptoms or syndromes listed that may characterize one of the 33 presenting problems.

STEP THREE: GOAL DEVELOPMENT

The next step in treatment plan development is to set broad goals for the resolution of the target problem. These statements need not be crafted in measurable terms but can be global, long-term goals that indicate a desired positive outcome to the treatment procedures. The Planner suggests several possible goal statements for each problem, but one statement is all that is required in a treatment plan.

STEP FOUR: OBJECTIVE CONSTRUCTION

In contrast to long-term goals, objectives must be stated in behaviorally measurable language. It must be clear when the client has achieved the established objectives; therefore, vague, subjective objectives are not acceptable. Review agencies (e.g., JCAHO), health maintenance organizations (HMOs), and managed care organizations) insist that psychological treatment outcomes be measurable. The objectives presented in this Planner are designed to meet this demand for accountability. Numerous alternatives are presented to allow construction of a variety of treatment plan possibilities for the same presenting problem. The clinician must exercise professional judgment as to which objectives are most appropriate for a given client.

Each objective should be developed as a step toward attaining the broad treatment goal. In essence, objectives can be thought of as a series of steps that, when completed, will result in the achievement of the long-term goal. There should be at least two objectives for each problem, but the clinician may construct as many as are necessary for goal achievement. Target attainment dates may be listed for each objective. New objectives should be added to the plan as the individual's treatment progresses. When all the necessary objectives have been achieved, the client should have resolved the target problem successfully.

STEP FIVE: INTERVENTION CREATION

Interventions are the actions of the clinician designed to help the client complete the objectives. There should be at least one intervention for every objective. If the client does not accomplish the objective after the initial intervention, new interventions should be added to the plan.

Interventions should be selected on the basis of the client's needs and the treatment provider's full therapeutic repertoire. This Planner contains interventions from a broad range of therapeutic approaches, including cognitive, dynamic, behavioral, pharmacologic, family-oriented, and solution-focused brief therapy. Other interventions may be written by the provider to reflect his or her own training and experience. The addition of new problems, definitions, goals, objectives, and interventions to those found in the Planner is encouraged because doing so adds to the database for future reference and use.

Some suggested interventions listed in the Planner refer to specific books that can be assigned to the client for adjunctive bibliotherapy. Appendix B contains a full bibliographic reference list of these materials. The books are arranged under each problem for which they are appropriate as assigned reading for clients. When a book is used as part of an intervention plan, it should be reviewed with the client after it is read, enhancing the application of the content of the book to the specific client's circumstances. For further information about self-help books, mental health professionals may wish to consult *The Authoritative Guide to Self-Help Books* (1994) by Santrock, Minnett, and Campbell (available from The Guilford Press, New York).

Assigning an intervention to a specific provider is most relevant if the client is being treated by a team in an inpatient, residential, or intensive outpatient setting. Within these settings, personnel other than the primary clinician may be responsible for implementing a specific intervention. Review agencies require that the responsible provider's name be stipulated for every intervention.

STEP SIX: DIAGNOSIS DETERMINATION

The determination of an appropriate diagnosis is based on an evaluation of the client's complete clinical presentation. The clinician must compare the behavioral, cognitive, emotional, and interpersonal symptoms that the client presents to the criteria for diagnosis of a mental illness condition as described in *DSM-IV-TR*. The issue of differential diagnosis is admittedly a difficult one that research has shown to have rather low inter-rater reliability. Psychologists have also been trained to think more in terms of maladaptive behavior than of disease labels. Despite these factors, diagnosis is a reality that exists in the world of mental health care and it is a necessity for third-party reimbursement. (However, recently, managed care agencies are more interested in behavioral indices that are exhibited by the client than in the actual diagnosis.) It is the clinician's thorough knowledge of *DSM-IV-TR* criteria and a complete understanding of the client assessment data that contribute to the most reliable, valid diagnosis. An accurate assessment of behavioral indicators will also contribute to more effective treatment planning.

HOW TO USE THIS PLANNER

Our experience has taught us that learning the skills of effective treatment plan writing can be a tedious and difficult process for many clinicians. It is more stressful to try to develop this expertise when under the pressure of increased client load and short time frames placed on clinicians today by managed care systems. The documentation demands can be overwhelming when we must move quickly from assessment to treatment plan to progress notes. In the process, we must be very specific about how and when objectives can be achieved, and how progress is exhibited in each client. *The Adolescent Psychotherapy Treatment Planner* was developed as a tool to aid clinicians in writing a treatment plan in a rapid manner that is clear, specific, and highly individualized according to the following progression:

1. Choose one presenting problem (Step One) you have identified through your assessment process. Locate the corresponding page number for that problem in the Planner's table of contents.
2. Select two or three of the listed behavioral definitions (Step Two) and record them in the appropriate section on your treatment plan form. Feel free to add your own defining statement if you determine that your client's behavioral manifestation of the identified problem is not listed. (Note that while our design for

treatment planning is vertical, it will work equally well on plan forms formatted horizontally.)

3. Select a single long-term goal (Step Three) and again write the selection, exactly as it is written in the Planner or in some appropriately modified form, in the corresponding area of your own form.

4. Review the listed objectives for this problem and select the ones that you judge to be clinically indicated for your client (Step Four). Remember, it is recommended that you select at least two objectives for each problem. Add a target date or the number of sessions allocated for the attainment of each objective.

5. Choose relevant interventions (Step Five). The Planner offers suggested interventions related to each objective in the parentheses following the objective statement. But do not limit yourself to those interventions. The entire list is eclectic and may offer options that are more tailored to your theoretical approach or preferred way of working with clients. Also, just as with definitions, goals, and objectives, there is space allowed for you to enter your own interventions into the Planner. This allows you to refer to these entries when you create a plan around this problem in the future. You will have to assign responsibility to a specific person for implementation of each intervention if the treatment is being carried out by a multidisciplinary team.

6. Several *DSM-IV-TR* diagnoses are listed at the end of each chapter that are commonly associated with a client who has this problem. These diagnoses are meant to be suggestions for clinical consideration. Select a diagnosis listed or assign a more appropriate choice from the *DSM-IV-TR* (Step Six).

Note: To accommodate those practitioners who tend to plan treatment in terms of diagnostic labels rather than presenting problems, Appendix C lists all of the *DSM-IV-TR* diagnoses that have been presented in the various presenting problem chapters as suggestions for consideration. Each diagnosis is followed by the presenting problem that has been associated with that diagnosis. The provider may look up the presenting problems for a selected diagnosis to review definitions, goals, objectives, and interventions that may be appropriate for their clients with that diagnosis.

Congratulations! You should now have a complete, individualized treatment plan that is ready for immediate implementation and presentation to the client. It should resemble the format of the first example, the Sample Standard Treatment Plan. The second example, the Sample Quantitative Treatment Plan, may serve as a better example for you to follow if you choose to revise the standard language of our treatment plan suggestions into more quantifiable terms.

A FINAL NOTE

One important aspect of effective treatment planning is that each plan should be tailored to the individual client's problems and needs. Treatment plans should not be mass produced, even if clients have similar problems. The individual's strengths and weaknesses, unique stressors, social network, family circumstances, and symptom patterns *must* be considered in developing a treatment strategy. Drawing upon our own years of clinical experience, we have put together a variety of treatment choices. These statements can be combined in thousands of permutations to develop detailed treatment plans. Relying on their own good judgment, clinicians can easily select the statements that are appropriate for the individuals they are treating. In addition, we encourage readers to add their own definitions, goals, objectives, and interventions to the existing samples. It is our hope that the *Adolescent Psychotherapy Treatment Planner,* third edition, will promote effective, creative treatment planning—a process that will ultimately benefit the client, clinician, and mental health community.

SAMPLE STANDARD TREATMENT PLAN

PROBLEM: ANGER MANAGEMENT

Definitions: Repeated angry outbursts that are out of proportion to the precipitating event.

Excessive screaming, cursing, or use of verbally abusive language when frustrated or stressed.

Persistent pattern of destroying property or throwing objects when angry.

Goals: Significantly reduce the intensity and frequency of angry verbal outbursts.

Parents establish and maintain appropriate parent-child boundaries, setting firm, consistent limits when the client reacts in a verbally or physically aggressive or passive-aggressive manner.

OBJECTIVES

1. Parents establish clearly defined rules and appropriate boundaries and follow through consistently with consequences for anger control problems.

2. Comply with rules at home and school without protesting or venting strong feelings of anger.

INTERVENTIONS

1. Assist the parents in establishing clearly defined rules, boundaries, and consequences for angry outbursts and acts of aggression or destruction.

2. Establish clear rules for the client at home or school; ask him/her to repeat rules to demonstrate an understanding of the expectations.

1. Establish clear rules for the client at home or school; ask him/her to repeat rules to demonstrate an understanding of the expectations.

2. Assign readings to parents that teach effective conflict resolution strategies and help diffuse the intensity of

the client's angry feelings (e.g., *Negotiating Parent / Adolescent Conflict* by Robin and Foster; *Parents, Teens and Boundaries* by Bluestein; *Get Out of My Life but First Could You Drive Me and Cheryl to the Mall* by Wolf).

3. Express anger through controlled, respectful verbalizations and healthy physical outlets.

1. Teach mediational and self-control strategies (e.g., "stop, look, listen, and think"; take deep breaths and count to 10) to help the client express anger through appropriate verbalizations and healthy physical outlets.

2. Train the client in the use of progressive relaxation or guided imagery techniques to help calm himself/herself and decrease intensity of angry feelings.

4. Reduce the frequency and intensity of angry verbal outbursts when frustrated or stressed.

1. Teach the client effective communication and assertiveness skills to express angry feelings in a controlled manner and meet his/her needs through constructive actions.

2. Inquire into what the client does differently on days when he/she controls anger and does not lash out verbally or physically toward siblings or peers; process his/her responses and reinforce any positive coping mechanisms used to manage anger.

5. Parents increase the frequency of praise and positive reinforcement of the client for demonstrating good control of anger.

1. Encourage the parents to provide frequent praise and positive reinforcement to the client for displaying good anger control in situations involving conflict or stress.

6. Increase verbalizations of empathy and concern for other people.

1. Assign the client the task of showing empathy, kindness, or sensitivity to the needs of others (e.g., assist younger sibling with homework, perform cleaning task for ailing family member).

Diagnosis: 312.81   Intermittent Explosive Disorder

SAMPLE QUANTITATIVE TREATMENT PLAN

PROBLEM: ANGER MANAGEMENT

BEHAVIORAL DEFINITIONS

1. Client (PA) is reported by his parents and school officials to demonstrate angry outbursts that are out of proportion to any precipitating events, and these outbursts occur 2 to 3 times per school day in various classes throughout the day, 3 to 8 times per day at home in the mornings before school and in the evenings after school, and 5 to 10 times on the weekend days or days without school.

2. PA screams, curses, or uses verbally abusive language toward others 75 percent of the time when he is frustrated or stressed. These behaviors occur two to five times per day at home and school.

3. PA breaks or destroys nearby objects or throws objects when he is angry two to four times per week in the home.

LONG-TERM GOALS

1. PA is to significantly reduce the intensity and frequency of angry verbal outbursts.

2. PA's parents shall establish and maintain appropriate parent-child boundaries, setting firm, consistent limits when he reacts in a verbally or physically aggressive manner.

SHORT-TERM OBJECTIVES

THERAPEUTIC INTERVENTIONS

1. By 03/05/05, PA's parents are to establish clearly defined rules and appropriate boundaries and consistently follow through with negative consequences (e.g., time-out, loss of allowance) for PA's anger control problems (e.g., loud anger outbursts; screaming, cursing, or being verbally abusive toward others; breaking or throwing objects) as well as reinforcing (e.g., praise, increased allowance) appropriate anger control (e.g., verbalizing anger calmly, using "I" messages, avoiding the use of cursing) with a 100 percent schedule of reinforcement for noted behaviors.

1. Assist the parents in establishing clearly defined rules, boundaries, and consequences for angry outbursts and acts of aggression or destruction.

2. Establish clear rules for the client at home or school; ask him/her to repeat these rules to demonstrate an understanding of the expectations.

2. By 03/20/05, PA is to comply with rules at home and school without protesting or venting strong feelings of anger at a level of 80 percent of the time.

1. Establish clear rules for the client at home or school; ask him/her to repeat these rules to demonstrate an understanding of the expectations.

2. Assign to the parents readings that teach effective conflict resolution strategies and that help to diffuse the intensity of the client's angry feelings (e.g., *Negotiating Parent/Adolescent Conflict* by Robin and Foster; *Parents, Teens and Boundaries* by Bluestein; *Get Out of My Life but First*

Could You Drive Me and Cheryl to the Mall? by Wolf).

3. By 03/30/05, PA is to express anger through controlled, respectful verbalizations (e.g., "It really makes me angry when _____"; "It would help me to cope better if you could _____"; and "I am getting angry. I need to have some time to myself, please"; or silently counting to 10 a few times) and healthy physical outlets (e.g., running, hitting a mattress or pillow, yelling into a pillow, biting a towel, sitting or lying down and flexing and relaxing major muscle groups) at a level of 66 percent of the time.

1. Teach mediational and self-control strategies (e.g., "stop, look, listen, and think"; take deep breaths and count to 10) to help the client express anger through appropriate verbalizations and healthy physical outlets.

2. Train the client in the use of progressive relaxation or guided imagery techniques to help calm himself/herself and decrease the intensity of his/her angry feelings.

4. By 04/15/05, PA is to reduce to 75 percent the frequency and intensity of angry, verbal outbursts (e.g., yelling or screaming, swearing at his parents, yelling aloud in class) when frustrated or stressed.

1. Teach the client effective communication and assertiveness skills to express angry feelings in a controlled manner and meet his/her needs through constructive actions.

2. Inquire into what the client does differently on days when he/she controls anger and does not lash out verbally or physically toward siblings or peers; process his/her responses and reinforce any positive coping mechanisms used to manage anger.

5. By 03/30/05, PA's parents shall increase to 100 percent the frequency of verbal praise and positive reinforcement (e.g., increased car driving time) for PA's demonstration of good control of anger during stress by using the skills he is being taught (e.g., using effective communication and assertiveness skills to express angry feelings in a controlled manner, implementing relaxation techniques when upset).

1. Encourage the parents to provide frequent praise and positive reinforcement to the client for displaying good anger control in situations involving conflict or stress.

6. By 03/03/05, PA is to increase verbalizations of empathy and concern for other people (e.g., asking about their feelings, using active listening, assisting a sibling with a difficult task) three times or more per week.

1. Assign the client the task of showing empathy, kindness, or sensitivity to the needs of others (e.g., assisting a younger sibling with homework, performing a cleaning task for an ailing family member).

DIAGNOSTIC SUGGESTIONS

Axis I: 312.34   Intermittent Explosive Disorder
Axis II: V71.09   No Diagnosis on Axis II

ACADEMIC UNDERACHIEVEMENT

BEHAVIORAL DEFINITIONS

1. History of academic performance that is below the expected level, given the client's measured intelligence or performance on standardized achievement tests.
2. Repeated failure to complete homework assignments on time.
3. Poor organization or study skills.
4. Frequent tendency to postpone doing homework assignments in favor of engaging in recreational and leisure activities.
5. Positive family history of members having academic problems, failures, or disinterest.
6. Feelings of depression, insecurity, and low self-esteem that interfere with learning and academic progress.
7. Recurrent pattern of engaging in acting-out, disruptive, and negative attention-seeking behaviors when encountering frustration in learning.
8. Heightened anxiety that interferes with performance during tests.
9. Parents place excessive or unrealistic pressure on the client to such a degree that it negatively affects the client's academic performance.
10. Decline in academic performance that occurs in response to environmental stress (e.g., parents' divorce, death of loved one, relocation, or move).

—. _____
_____

—. _____
_____

—. _____
_____

LONG-TERM GOALS

1. Attain and maintain a level of academic performance that is commensurate with intellectual ability.
2. Complete school and homework assignments on a regular and consistent basis.
3. Achieve and maintain a healthy balance between accomplishing academic goals and meeting social and emotional needs.
4. Stabilize mood and build self-esteem sufficiently to cope effectively with the frustration associated with academic pursuits.
5. Eliminate pattern of engaging in acting-out, disruptive, or negative attention-seeking behaviors when confronted with frustration in learning.
6. Significantly reduce the level of anxiety related to taking tests.
7. Parents establish realistic expectations of the client's learning abilities.
8. Parents implement effective intervention strategies at home to help the client achieve academic goals.
9. Remove emotional impediments or resolve family conflicts and environmental stressors to allow for improved academic performance.

—. _____

_____

—. _____

_____

—. _____

_____

SHORT-TERM OBJECTIVES	THERAPEUTIC INTERVENTIONS
1. Complete a psychoeducational evaluation. (1)	1. Arrange for psychoeducational testing to evaluate the presence of a learning disability and to determine whether the client is eligible to receive special education services; provide feedback to the client, his/her family, and school officials regarding the psychoeducational evaluation.

2. Complete psychological testing. (2)

2. Arrange for psychological testing to assess whether possible Attention-Deficit/ Hyperactivity Disorder (ADHD) or emotional factors are interfering with the client's academic performance; provide feedback to the client, his/her family, and school officials regarding the psychological evaluation.

3. Parents and client provide psychosocial history information. (3)

3. Gather psychosocial history information that includes key developmental milestones and a family history of educational achievements and failures.

4. Cooperate with a hearing, vision, or medical examination. (4)

4. Refer the client for a hearing, vision, or medical examination to rule out possible hearing, visual, or health problems that are interfering with school performance.

5. Comply with the recommendations made by the multidisciplinary evaluation team at school regarding educational interventions. (5)

5. Attend an individualized educational planning committee (IEPC) meeting with the parents, teachers, and school officials to determine the client's eligibility for special education services, design educational interventions, and establish education goals.

6. Parents and teachers implement educational strategies that maximize the client's learning strengths and compensate for learning weaknesses. (6, 7)

6. Based on the IEPC goals and recommendations, move the client to an appropriate classroom setting to maximize his/her learning.

7. Participate in outside tutoring to increase knowledge and skills in the area of academic weakness. (8, 9, 10)

8. Implement effective study skills, which increase the frequency of completion of school assignments and improve academic performance. (11, 12)

7. Consult with the client, parents, and school officials about designing effective learning programs or intervention strategies that build on the client's strengths and compensate for his/her weaknesses.

8. Recommend that the parents seek privately contracted tutoring for the client after school to boost his/her skills in the area of his/her academic weakness (i.e., reading, mathematics, or written expression).

9. Refer the client to a private learning center for extra tutoring in the areas of academic weakness and assistance in improving study and test-taking skills.

10. Help the client to identify specific academic goals and steps needed to accomplish goals.

11. Teach the client more effective study skills (e.g., remove distractions, study in quiet places, develop outlines, highlight important details, schedule breaks).

12. Consult with teachers and parents about using a peer tutor to assist the client in his/her area of academic weakness and help improve study skills.

9. Implement effective test-taking strategies, which decrease anxiety and improve test performance. (13, 14)

13. Teach the client more effective test-taking strategies (e.g., study in small segments over an extended period of time, review material regularly, read directions twice, recheck work).

14. Train the client in the use of guided imagery or relaxation techniques to reduce anxiety before or during the taking of tests.

10. Parents maintain regular communication (i.e., daily to weekly) with teachers. (15)

15. Encourage the parents to maintain regular (daily or weekly) communication with teachers to help the client remain organized and keep up with school assignments.

11. Use self-monitoring checklists, planner, or calendars to remain organized and help complete school assignments. (16, 17, 18)

16. Encourage the client to use self-monitoring checklists to increase completion of school assignments and improve academic performance.

17. Direct the client to use planners or calendars to record school or homework assignments and plan ahead for long-term projects.

18. Utilize the "Break It Down into Small Steps" program in the *Brief Adolescent Therapy Homework Planner* (Jongsma, Peterson, and McInnis) to help the client complete projects or long-term assignments on time.

12. Establish a regular routine that allows time to engage in leisure or recreational activities, spend quality time with the family, and complete homework assignments. (19)

13. Parents and teachers increase praise and positive reinforcement toward the client for improved school performance. (20, 21, 22)

14. Identify and remove all emotional or family conflicts that may be a hindrance to learning. (23, 24)

19. Assist the client and his/her parents in developing a routine daily schedule at home that allows him/her to achieve a healthy balance of completing school/homework assignments, engaging in leisure activities, and spending quality time with family and peers.

20. Encourage the parents and teachers to give frequent praise and positive reinforcement for the client's effort and accomplishment on academic tasks.

21. Assign the parents to observe and record responsible behaviors by the client between therapy sessions that pertain to schoolwork. Reinforce responsible behaviors to encourage the client to continue to engage in those behaviors in the future.

22. Help the client identify what rewards would increase his/her motivation to improve academic performance and then make these reinforcers contingent on academic success.

23. Conduct family sessions to identify any family or marital conflicts that may be inhibiting the client's academic performance; assist the family in resolving conflicts.

24. Conduct individual therapy sessions to help the client work through and resolve painful emotions, core conflicts, or stressors that impede academic performance.

15. Parents increase time spent involved with the client's homework. (25, 26, 27)

25. Encourage the parents to demonstrate and/or maintain regular interest and involvement in the client's homework (i.e., attend school functions, review planners or calendars to see if the client is staying caught up with schoolwork).

26. Design and implement a reward system and/or contingency contract to help the parents reinforce the client's responsible behaviors, completion of school assignments, and academic success.

27. Assign the parents to observe and record responsible behaviors by the client between therapy sessions that pertain to schoolwork; urge them to reinforce responsible behaviors to encourage the client to continue to engage in those behaviors in the future.

16. Parents decrease the frequency and intensity of arguments with the client over issues related to school performance and homework. (28, 29)

28. Conduct family therapy sessions to assess whether the parents have developed unrealistic expectations or are placing excessive pressure on the client to perform; confront and challenge the parents about placing excessive pressure on the client.

29. Encourage the parents to set firm, consistent limits and utilize natural, logical consequences for the client's noncompliance or refusal to do homework; instruct the parents to avoid unhealthy power struggles or lengthy arguments over the client's homework each night.

17. Parents verbally recognize that their pattern of over-protectiveness interferes with the client's academic growth and assumption of responsibility. (30, 31)

30. Assess the parent-child relationship to help determine whether the parents' overprotectiveness and/or overindulgence of the client contributes to his/her academic underachievement; assist the parents in developing realistic expectations of the client's learning potential.

31. Encourage the parents not to protect the client from the natural consequences of poor academic performance (e.g., loss of credits, detention, delayed graduation, inability to take driver training, higher cost of car insurance) and allow him/her to learn from mistakes or failures.

18. Increase the frequency of on-task behaviors at school, completing school assignments without expressing the desire to give up. (32)

32. Consult with school officials about ways to improve the client's on-task behaviors (e.g., sit the client toward the front of the class or near positive peer role models, call on the client often, provide frequent feedback, break larger assignments into a series of small steps).

19. Increase the frequency of positive statements about school experiences and about confidence in the ability to succeed academically. (33, 34, 35)

33. Reinforce the client's successful school experiences and positive statements about school and confront the client's self-disparaging remarks and expressed desire to give up on school assignments.

34. Consult with the teachers to assign the client a task at school (e.g., giving announcements over the intercom; tutoring another student in his/her area of interest or strength) to demonstrate confidence in his/her ability to act responsibly.

35. Assign the client the task of making one positive statement daily to himself/herself about school and his/her ability and recording it in a journal or writing it on a sticky note and posting it in the bedroom or kitchen.

20. Decrease the frequency and severity of acting-out behaviors when encountering frustration with school assignments. (36)

36. Teach the client positive coping strategies (e.g., deep breathing and relaxation skills, positive self-talk, "stop, look, listen, and think") to inhibit the impulse to act out or engage in negative attention-seeking behaviors when he/she encounters frustration with schoolwork.

21. Identify and verbalize how specific responsible actions lead to improvements in academic performance. (37, 38, 39)

37. Explore for periods of time when the client completed schoolwork regularly and achieved academic success; identify and encourage

him/her to use similar strategies to improve his/her current academic functioning.

38. Examine coping strategies that the client has used to solve other problems. Encourage him/her to use similar coping strategies to overcome his/her problems associated with learning.

39. Give the client a homework assignment of identifying three to five role models and listing reasons he/she admires each role model. Explore in the next session the factors that contributed to each role model's success; encourage the client to take similar positive steps to achieve academic success.

22. Develop a list of resource people within the school setting who can be turned to for support, assistance, or instruction for learning problems. (40)

40. Identify a list of individuals within the school to whom the client can turn for support, assistance, or instruction when he/she encounters difficulty or frustration with learning.

__. _____

_____

__. _____

_____

__. _____

_____

__. _____

_____

__. _____

_____

__. _____

_____

DIAGNOSTIC SUGGESTIONS

Axis I:

315.00	Reading Disorder
315.1	Mathematics Disorder
315.2	Disorder of Written Expression
V62.3	Academic Problem
314.01	Attention-Deficit/Hyperactivity Disorder, Combined Type
314.00	Attention-Deficit/Hyperactivity Disorder, Predominantly Inattentive Type
300.4	Dysthymic Disorder
313.81	Oppositional Defiant Disorder
312.9	Disruptive Behavior Disorder NOS
_____	_____
_____	_____

Axis II:

317	Mild Mental Retardation
V62.89	Borderline Intellectual Functioning
_____	_____
_____	_____

ADOPTION

BEHAVIORAL DEFINITIONS

1. Questions are arising regarding family of origin or biological parents.
2. Confusion regarding identity linked to adoption.
3. Statements that reflect a feeling of not being a part of the family (e.g., "I don't fit here," or "I'm different.").
4. Asking to make a search to get additional information about or make contact with biological parents.
5. Marked shift in interests, dress, and peer group, all of which are contrary to the adoptive family's standards.
6. Exhibiting excessive clingy and helpless behavior that is inappropriate for developmental level.
7. Extreme testing of all limits (e.g., lying, breaking rules, academic underachievement, truancy, stealing, drug and alcohol experimentation/use, verbal abuse of parents and other authority, promiscuity).
8. Adoptive parents express anxiety and fearfulness because the child wants to meet his/her biological parents.
9. The adoption of an older special-needs child or sibset.
10. Parents express frustration with the adopted child's development and level of achievement.

__. _____
   _____
__. _____
   _____
__. _____
   _____

LONG-TERM GOALS

1. Termination of self-defeating, acting-out behaviors and acceptance of self as loved and lovable within an adopted family.
2. The weaving of an acceptable self-identify that includes self, biological parents, and adoptive parents.
3. Resolution of the loss of a potential relationship with the biological parents.
4. Completion of the search process that results in reconnection with the biological parent(s).
5. Successful working through of all unresolved issues connected with being adopted.
6. Resolution of the question, "Who am I?"

—. _____
   _____
—. _____
   _____
—. _____
   _____

SHORT-TERM OBJECTIVES

1. Develop a trusting relationship with the therapist in which feelings and thoughts can be openly communicated. (1)

2. Family members commit to attending and actively participating in family sessions that address issues related to adoption. (2, 3)

THERAPEUTIC INTERVENTIONS

1. Actively build the level of trust with the client in individual and family sessions through consistent eye contact, active listening, and unconditional acceptance to increase his/her ability to express thoughts and feelings regarding his/her adoption.

2. Solicit a commitment from all family members to regularly attend and participate in family therapy sessions.

3. Create a genogram in a family session, listing all

family members and what
is known about each. Ask
the child and the parents
what they know or have
been told about the biological parents and their families.

3. Verbally identify all the
losses related to being
adopted. (4)

4. Ask the client to identify
losses connected to being
adopted and to process
them with the therapist.

4. Express feelings of grief
connected to the losses associated with being adopted.
(5, 6)

5. Assist, guide, and support
the client in working
through the process of
grieving each identified
loss associated with being
adopted.

6. Assign the client to read
*Common Threads of
Teenage Grief* (Tyson) and
to process the key concepts
he/she gains from the reading with the therapist.

5. Report decreased feelings of
guilt, shame, abandonment,
and rejection. (7, 8, 9, 10)

7. Help the client identify and
verbally express feelings
connected to issues of rejection or abandonment.

8. Assign the client to read
Why Didn't She Keep Me?
(Burlingham-Brown) to
help him/her resolve feelings of rejection, abandonment, and guilt/shame.

9. Ask the client to read *How
It Feels to Be Adopted* (Krementz) and list the key
items from each vignette
that he/she identifies with.
Process completed list.

10. Assist the client in identifying irrational thoughts and beliefs (e.g., "I must have been bad for Mom to have released me for adoption," "I must have been a burden") that contribute to his/her feelings of shame and guilt. Then assist him/her in replacing the irrational thoughts and beliefs with healthy, rational ones.

6. Attend an adoption support group. (11)

11. Refer the client and/or parents to an adoption support group.

7. Identify positive aspects of self. (12, 13)

12. Explore with the client what aspects of himself/herself he/she would like to change and develop an action plan to achieve those goals (or assign the exercise "Three Ways to Change Yourself" in the *Brief Adolescent Therapy Homework Planner* by Jongsma, Peterson, and McInnis).

13. Assign a self-esteem-building exercise from *SEALS & PLUS* (Korb-Khalsa, Azok, and Leutenberg) to help the client develop self-knowledge, acceptance, and confidence.

8. Verbalize a decrease in confusion regarding self-identify. (14, 15)

14. Provide education to the client about his/her "true and false self or artificial and forbidden self" (see *Journey of the Adopted Self* by Lifton) to give him/her direction and permission to

pursue exploring who he/she is.

15. Assign the client the task of creating a list that responds to the question, "Who am I?" Ask him/her to add daily to the list and to share the list with the therapist each week for processing.

9. Parents verbalize an understanding of the dynamics of the struggle with adoption status by adolescents who are searching for identity developmentally. (16, 17)

16. Encourage the parents to read material to increase their knowledge and understanding of the adopted child in adolescence (e.g., *The Whole Life Adoption Book* by Schooler or *Making Sense of Adoption* by Melina).

17. Teach the parents about the developmental task of adolescence that is focused on searching for an independent identity and how this is complicated for an adopted adolescent.

10. Parents report reduced level of fear of the client's interest in and search for information and possible contact with biological parents. (18)

18. Conduct a session with the adoptive parents in which their fears and concerns are discussed regarding the client searching for and possibly meeting the biological parents. Confirm the parents' rights and empower them to support, curtail, or postpone the client's search.

11. Parents verbalize support for the client's search for biological parents. (19)

19. Hold a family session in which the client's desire to search for his/her biological parents is the issue. If the parents give support to the search, ask them to state verbally their

encouragement in going forward. Then elicit from the client a commitment to keep his/her parents informed about the search at a mutually agreed-upon level.

12. Parents verbalize refusal to support a search for the biological parents and insist it be postponed until the client is 18 or older. (20)

20. Hold a family session in which the client's desire to search for his/her biological parents is the issue. If the parents are opposed, support their right, since the child is a minor, and ask them to state their rationale. Affirm the client's right to search after he/she is 18 if he/she still desires to.

13. Verbalize an acceptance of the need to delay the search for the biological parents until age 18. (20, 21)

20. Hold a family session in which the client's desire to search for his/her biological parents is the issue. If the parents are opposed, support their right, since the child is a minor, and ask them to state their rationale. Affirm the client's right to search after he/she is 18 if he/she still desires to.

21. Affirm the parents' right to refuse to support a search for the client's biological parents at present, and assist the client in working to a feeling of acceptance of this decision.

14. Verbalize anxieties associated with the search for the biological parents. (22, 23, 24)

22. Locate an adult who is adopted and who would agree to meet with the client and the therapist to tell of his/her search experience

and answer any questions that the client has.

23. Prepare the client for the search by probing and affirming his/her fears, hopes, and concerns. Develop a list of questions about the biological parents that he/she would like to have answered.

24. Ask the client and the parents to read *Searching for a Past* (Schooler) to expand their knowledge and understanding of the search process.

15. Create an album of life experiences that could be shared with the biological parents. (25)

25. Have the client review his/her "life book" filled with pictures and mementos; if he/she does not have one, help him/her construct one to add to the search/reunion process.

16. Begin the search for the biological parents. (26)

26. Refer the client to the agency that did his/her adoption or to an adoption agency that has postadoption services to begin the search process.

17. Share any increased knowledge of the biological parents and their backgrounds that is attained from the search. (27)

27. Debrief the client on the information he/she receives from the search. Identify and support his/her feelings around what is revealed.

18. Verbalize and resolve feelings associated with not being able to contact the biological parents. (28)

28. Assist the client in working through his/her feelings of disappointment, anger, or loss connected to a dead end regarding possible contact with the biological parents.

19. Inform the adoptive parents of information discovered about the biological parents and feelings about it. (29)

20. Make a decision to pursue or not pursue a reunion with the biological parents. (24, 30)

21. Identify and express expectations and feelings around impending reunion with the biological parents. (31, 32)

22. Attend and participate in a meeting with the biological parents. (33)

29. Monitor the client's communication to the adoptive parents of information regarding the search to make sure it is occurring at the agreed-upon level.

24. Ask the client and the parents to read *Searching for a Past* (Schooler) to expand their knowledge and understanding of the search process.

30. Help the client reach a decision to pursue or postpone contact or reunion with the biological parents, reviewing the pros and cons of each alternative.

31. Prepare the client to have contact with the biological parents by examining his/her expectations to make them as realistic as possible and to seed and reinforce the message to let the relationship build slowly.

32. Role-play with the client a first meeting with the biological parents and process the experience.

33. Arrange for and conduct a meeting with the client and the biological parents facilitating a complete expression of feelings by all family members; explore with all parties the next possible steps.

23. Verbalize feelings regarding first contact with the biological parents and expectations regarding the future of the relationship. (34)

24. Reassure the adoptive parents of love and loyalty to them that is not compromised by contact with the biological parents. (35)

25. Verbalize a realistic plan for a future relationship with the biological parents. (33, 36)

34. Process with the client his/her first contact with the biological parents and explore the next step he/she would like to make in terms of a future relationship.

35. Assist the client in creating a plan for further developing his/her new relationship with the biological parents, with emphasis on taking things slowly, keeping expectations realistic, and being sensitive to the feelings of the adoptive parents who have provided consistent love and nurturing.

33. Arrange for and conduct a meeting with the client and the biological parents facilitating a complete expression of feelings by all family members; explore with all parties the next possible steps.

36. Conduct a family session with the client and the adoptive parents to update them on the meeting with the biological parents and the next possible steps. Offer appropriate affirmation and explore how the new family arrangement might work.

—. _____
    _____

—. _____
    _____

—. _____
    _____

—. _____
    _____

—. _____
    _____

—. _____
    _____

DIAGNOSTIC SUGGESTIONS

Axis I:

309.0	Adjustment Disorder With Depressed Mood
309.4	Adjustment Disorder With Mixed Disturbance of Emotions and Conduct
308.90	Alcohol Dependence
300.4	Dysthymic Disorder
312.81 or 2	Conduct Disorder, Child and Adolescent Onset
313.81	Oppositional Deficit Disorder
314.01	Attention-Deficit/Hyperactivity Disorder, Combined Type
_____	_____
_____	_____

Axis II:

799.9	Diagnosis Deferred
V71.09	No Diagnosis
_____	_____
_____	_____

ANGER MANAGEMENT

BEHAVIORAL DEFINITIONS

1. Repeated angry outbursts that are out of proportion to the precipitating event.
2. Excessive screaming, cursing, or use of verbally abusive language when frustrated or stressed.
3. Frequent fighting, intimidation of others, and acts of cruelty or violence toward people or animals.
4. Verbal threats of harm to parents, adult authority figures, siblings, or peers.
5. Persistent pattern of destroying property or throwing objects when angry.
6. Consistent failure to accept responsibility for loss of control, accompanied by repeated pattern of blaming others for his/her anger control problems.
7. History of engaging in passive-aggressive behaviors (e.g., forgetting, pretending not to listen, dawdling, procrastinating, stubborn refusal to comply with reasonable requests or rules) to frustrate or annoy other family members, adults, or peers.
8. Strained interpersonal relationships with peers due to anger control problems and aggressive or destructive behaviors.
9. Underlying feelings of depression, anxiety, or insecurity that contribute to angry outbursts and aggressive behaviors.

__. _____
   _____
__. _____
   _____
__. _____
   _____

LONG-TERM GOALS

1. Express anger through appropriate verbalizations and healthy physical outlets.
2. Significantly reduce the intensity and frequency of angry verbal outbursts.
3. Terminate all acts of violence or cruelty toward people or animals and destruction of property.
4. Interact consistently with adult authority figures in a mutually respectful manner.
5. Markedly reduce the frequency of passive-aggressive behaviors by expressing anger and frustration through controlled, respectful, and direct verbalizations.
6. Resolve the core conflicts that contribute to the emergence of anger control problems.
7. Parents establish and maintain appropriate parent-child boundaries, setting firm, consistent limits when the client reacts in a verbally or physically aggressive or passive-aggressive manner.
8. Demonstrate marked improvement in the ability to listen and respond empathetically to the thoughts, feelings, and needs or others.

—. _____

   _____

—. _____

   _____

   _____

—. _____

   _____

SHORT-TERM OBJECTIVES	THERAPEUTIC INTERVENTIONS
1. Complete psychological testing. (1)	1. Arrange for psychological testing to assess whether emotional factors or Attention-Deficit/Hyperactivity Disorder (ADHD) are contributing to anger control problems; provide feedback to the client and parents.

2. Complete a substance abuse evaluation and comply with the recommendations offered by the evaluation findings. (2)

3. Cooperate with the recommendations or requirements mandated by the criminal justice system. (3, 4, 5)

4. Parents establish clearly defined rules and appropriate boundaries and follow through consistently with consequences for anger control problems. (6, 7, 8)

2. Arrange for a substance abuse evaluation and/or treatment for the client.

3. Consult with criminal justice officials about the appropriate consequences for the client's destructive or aggressive behaviors (e.g., pay restitution, community service, probation, intensive surveillance).

4. Consult with parents, school officials, and criminal justice officials about the need to place the client in an alternative setting (e.g., foster home, group home, residential program, or juvenile detention facility).

5. Encourage and challenge the parents not to protect the client from the natural or legal consequences of his/her destructive or aggressive behaviors.

6. Assist the parents in establishing clearly defined rules, boundaries, and consequences for angry outbursts and acts of aggression or destruction.

7. Establish clear rules for the client at home or school; ask him/her to repeat rules to demonstrate an understanding of the expectations.

8. Assign readings to parents that teach effective conflict resolution strategies and help diffuse the intensity of the client's angry feelings (e.g., *Negotiating Parent / Adolescent Conflict* by Robin and Foster; *Parents, Teens and Boundaries* by Bluestein; *Get Out of My Life but First Could You Drive Me and Cheryl to the Mall* by Wolf).

5. Increase the number of verbalizations that reflect the acceptance of responsibility for angry outbursts and destructive or aggressive behaviors. (9, 10)

9. Firmly confront the client about the impact of his/her angry outbursts and destructive or aggressive behaviors, pointing out consequences for himself/herself and others.

10. Confront statements in which the client blames others for his/her anger control problems and fails to accept responsibility for his/her destructive or aggressive behaviors.

6. Express anger through controlled, respectful verbalizations and healthy physical outlets. (11, 12)

11. Teach mediational and self-control strategies (e.g., "stop, look, listen, and think"; take deep breaths and count to 10) to help the client express anger through appropriate verbalizations and healthy physical outlets.

12. Train the client in the use of progressive relaxation or guided imagery techniques to help calm himself/herself and decrease intensity of angry feelings.

7. Reduce the frequency and intensity of angry verbal outbursts when frustrated or stressed. (13, 14)

8. Parents agree to and follow through with the implementation of a reward system contingency contract or token economy to reinforce positive control of anger. (15, 16, 17)

13. Teach the client effective communication and assertiveness skills to express angry feelings in a controlled manner and meet his/her needs through constructive actions.

14. Inquire into what the client does differently on days when he/she controls anger and does not lash out verbally or physically toward siblings or peers; process his/her responses and reinforce any positive coping mechanisms used to manage anger.

15. Design a reward system and/or contingency contract for the client to reinforce good anger control and deter destructive or aggressive behaviors.

16. Design and implement a token economy to increase the client's positive social behaviors, improve his/her anger control, and deter destructive or aggressive behaviors.

17. Assign a homework exercise designed to help the client learn to express anger in a controlled manner (or assign the "Anger Control" exercise in the *Brief Adolescent Therapy Homework Planner* by Jongsma, Peterson, and McInnis).

9. Parents increase the frequency of praise and positive reinforcement of the client for demonstrating good control of anger. (18)

10. Recognize and verbalize how feelings of insecurity or other painful emotions are connected to anger control problems. (19, 20, 21)

11. Identify targets or triggers for angry outbursts and aggressive behavior. (22, 23, 24, 25)

18. Encourage the parents to provide frequent praise and positive reinforcement to the client for displaying good anger control in situations involving conflict or stress.

19. Assist the client in making a connection between underlying painful emotions (e.g., depression, anxiety, helplessness) and angry outbursts or aggressive behaviors.

20. Help the client recognize how his/her underlying emotional pain contributes to angry outbursts (or utilize the "Surface Behavior/ Inner Feelings" exercise in the *Brief Adolescent Therapy Homework Planner* by Jongsma, Peterson, and McInnis).

21. Assign the client to read material to help him/her manage anger more effectively (e.g., *S.O.S. Help for Emotions* by Clark); process reading with the client.

22. Direct the client to develop a thorough list of all targets and causes of anger.

23. Ask the client to keep a daily journal in which he/she documents persons and situations that evoke strong feelings of anger.

24. Assign the client to list significant life experiences that have produced strong

feelings of anger, hurt, or disappointment.

25. Utilize the family-sculpting technique, in which the client defines the roles and behaviors of each family member in a scene of his/her choosing, to assess family dynamics that may contribute to the emergence of his/her anger control problems.

12. Identify and verbalize unmet emotional needs directly to significant others. (26)

13. Identify and verbally express feelings associated with past neglect, abuse, separation, or abandonment. (27, 28, 29, 30)

26. Assist the client in first identifying unmet needs and then expressing them to significant others.

27. Explore the client's family background for a history of physical, sexual, or substance abuse, which may contribute to his/her anger control problems.

28. Encourage and support the client in expressing feelings associated with neglect, abuse, separations, or abandonment.

29. Assign the client the task of writing a letter to the absent or abusive parent. Process the content of the letter to help him/her express and work through feelings of anger, sadness, and helplessness about past abandonment or abuse.

30. Use the empty chair technique to coach the client in expressing angry feelings in a constructive manner

14. Uninvolved or detached parent(s) increase time spent with client in recreational, school, or work activities. (31)

15. Express and verbalize forgiveness to perpetrator or target of anger. (32, 33)

16. Identify and replace the irrational beliefs or maladaptive thoughts that contribute to the emergence of destructive or aggressive behaviors. (34)

17. Participate in anger control group therapy. (35)

18. Establish and maintain steady employment to deter aggressive or destructive behaviors. (36)

toward the absent or abusive parent.

31. Give a directive to uninvolved or disengaged parents to spend more time with the client in leisure, school, or work activities.

32. Explore and discuss the client's willingness to forgive the perpetrators of emotional or physical pain as a process of letting go of anger.

33. Instruct the client to write a letter of forgiveness to a target of anger as a step toward letting go of his/her anger; process the letter in session and discuss what to do with the letter.

34. Identify and confront irrational thoughts that contribute to the emergence of anger control problems; replace irrational thoughts with more adaptive ways of thinking to help control anger.

35. Refer the client to an anger management group.

36. Instruct the client to seek and secure employment in order to have funds available to make restitution for aggressive or destructive acts, to assume responsibility, and to gain income to meet his/her needs in an adaptive manner.

19. Increase the frequency of positive interactions with parents, adult authority figures, siblings, and peers. (37, 38, 39)

37. Utilize The Self-Control Game (Shapiro; available from Childswork/Childsplay, LLC) in session to help the client develop problem-solving skills and improve self-control.

38. Assist the client in identifying more age-appropriate ways of establishing control and/or power than through intimidating or bullying others.

39. Assign the client the task of showing empathy, kindness, or sensitivity to the needs of others (e.g., assist younger sibling with homework, perform cleaning task for ailing family member).

20. Express feelings of anger through the medium of art. (40, 41)

40. Direct the client to draw pictures of three events or situations that commonly evoke feelings of anger; process his/her thoughts and feelings after he/she completes drawings.

41. Tell the client to draw on outline of a human body on a large piece of paper or poster board; then ask him/her to fill in the mural with objects, symbols, or pictures that reflect who or what the client is angry about in his/her life. Process the content of the artwork in session.

21. Take medication as prescribed by the physician. (42)

42. Refer the client for medication evaluation to help stabilize moods and improve his/her anger control.

___. _____   ___. _____
      _____   _____
                    .   _____
___. _____   ___. _____
      _____   _____
___. _____   ___. _____
      _____   _____

DIAGNOSTIC SUGGESTIONS

Axis I: 313.81   Oppositional Defiant Disorder
313.34   Intermittent Explosive Disorder
312.30   Impulse-Control Disorder NOS
312.8   Conduct Disorder/Adolescent-Onset Type
312.9   Disruptive Behavior Disorder NOS
314.01   Attention-Deficit/Hyperactive Disorder,
         Predominantly Hyperactive-Impulsive Type
314.9   Attention-Deficit/Hyperactivity Disorder NOS
V71.02   Adolescent Antisocial Behavior
V61.20   Parent-Child Relational Problem

_____   _____

Axis II: 799.9   Diagnosis Deferred
V71.09   No Diagnosis on Axis II

_____   _____

_____   _____

ANXIETY

BEHAVIORAL DEFINITIONS

1. Excessive anxiety, worry, or fear that markedly exceeds the normal level for the client's stage of development.
2. High level of motor tension, such as restlessness, tiredness, shakiness, or muscle tension.
3. Autonomic hyperactivity (e.g., rapid heartbeat, shortness of breath, dizziness, dry mouth, nausea, or diarrhea).
4. Hypervigilance, such as feeling constantly on edge, concentration difficulties, trouble falling or staying asleep, and a general state of irritability.
5. A specific fear that has become generalized to cover a wide area and has reached the point where it significantly interferes with the client's and the family's daily life.
6. Excessive anxiety or worry due to parent's threat of abandonment, overuse of guilt, denial of autonomy and status, friction between parents, or interference with physical activity.

__. _____
   _____
__. _____
   _____
__. _____
   _____

LONG-TERM GOALS

1. Reduce the overall frequency and intensity of the anxiety response so that daily functioning is not impaired.

2. Stabilize the anxiety level while increasing the ability to function on a daily basis.
3. Resolve the key issue that is the source of the anxiety or fear.
4. Interact with the world without excessive fear, worry, or anxiety.

—. _____
   _____

—. _____
   _____

—. _____
   _____

SHORT-TERM OBJECTIVES

1. Verbally identify specific fears, worries, and anxieties. (1, 2, 3, 4)

THERAPEUTIC INTERVENTIONS

1. Actively build the level of trust with the client though consistent eye contact, active listening, unconditional positive regard, and warm acceptance to help increase his/her ability to identify and express specific anxieties.

2. Use a therapeutic game (The Talking, Feeling, and Doing Game by Gardner, available from Creative Therapeutics, or the Ungame by Zakich, available from The Ungame Company) to expand the client's awareness of feelings, self, and others.

3. Have the client read the chapter "Understanding Anxiety" from *The Feeling Good Handbook* (Burns) and select five key ideas to discuss.

4. Play the *My Home and Places* game (Flood) with the client to reduce resistance and to facilitate talking and identification of what makes him/her anxious.

2. Implement positive self-talk to reduce or eliminate anxiety. (5, 6)

5. Explore distorted cognitive messages that mediate the client's anxiety response.

6. Help the client develop reality-based cognitive messages that will increase self-confidence in coping with fears and anxieties.

3. Complete homework assignments designed to reduce anxiety. (7, 8, 9)

7. Ask the client to complete several anxiety reduction assignments in *Anxiety and Phobia Workbook* (Bourne); process each assignment.

8. Assign the client to complete the anxiety section exercises in *Ten Days to Self-Esteem* (Burns); process the completed exercises.

9. Explore the nature of the client's responses to experiencing anxiety symptoms as to whether they are beneficial or dysfunctional (or assign the exercise "Finding and Losing Your Anxiety" from the *Brief Adolescent Therapy Homework Planner* by Jongsma, Peterson, and McInnis).

4. Identify areas of conflict that precipitate anxiety. (10, 11)

10. Ask the client to develop a list of key past and present conflicts within the family and with peers that trigger

worry. Process this list with the therapist.

11. Assist the client in working toward resolution (e.g., using problem solving, assertiveness, acceptance, cognitive restructuring) of key past and present conflicts.

5. Increase participation in daily social and academic activities. (12, 13)

12. Teach the client behavioral anxiety coping strategies that create distraction from the anxiety preoccupation (e.g., increased social involvement, participation in school-related activities) and contract for implementations.

13. Encourage the parents to seek an experiential camp or weekend experience for the client that will focus on the issues of fears, taking risks, and building confidence. Process the experience with the client and his/her parents.

6. State a connection between anxiety and underlying, previously unexpressed wishes or thoughts. (14)

14. Utilize an interpretive interview method in which the therapist interviews the client to help him/her express motivation and feelings. Then assist the client in making a connection between fears or anxieties and unexpressed or unacceptable wishes or "bad" thoughts.

7. Implement appropriate relaxation activities to decrease the level of anxiety. (15)

15. Teach deep muscle relaxation, deep breathing, and positive imagery as anxiety coping skills.

8. Identify new coping strategies for anxiety management. (3, 7, 8, 16)

3. Have the client read the chapter "Understanding Anxiety" from *The Feeling Good Handbook* (Burns) and select five key ideas to discuss.

7. Ask the client to complete several anxiety reduction assignments in *Anxiety and Phobia Workbook* (Bourne); process each assignment.

8. Assign the client to complete the anxiety section exercises in *Ten Days to Self-Esteem* (Burns); process the completed exercises.

16. Play The Stress and Anxiety Game (Berg) with the client to help expand his/her skills at handling situations that cause anxiety and/or stress.

9. Set aside time for overthinking about anxieties. (17)

17. Advocate and encourage overthinking about anxiety trigger situations (i.e., help the client explore and prepare for every conceivable thing that could possibly happen when facing a new or anxiety-producing situation). Monitor weekly results and redirect as needed.

10. Parents verbalize an understanding of the client's anxieties and fears. (18, 19, 20)

18. Teach the client's parents which fears and anxieties are developmentally normal for various stages of adolescent behavior.

19. Assign the client's parents to read books related to

child development and parenting (e.g., *Between Parent and Teenager* by Ginott or *How to Talk So Kids Will Listen and Listen So Kids Will Talk* by Faber and Mazlish).

20. Refer the client's parents to a parenting class or support group.

11. Parents verbalize constructive ways to respond to the client's anxiety. (21)

21. Assist the parents in developing their skills in effectively responding to the client's fears and anxieties with calm confidence (e.g., parents remind the client of a time he/she effectively handled a fearful situation, or parents express confidence in the client's ability to face his/her fear) rather than fearful reactivity.

12. Participate in family therapy sessions that identify and resolve conflicts between family members. (22, 23)

22. Conduct a family session in which the system is probed to determine the level of fear or anxiety that is present or to bring to the surface underlying conflicts.

23. Conduct family sessions to resolve conflicts and to increase the family's level of healthy functioning.

13. Parents reduce their attempts to control the client. (24, 25)

24. Use a structural approach in the family session in which roles are adjusted to encourage the parents to work less at controlling the teen and to allow age-appropriate levels of freedom.

25. Conduct family sessions in which strategic directions

14. Identify specific parameters of anxiety occurrence and implement an adaptive solution to reduce anxiety. (26)

15. Identify instances from the past when anxiety has been absent or successfully overcome. (27)

16. Utilize an Ericksonian tale to cope with anxiety. (28)

17. Complete a medication evaluation. (29)

that are designed to increase the physical freedom of the children and to adjust the parental control of the system are developed and given to the family.

26. Use a brief therapy approach of "mapping patterns" (O'Hanlon and Beadle) by asking questions of how, where, when, or with whom anxiety occurs in order to locate several points to intervene. Then develop from these points a solution and get the client to buy into implementing.

27. Assist the client in tapping his/her own internal or external skills and resources to handle the anxiety by utilizing a brief solution-focused technique such as "Finding Times without the Problem," "Finding What Worked," "Finding Competence," and have the client implement the solution (see *A Guide to Possibility Land* by O'Hanlon and Beadle).

28. Create and tell a teaching tale in the Ericksonian model around an aspect of anxiety. Tape-record the story for the client to take and play during the week when he/she feels anxious. Repeat as needed.

29. Refer the client to a psychiatrist for a medication consultation; confer with the psychiatrist before and

18. Take medication as prescribed and report as to effectiveness and side effects. (30)

___. _____
    _____

___. _____
    _____

___. _____
    _____

upon the completion of the evaluation.

30. Monitor the client for psychotropic medication prescription compliance, side effects, and effectiveness.

___. _____
    _____

___. _____
    _____

___. _____
    _____

DIAGNOSTIC SUGGESTIONS

Axis I: 300.02   Generalized Anxiety Disorder
              300.00   Anxiety Disorder NOS
              314.01   Attention-Deficit/Hyperactivity Disorder, Combined Type

              _____   _____

Axis II: 799.9   Diagnosis Deferred
              V71.09   No Diagnosis

              _____   _____
              _____   _____

ATTENTION-DEFICIT/HYPERACTIVITY DISORDER (ADHD)

BEHAVIORAL DEFINITIONS

1. Short attention span; difficulty sustaining attention on a consistent basis.
2. Susceptibility to distraction by extraneous stimuli and internal thoughts.
3. Gives impression that he/she is not listening well.
4. Repeated failure to follow through on instructions or complete school assignments or chores in a timely manner.
5. Poor organizational skills as demonstrated by forgetfulness, inattention to details, and losing things necessary for tasks.
6. Hyperactivity as evidenced by a high energy level, restlessness, difficulty sitting still, or loud or excessive talking.
7. Impulsivity as evidenced by difficulty awaiting turn in group situations, blurting out answers to questions before the questions have been completed, and frequent intrusions into others' personal business.
8. Frequent disruptive, aggressive, or negative attention-seeking behaviors.
9. Tendency to engage in carelessness or potentially dangerous activities.
10. Difficulty accepting responsibility for actions; history of projecting blame for problems onto others; failing to learn from experience.
11. Low self-esteem and poor social skills.

—. _____
   _____
—. _____
   _____

—. _____
   _____

LONG-TERM GOALS

1. Sustain attention and concentration for consistently longer periods of time.
2. Increase the frequency of on-task behaviors.
3. Demonstrate marked improvement in impulse control.
4. Regularly take medication as prescribed to decrease impulsivity, hyperactivity, and distractibility.
5. Parents and/or teachers successfully utilize a reward system, contingency contract, or token economy to reinforce positive behaviors and deter negative behaviors.
6. Parents set firm, consistent limits and maintain appropriate parent-child boundaries.
7. Improve self-esteem.
8. Develop positive social skills to help maintain lasting peer friendships.

—. _____
   _____
   _____

—. _____
   _____
   _____

—. _____
   _____

SHORT-TERM OBJECTIVES

THERAPEUTIC INTERVENTIONS

1. Complete psychological testing to confirm the diagnosis of ADHD and/or rule out emotional factors. (1)

1. Arrange for psychological testing to confirm the presence of ADHD and/or rule out emotional problems that may be contributing to the client's inattentiveness, impulsivity, and hyperactivity; give feedback to the client and his/her parents regarding the testing results.

2. Take prescribed medication as directed by the physician. (2, 3)

    2. Arrange for a medication evaluation for the client.

    3. Monitor the client for psychotropic medication prescription compliance, side effects, and effectiveness; consult with the prescribing physician at regular intervals.

3. Parents and the client increase knowledge about ADHD symptoms. (4, 5, 6)

    4. Educate the client's parents and siblings about the symptoms of ADHD.

    5. Assign the parents readings to increase their knowledge about symptoms of ADHD (e.g., *Taking Charge of ADHD* by Barkley, *ADHD and Teens* by Alexander-Roberts, and *Teenagers with ADD* by Dendy-Zeigler).

    6. Assign the client readings to increase his/her knowledge about ADHD and ways to manage symptoms (e.g., *Adolescents and ADD* by Quinn, and *ADHD—A Teenager's Guide* by Crist).

4. Parents develop and utilize an organized system to keep track of the client's school assignments, chores, and household responsibilities. (7, 8)

    7. Assist the parents in developing and implementing an organizational system to increase the client's on-task behaviors and completion of school assignments, chores, or household responsibilities (e.g., using calendars, charts, notebooks, and class syllabi).

    8. Assist the parents in developing a routine schedule to increase the client's compliance with school,

5. Parents maintain communication with the school to increase the client's compliance with completion of school assignments. (9)

6. Utilize effective study skills on a regular basis to improve academic performance. (10, 11)

7. Increase frequency of completion of school assignments, chores, and household responsibilities. (8, 12, 13)

household, or work-related responsibilities.

9. Encourage the parents and teachers to maintain regular communication about the client's academic, behavioral, emotional, and social progress.

10. Teach the client more effective study skills (e.g., clearing away distractions, studying in quiet places, scheduling breaks in studying).

11. Assign the client to read *13 Steps to Better Grades* (Silverman) to improve organizational and study skills.

8. Assist the parents in developing a routine schedule to increase the client's compliance with school, chores, or household responsibilities.

12. Consult with the client's teachers to implement strategies to improve school performance (e.g., sitting in the front row during class, using a prearranged signal to redirect the client back to task, scheduling breaks from tasks, providing frequent feedback, calling on the client often, arranging for a listening buddy).

13. Encourage the parents and teachers to utilize a school contract and reward system to reinforce completion of the client's assignments (or employ the "Getting It

Done" program in the *Brief Adolescent Therapy Homework Planner* by Jongsma, Peterson, and McInnis).

8. Implement effective test-taking strategies on a consistent basis to improve academic performance. (14)

14. Teach the client more effective test-taking strategies (e.g., reviewing material regularly, reading directions twice, rechecking work).

9. Delay instant gratification in favor of achieving meaningful long-term goals. (15, 16)

15. Teach the client mediational and self-control strategies (e.g., "stop, look, listen, and think") to delay the need for instant gratification and inhibit impulses to achieve more meaningful, longer-term goals.

16. Assist the parents in increasing structure to help the client learn to delay gratification for longer-term goals (e.g., completing homework or chores before playing basketball).

10. The client and his/her parents comply with the implementation of a reward system, contingency contract, or token economy to reduce the frequency of impulsive, disruptive, and negative attention-seeking behaviors. (17, 18, 19)

17. Identify a variety of positive reinforcers or rewards to maintain the client's interest or motivation in achieving desired goals or changes in behavior.

18. Design a reward system and/or contingency contract to reinforce the client's desired positive behaviors and deter impulsive behaviors.

19. Design and implement a token economy to improve the client's academic performance, social skills, and impulse control.

11. Parents set firm limits and use natural, logical consequences to deter the client's impulsive behaviors. (20, 21)

20. Establish clear rules for the client at home and school; ask him/her to repeat the rules to demonstrate an understanding of the expectations.

21. Encourage the parents to use natural, logical consequences for the client's disruptive and negative attention-seeking behaviors.

12. Express feelings through controlled, respectful verbalizations and healthy physical outlets. (22, 23)

22. Teach the client effective communication and assertiveness skills to express feelings in a controlled fashion and meet his/her needs through more constructive actions.

23. Train the client in the use of guided imagery or relaxation techniques to help control anger.

13. Identify and implement effective problem-solving strategies. (24, 25)

24. Teach the client effective problem-solving skills (e.g., identifying the problem, brainstorming alternative solutions, selecting an option, implementing a course of action, and evaluating).

25. Utilize role playing and modeling to teach the client how to implement effective problem-solving techniques in his/her daily life (or assign the "Stop, Think and Act" exercise in the *Brief Adolescent Therapy Homework Planner* by Jongsma, Peterson, and McInnis).

14. Increase verbalizations of acceptance of responsibility for misbehavior. (26, 27, 28)

26. Assign the client's parents to read material on resolving conflict with adolescents more effectively by placing more responsibility on them (e.g., *Negotiating Parent/ Adolescent Conflict* by Robin and Foster).

27. Firmly confront the client's impulsive behaviors, pointing out consequences for himself/herself and others.

28. Confront statements in which the client blames others for his/her annoying or impulsive behaviors and fails to accept responsibility for his/her actions.

15. Identify stressors or painful emotions that trigger increase in hyperactivity and impulsivity. (29, 30)

29. Explore and identify stressful events or factors that contribute to an increase in impulsivity, hyperactivity, and distractibility. Help the client and parents develop positive coping strategies (e.g., "stop, look, listen, and think," relaxation techniques, and positive self-talk) to manage stress more effectively.

30. Explore possible stressors, roadblocks, or hurdles that might cause impulsive and acting-out behaviors to increase in the future. Identify coping strategies (e.g., "stop, look, listen, and think," guided imagery, utilizing "I" messages to communicate needs) that the client and his/her family can use to cope with or

16. Increase the frequency of positive interactions with parents. (31, 32, 33)

17. Parents and the client regularly attend and actively participate in group therapy. (34, 35)

18. Increase the frequency of socially appropriate behaviors with siblings and peers. (36, 37, 38)

overcome stressors, roadblocks, or hurdles.

31. Explore for periods of time when the client demonstrated good impulse control and engaged in fewer disruptive behaviors; process his/her responses and reinforce positive coping mechanisms that he/she used to deter impulsive or disruptive behaviors.

32. Instruct the parents to observe and record three to five positive behaviors by the client in between therapy sessions; reinforce positive behaviors and encourage him/her to continue to exhibit these behaviors.

33. Encourage the parents to spend 10 to 15 minutes daily of one-on-one time with the client to create a closer parent-child bond. Allow the client to take the lead in selecting the activity or task.

34. Arrange for the client to attend group therapy to build social skills.

35. Encourage the client's parents to participate in an ADHD support group.

36. Identify and reinforce positive social behaviors to assist the client in establishing and maintaining friendships.

	37. Give homework assignments where the client identifies 5 to 10 strengths or interests; review the list in the following session and encourage him/her to utilize strengths or interests to establish friendships.
	38. Assign the client the task of showing empathy, kindness, or sensitivity to the needs of others (e.g., allowing sibling or peer to take first turn in a video game, helping with a school fundraiser).
19. Identify and list constructive ways to utilize energy. (39)	39. Give a homework assignment where the client lists the positive and negative aspects of his/her high energy level. Review the list in the following session and encourage him/her to channel energy into healthy physical outlets and positive social activities.
20. Express feelings through artwork. (40)	40. Instruct the client to draw a picture reflecting what it feels like to have ADHD; process content of the drawing with the therapist.
21. Implement a process of monitoring and assessing behavior. (41)	41. Encourage the client to use self-monitoring checklists to improve his/her attention and social skills (or assign the "Social Skills Exercise" in the *Brief Adolescent Therapy Homework Planner* by Jongsma, Peterson, and McInnis).

22. Increase brain wave control, which results in improved attention span and decreased impulsivity and hyperactivity. (42, 43)

42. Use brain wave biofeedback techniques to improve the client's attention span, impulse control, and ability to relax, encouraging the client to transfer the biofeedback training skills of relaxation and cognitive focusing to everyday situations (e.g., classroom and home).

43. Use Heartbeat Audiotapes (Lamb, available from Childswork/Childsplay) that play background music at 60 beats per minute to help calm the client and improve concentration while studying or learning new material.

__. _____
_____
__. _____
_____
__. _____
_____

__. _____
_____
__. _____
_____
__. _____
_____

DIAGNOSTIC SUGGESTIONS

Axis I:	314.01	Attention-Deficit/Hyperactivity Disorder, Combined Type
	314.00	Attention-Deficit/Hyperactivity Disorder, Predominantly Inattentive Type
	314.01	Attention-Deficit/Hyperactivity Disorder, Predominantly Hyperactive-Impulsive Type
	314.9	Attention-Deficit/Hyperactivity Disorder NOS
	312.81	Conduct Disorder/Childhood-Onset Type
	312.81	Conduct Disorder/Adolescent-Onset Type
	313.81	Oppositional Defiant Disorder

	312.9	Disruptive Behavior Disorder NOS
	296.xx	Bipolar I Disorder
	____	_____
	____	_____
Axis II:	799.9	Diagnosis Deferred
	V71.09	No Diagnosis on Axis II
	____	_____
	____	_____

AUTISM/PERVASIVE DEVELOPMENTAL DISORDER

BEHAVIORAL DEFINITIONS

1. Pervasive lack of interest in or responsiveness to other people.
2. Chronic failure to develop social relationships appropriate to the developmental level.
3. Lack of spontaneity and emotional or social reciprocity.
4. Significant delays in or total lack of spoken language development.
5. Impairment in sustaining or initiating conversation.
6. Oddities in speech and language as manifested by echolalia, pronominal reversal, or metaphorical language.
7. Inflexible adherence to repetition of nonfunctional rituals or stereotyped motor mannerisms.
8. Persistent preoccupation with objects, parts of objects, or restricted areas of interest.
9. Marked impairment or extreme variability in intellectual and cognitive functioning.
10. Extreme resistance or overreaction to minor changes in routines or environment.
11. Emotional constriction or blunted affect.
12. Recurrent pattern of self-abusive behaviors (e.g., head banging or biting or burning self).

__. _____
   _____
   _____
__. _____
   _____
   _____
__. _____
   _____

LONG-TERM GOALS

1. Develop basic language skills and the ability to communicate simply with others.
2. Establish and maintain a basic emotional bond with primary attachment figures.
3. Achieve the educational, behavioral, and social goals identified on the individualized educational plan (IEP).
4. Family members develop acceptance of the client's overall capabilities and place realistic expectations on his/her behavior.
5. Engage in reciprocal and cooperative interactions with others on a regular basis.
6. Stabilize mood and tolerate changes in routine or environment.
7. Eliminate all self-abusive behaviors.
8. Attain and maintain the highest realistic level of independent functioning.

__. _____

_____

__. _____

_____

__. _____

_____

SHORT-TERM OBJECTIVES	THERAPEUTIC INTERVENTIONS
1. Cooperate with and complete all recommended evaluations and testing. (1, 2, 3, 4)	1. Arrange for an intellectual and cognitive assessment to gain greater insights into the client's strengths and weaknesses; provide feedback to the parents.
	2. Refer the client for a speech/language evaluation; consult with the speech/language pathologist about the evaluation findings.
	3. Arrange for a neurological evaluation or neuropsychological testing of the client

to rule out organic factors.

4. Arrange for a psychiatric evaluation of the client.

2. Comply fully with the recommendations offered by the assessment(s) and individualized educational planning committee (IEPC). (5)

5. Attend an IEPC review to establish the client's eligibility for special education services, to update and revise educational interventions, and to establish new behavioral and educational goals.

3. Comply with the move to an appropriate classroom setting. (6)

6. Consult with the parents, teachers, and other appropriate school officials about designing effective learning programs, classroom assignments, or interventions that build on the client's strengths and compensate for weaknesses.

4. Comply with the move to an appropriate alternative residential placement setting. (7)

7. Consult with the parents, school officials, and mental health professionals about the need to place the client in an alternative residential setting (e.g., foster care, group home, or residential program).

5. Attend speech and language therapy sessions. (8)

8. Refer the client to a speech/language pathologist for ongoing services to improve his/her speech and language abilities.

6. Increase the frequency of appropriate, spontaneous verbalizations toward the therapist, family members, and others. (9, 10, 11)

9. Actively build the level of trust with the client through consistent eye contact, frequent attention and interest, unconditional positive regard, and warm acceptance to facilitate increased communication.

10. Employ frequent use of praise and positive reinforcement to increase the client's initiation of verbalizations as well as acknowledgment of and responsiveness to others' verbalizations.

11. Provide the parents with encouragement, support, and reinforcement or modeling methods to foster the client's language development.

7. Decrease oddities or peculiarities in speech and language. (12)

12. In conjunction with the speech therapist, design and implement a response-shaping program using positive reinforcement principles to facilitate the client's language development and decrease oddities or peculiarities in speech and language.

8. Decrease the frequency and severity of temper outbursts and aggressive and self-abusive behaviors. (13, 14, 15, 16, 17)

13. Teach the parents behavior management techniques (e.g., time-out, response cost, overcorrection, removal of privileges) to decrease the client's idiosyncratic speech, excessive self-stimulation temper outbursts, and self-abusive behaviors.

14. Design a token economy for use in the home, classroom, or residential program to improve the client's social skills, anger management, impulse control, and speech/language abilities.

15. Develop a reward system or contingency contract to improve the client's social skills and anger control.

16. Teach the proper use of aversive therapy techniques to stop or limit the client's self-abusive or self-stimulating behaviors.

17. Counsel the parents to develop interventions to manage the client's self-abusive behaviors, including positive reinforcement, response cost, and, if necessary, physical restraint.

9. Parents verbalize increased knowledge and understanding of autism and pervasive developmental disorders. (18)

18. Educate the client's parents and family members about the maturation process in individuals with autism or pervasive developmental disorders and the challenges that this process presents.

10. Parents increase social support network. (19, 20)

19. Direct the parents to join the Autism Society of America to expand their social network, to gain additional knowledge of the disorder, and to give them support and encouragement.

20. Refer the client's parents to a support group for parents of autistic children.

11. Parents utilize respite care to reduce stress related to being caregiver(s). (21)

21. Refer the parents to, and encourage them to use, respite care for the client on a periodic basis.

12. Demonstrate essential self-care and independent living skills. (22, 23, 24)

22. Counsel the parents about teaching the client essential self-care skills (e.g., combing hair, bathing, brushing teeth).

23. Monitor and provide frequency feedback to the client regarding his/her progress toward developing self-care skills.

24. Use operant conditioning principles and response-shaping techniques to help the client develop self-help skills (e.g., dressing self, making bed, fixing sandwich) and improve personal hygiene.

13. Parent and siblings report feeling a closer bond with the client. (25, 26)

25. Conduct family therapy sessions to provide the parents and siblings with the opportunity to share and work through their feelings pertaining to the client's autism or pervasive developmental disorder.

26. Assign the client and his/her parents a task (e.g., swimming, riding a bike) that will help build trust and mutual dependence.

14. Increase the frequency of positive interactions with parents and siblings. (27, 28)

27. Encourage the family members to regularly include the client in structured work or play activities for 20 minutes each day.

28. Encourage detached parents to increase their involvement in the client's daily life, leisure activities, or schoolwork.

15. Channel strengths or areas of interest into a positive, constructive activity. (29, 30)

29. Redirect the client's preoccupation with a single object or restricted area of interest to turn it into a productive activity (e.g., learning to tune instruments or using interest with numbers to learn how to budget allowance money).

30. Employ applied behavior analysis in home, school, or residential setting to alter maladaptive behaviors. First, define and operationalize target behaviors. Next, select antecedents and consequences for specific behaviors. Then, observe and record the client's response to reinforcement interventions. Finally, analyze data to assess treatment effectiveness.

16. Increase the frequency of social contacts with peers. (31, 32)

31. Consult with the client's parents and teachers about increasing the frequency of the client's social contacts with his/her peers (working with student aide in class, attending Sunday school, participating in Special Olympics).

32. Refer the client to a summer camp program to foster social contacts.

17. Attend vocational training sessions. (33, 34)

33. Refer the client to a sheltered workshop or vocational training program to develop basic job skills.

34. Help the family to arrange an interview for the client's

18. Attend a program to build skills for independent activities of daily living. (35)

19. Parents verbalize their fears regarding the client living independent of them. (36)

20. Parents develop and implement a step program for moving the client toward establishing independent status. (37, 38, 39)

possible placement in a school-based vocational training program.

35. Refer the client to a life or daily skills program that builds competency in budgeting, cooking, shopping, and other skills required to maintain an independent living arrangement.

36. Help the parents and family process their concerns and fears about the client living independently from them.

37. Work with the family and parents to develop a step program that will move the client toward working and living independently.

38. Coach and monitor the parents and the client in implementing a plan for the client to live independently.

39. Assist the family in finding a group home or supervised living program (e.g., an apartment with an on-site manager) for the client to establish his/her independence from the family.

__. _____   __. _____
    _____   _____

__. _____   __. _____
    _____   _____

__. _____   __. _____
    _____   _____

DIAGNOSTIC SUGGESTIONS

Axis I:

299.00	Autistic Disorder
299.80	Pervasive Developmental Disorder NOS
299.80	Rett's Disorder
299.10	Childhood Disintegrative Disorder
299.80	Asperger's Disorder
307.3	Stereotypic Movement Disorder
295.xx	Schizophrenia
_____	_____
_____	_____

Axis II:

317	Mild Mental Retardation
319	Mental Retardation, Severity Unspecified
799.9	Diagnosis Deferred
V71.09	No Diagnosis on Axis II
_____	_____
_____	_____

BLENDED FAMILY

BEHAVIORAL DEFINITIONS

1. Children from a previous union of respective parents are brought into a single family unit, resulting in interpersonal conflict, anger, and frustration.
2. Resistance and defiance on the part of a child toward his/her new stepparent.
3. Open conflict between siblings with different parents now residing as siblings in the same family system.
4. Overt or covert defiance of the stepparent by one or several siblings.
5. Verbal threats to the biological parent of going to live with the other parent, report abuse, and so on.
6. Interference from ex-spouse in the daily life of the new family system.
7. Anxiety and concern by both new partners regarding bringing their two families together.
8. No clear lines of communication or responsibilities assigned within the blended family, making for confusion, frustration, and unhappiness.
9. Internal conflicts regarding loyalty to the noncustodial parent result in distance from the stepparent.

—. _____
   _____
—. _____
   _____
—. _____
   _____

LONG-TERM GOALS

1. Achieve a reasonable level of family connectedness and harmony whereby members support, help, and are concerned for each other.
2. Become an integrated blended family system that is functional and in which members are bonded to each other.
3. Attain a level of peaceful coexistence where daily issues can be negotiated without becoming ongoing conflicts.
4. Accept the stepparent and/or stepsiblings and treat them with respect, kindness, and cordiality.
5. Establish a new family identity in which each member feels he/she belongs and is valued.
6. Accept the new blended family system as not inferior to the nuclear family, just different.
7. Establish a strong bond between the couple as a parenting team that is free from triangulation and is able to bring stabilization to the family.

—. _____
_____
_____

—. _____
_____
_____

—. _____
_____

SHORT-TERM OBJECTIVES	THERAPEUTIC INTERVENTIONS
1. Each family member openly shares thoughts and feelings regarding the blended family. (1)	1. Actively build the level of trust with each family member within family therapy sessions through consistent eye contact, active listening, unconditional positive regard, and acceptance to allow each family member to identify and express openly his/her thoughts and feelings regarding the blended family.

2. Attend and actively take part in family or sibling group sessions. (2, 3)

2. Conduct family, sibling, and marital sessions to address the issues of loss, conflict negotiation, parenting, stepfamily psychoeducation, joining, rituals, and relationship building.

3. Utilize an exercise with a set of markers and a large sheet of drawing paper in a family session. The therapist indicates that everyone is going to make a drawing and begins by making a scribble line on the paper, then has each family member add to the line using a colored marker of his/her choice. When the drawing is complete, the family is given the chance to either interpret the drawing individually or develop a mutual story based on the drawing (see Lowe in *101 Favorite Play Therapy Techniques* by Kaduson and Schaefer).

3. Family members verbalize realistic expectations and rejection of myths regarding stepfamilies. (4, 5, 6)

4. Within a family session, ask each member to list his/her expectations for the new family. Members will share and process their lists with the whole family and the therapist.

5. Remind family members that "instant love" of new family members is a myth. It is unrealistic to expect children to immediately like

4. Family members identify losses/changes in each of their lives. (2, 7, 8)

5. Family members demonstrate increased skills in recognizing and expressing feelings. (9, 10, 11)

(and certainly to love) the partner who is serving in the new-parent role.

6. Help family members accept the position that siblings from different biological families need not like or love one another, but that they should be mutually respectful and kind.

2. Conduct family, sibling, and marital sessions to address the issues of loss, conflict negotiation, parenting, stepfamily psychoeducation, joining, rituals, and relationship building.

7. Assign siblings to complete a list of losses and changes each has experienced for the last year and then for all years. Give empathetic confirmation while they share their lists in session and help them see the similarity in their experiences to those of the other siblings.

8. Ask the family to read *Changing Families: An Interactive Guide for Kids and Grownups* (Fassler, Lash, and Ives) to help them identify the changes within the family and give them ways to adjust and thrive.

9. Have the family or siblings play The Ungame (Zakich; available from The Ungame Company) or The Talking,

Feeling, and Doing Game (Gardner; available from Childswork/Childsplay) to promote family members' awareness of self and their feelings.

10. Provide education to the family on identifying, labeling, and expressing feelings appropriately.

11. Help the family practice identifying and expressing feelings by doing a feelings exercise (e.g., "I feel sad when _____," "I feel excited when _____") in a family session. The therapist models affirming and acknowledging each member as he/she shares during the exercise.

6. Family members verbalize expanded knowledge of stepfamilies. (12, 13, 14)

12. Suggest that the parents and teen read material to expand their knowledge of stepfamilies and their development (e.g., *Stepfamily Realities* by Newman) or *Stepfamilies Stepping Ahead* by Burt).

13. Refer parents to the Stepfamily Association of America (1-800-735-0329) to obtain additional information and resources on stepfamilies.

14. Assign the parents to read *How to Win as a Stepfamily* (Visher and Visher) and process the key concepts they gather from the reading.

7. Family members demonstrate increased negotiating skills. (15, 16)

8. Family members report a reduced level of tension between all members. (17, 18, 19)

15. Train family members in building negotiating skills (e.g., problem identification, brainstorming solutions, evaluating pros and cons, compromising, agreeing on a selected solution, making an implementation plan) and have them practice these skills on issues that present in family sessions.

16. Ask siblings to specify their conflicts and suggest solutions (or assign the exercise "Negotiating a Peace Treaty" from the *Brief Adolescent Therapy Homework Planner* by Jongsma, Peterson, and McInnis).

17. Inject humor whenever appropriate in family or sibling sessions to decrease tensions and conflict and to model balance and perspective. Give positive feedback to members who create appropriate humor.

18. Hold a family sibling session in which each child lists and verbalizes an appreciation of each sibling's unique traits or abilities (or assign the exercise "Cloning the Perfect Sibling" from the *Brief Adolescent Therapy Homework Planner* by Jongsma, Peterson, and McInnis).

19. Utilize a brief solution-focused intervention of reframing or normalizing the

conflictual situation as a stage that the family needs to get through. Identify the next stage as the coming together stage, and talk about when they might be ready to move there and how they could start to head there (see *A Guide to Possibility Land* by O'Hanlon and Beadle).

9. Family members report increased trust of each other. (20, 21)

20. Read and process with the family the story *Stone Soup* (Brown), focusing on the issues of risk, mistrust, and cooperation.

21. Read Dr. Seuss's *The Sneetches* in a family session to seed with members the folly of top dog, low dog, one-upmanship, and insider-outsider attitudes.

10. Each parent takes primary role of discipline with own children. (22)

22. Encourage each parent to take the primary role in disciplining his/her own children and refrain from all negative references to ex-spouses.

11. The parents attend a step-parenting didactic group to increase parenting skills. (23)

23. Refer the parents to a parenting group for stepparents.

12. Family members attend weekly family meeting in the home to express feelings and voice issues. (24)

24. Assist the parents in implementing a once-a-week family meeting in which issues can be raised and resolved and where members are encouraged to share their thoughts, complaints, and compliments.

13. The parents create and institute new family rituals. (25, 26, 27)

14. The parents identify and eliminate triangulation within the system. (28)

15. The parents report a strengthening of their marital bond. (29, 30, 31)

25. Encourage the parents to create and implement daily rituals (e.g., mealtimes, bedtime stories, household chores, time alone with parents, and time together) in order to give structure and connection to the system.

26. Conduct a family session where rituals from both former families are examined. Then work with the family to retain the rituals that are appropriate and will work in the new system and create the necessary new ones to fill in any gaps.

27. Give the family the assignment to create birthday rituals for their new blended unit in a family session.

28. Provide education to the parents on patterns of interactions within families, focusing on the pattern of triangulation and its dysfunctional aspects.

29. Refer the couple to skills-based marital therapy based on strengthening avenues of responsibilities, communication, and conflict resolution (see *PREP— Fighting for Your Marriage* by Markman, Stanley, and Blumberg).

30. Work with the parents in conjoint sessions to deal with issues of time away

alone, privacy, and individual space; develop specific ways for these things to regularly occur.

31. Hold conjoint sessions with the parents to process the issue of showing affection toward each other. Help the parents develop appropriate boundaries and ways of showing affection that do not give rise to unnecessary anger in their children.

16. The parents spend one-on-one time with each child. (32)

32. Work with the parents to build into each of their schedules one-on-one time with each child and stepchild in order to give each child undivided attention and to build and maintain relationships.

17. Family members report a slow development of bonds between each member. (33, 34, 35)

33. Refer the family members to an initiatives camp weekend to increase their skills in working cooperatively and conflict resolution and their sense of trust. Process the experience with the family in the next family session.

34. Complete and process with the siblings a cost-benefit analysis (see *Ten Days to Self-Esteem* by Burns) to evaluate the pluses and minuses of becoming a family or resisting. Use a positive outcome to move beyond resistance to begin the process of joining.

35. Emphasize and model in family, sibling, and couple sessions the need for family members to build their new relationships slowly, allowing everyone time and space to adjust and develop a level of trust with each other.

18. Family members report an increased sense of loyalty and connectedness. (33, 36, 37)

33. Refer the family members to an initiatives camp weekend to increase their skills in working cooperatively and conflict resolution and their sense of trust. Process the experience with the family in the next family session.

36. Conduct family sessions in which a genogram is developed for the entire new family system to show everyone how they are connected.

37. Give a family session assignment to design a family coat of arms on poster board. The coat of arms is to reflect where the family members came from and where they are now. Process this experience when completed, and then have the family display the poster at home.

__. _____
   _____
__. _____
   _____
__. _____
   _____

__. _____
   _____
__. _____
   _____
__. _____
   _____

DIAGNOSTIC SUGGESTIONS

Axis I:	309.0	Adjustment Disorder With Depressed Mood
	309.3	Adjustment Disorder With Disturbance of Conduct
	309.24	Adjustment Disorder With Anxiety
	309.81	Posttraumatic Stress Disorder
	300.4	Dysthymic Disorder
	V62.81	Relational Problem NOS
	_____	_____
	_____	_____
Axis II:	799.9	Diagnosis Deferred
	V71.09	No Diagnosis
	_____	_____
	_____	_____

CHEMICAL DEPENDENCE

BEHAVIORAL DEFINITIONS

1. Self-report of almost daily use of alcohol or illicit drugs or regularly using until intoxicated.
2. Caught or observed intoxicated and/or high on two or more occasions.
3. Changing peer groups to one that is noticeably oriented toward regular use of alcohol and/or illicit drugs.
4. Drug paraphernalia and/or alcohol found in the client's possession or in his/her personal area (e.g., bedroom, car, school locker, backpack).
5. Marked change in behavior (e.g., isolation or withdrawal from family and close friends, loss of interest in activities, low energy, sleeping more, or a drop in school grades).
6. Physical withdrawal symptoms (shaking, seizures, nausea, headaches, sweating, anxiety, insomnia, and/or depression).
7. Continued substance use despite persistent physical, legal, financial, vocational, social, or relationship problems that are directly caused by the substance use.
8. Mood swings.
9. Absent, tardy, or skipping school on a regular basis.
10. Poor self-image as evidenced by describing self as a loser or a failure, and rarely making eye contact when talking to others.
11. Predominately negative or hostile outlook on life and other people.
12. Has been caught stealing alcohol from a store, the home of friends, or parents.
13. Has been arrested for minor in possession, driving under the influence, or drunk and disorderly charges.

14. Positive family history of chemical dependence.

__. _____

_____

__. _____

_____

__. _____

_____

LONG-TERM GOALS

1. Confirm or rule out the existence of chemical dependence.
2. Maintain total abstinence from all mood-altering substances while developing an active recovery program.
3. Reestablish sobriety while developing a plan for addressing relapse issues.
4. Confirm and address chemical dependence as a family issue.
5. Develop the skills that are essential to maintaining a drug-free life.
6. Reduce level of family stress related to chemical dependence.
7. Reestablish connections with relationships and groups that will support and enhance ongoing recovery from chemical dependence.
8. Develop an understanding of the pattern of relapse and strategies for coping effectively to help sustain long-term recovery.

__. _____

_____

__. _____

_____

__. _____

_____

SHORT-TERM OBJECTIVES

1. Complete an evaluation for chemical dependence and comply with all the recommendations of the evaluation. (1, 2)

2. Sign a written agreement to refrain from the use of all alcohol and illicit chemicals. (3)

3. Comply with any requests for drug screens. (4)

4. Acknowledge honestly (without denial) the destructive pattern of chemical usage and the life problems it causes. (5, 6, 7)

THERAPEUTIC INTERVENTIONS

1. Conduct or arrange for a complete chemical dependence evaluation that assesses substance abuse history, frequency, nature of the drug used, peer use, physiological dependence signs, family use, and so on.

2. Present findings and recommendations of the substance abuse evaluation to the client and family; encourage compliance and assist them in finding an appropriate program and support groups for their recovery.

3. Assist the client and family in developing an agreement for the client to refrain from all substance use. Then ask the client to assent to the agreement by signing it.

4. Arrange for drug screens through laboratory tests and monitor them.

5. Explore with the client his/her history, frequency, and pattern of substance use in individual or group sessions.

6. Confront denial with the facts of use and its negative consequences until the client comes to an acceptance of his/her chemical dependence.

7. Assign the client to complete an Alcoholics Anonymous (AA) first-step paper and present it to the group or the therapist for feedback.

5. Complete a genogram that identifies members who are chemically dependent and family relationship patterns. (8)

8. Conduct a session that develops a genogram for the client and his/her family, focusing on the existence of chemical dependence and/or mood disorders in the immediate and extended family.

6. Acknowledge negative consequences of alcohol and/or drug use as seen by others. (9)

9. Assign the client to ask two or three people who are close to him/her to write letters to the therapist in which they identify how they saw the client's chemical dependence negatively impacting his/her life.

7. Verbally acknowledge and accept being chemically dependent and in need of help. (7, 10)

7. Assign the client to complete an AA first-step paper and present it to the group or the therapist for feedback.

10. Ask the client to make a list of the ways that chemical use has negatively impacted his/her life; process the list with the client.

8. Verbalize increased knowledge of the addiction and the recovery process. (11, 12, 13)

11. Assign the client to read pages 1 to 52 of *Alcoholics Anonymous: the Big Book* (Alcoholics Anonymous) to teach the client the terminology of addiction and the process of recovery (and/or assign the exercise "Welcome to Recovery" from the

Brief Adolescent Therapy Homework Planner by Jongsma, Peterson, and McInnis).

12. Require the client to attend all chemical dependence didactics and to identify, with the therapist, several key points attained from each didactic and process point.

13. Ask the client to read *POT* by Ohm or another specific cannabis article and process with the therapist five key points gained from the reading.

9. Write a good-bye letter to the drug of choice. (14)

14. Direct the client to write a good-bye letter to the drug of choice; read it and process the related feelings with the therapist.

10. Establish regular attendance at support group meetings. (15, 16)

15. Recommend that the client attend Narcotics Anonymous (NA) or Young People's AA meetings and report to the therapist the impact of the meetings.

16. Assign the client to meet with an NA or AA member who has been working with a 12-step program for several years and find out specifically how the program helped him/her stay sober. Afterward, process the meeting with the therapist.

11. Solicit the services of two AA sponsors and meet with them weekly. (17)

17. Encourage the client to find two temporary sponsors and meet with them weekly. The therapist will monitor and process the results.

12. Identify any signs or symptoms of depression that predate substance abuse. (18, 19)

18. Assess the client's feelings of depression and low self-esteem that may underlie chemical abuse; conduct or refer for treatment of mood disorder if indicated (see Depression chapter in this Planner).

19. Refer the client to a psychiatrist for evaluation for an antidepressant or other appropriate medication that may assist him/her in staying sober by treating an underlying mood disorder or by reducing impulsivity.

13. Identify positive traits about self. (20, 21)

20. Ask the client to obtain three letters of recommendation from adults he/she knows. The letters are to be sent directly to the therapist (who provides three addressed, stamped envelopes). Each is then opened and read with the therapist.

21. Assign a mirror exercise in which the client looks daily into a mirror for two minutes and then records all that he/she sees there. Repeat the exercise the second week, increasing the daily time to four minutes, and have the client look for and record only the positive things he/she sees. Process the recordings and the experience afterward with the therapist.

14. Practice stopping, thinking, listening, and planning before acting. (22)

22. Use modeling, role playing, and behavioral rehearsal to teach the client how to implement the "stop, think, listen, and plan before acting" technique in day-to-day situations. Review its use by the client in day-to-day life, identifying the positive results.

15. Verbally identify several occasions when impulsive action led to substance abuse and subsequent negative consequences. (23, 24)

23. Assign the client to write a list of negative consequences that occurred because of impulsivity and substance abuse. Then help him/her make key connections between impulsivity, substance abuse, and negative consequences.

24. Explore the client's history of impulsive actions that have resulted in substance abuse and negative consequences, helping him/her to see how dangerous it is to act impulsively.

16. Cooperate with a referral for acupuncture treatment. (25)

25. Refer the client to an acupuncturist for treatment on a regular basis and monitor its effectiveness.

17. Complete a psychiatric evaluation for psychotropic medications. (19)

19. Refer the client to a psychiatrist for evaluation for an antidepressant or other appropriate medication that may assist him/her in staying sober by treating an underlying mood disorder or by reducing impulsivity.

18. Take medication as directed by the physician and report any side effects. (26)

26. Monitor the client for medication compliance, side effects, and effectiveness.

Answer any questions regarding the medication that the client has, and confer with the prescribing psychiatrist.

19. Break ties with friends who use mood-altering substances and develop new friendships with those peers who will support and encourage sobriety. (27, 28)

27. Assist the client in developing social skills that will help him/her make friendships with drug-free peers. Use role plays and one-to-one dialogues to give him/her experience and to enhance his/her confidence level.

28. Encourage the client's involvement in extracurricular social, athletic, or artistic activities with a positive peer group that expands interests beyond hanging out.

20. Identify family dynamics and interpersonal stressors that are relapse triggers. (29, 30)

29. Process feelings of rejection from the client's family and/or friends that could cause escape into chemical dependence.

30. Assist the client in developing strategies to cope effectively with family dynamics that trigger use.

21. Develop a list of personal relapse triggers and strategies for coping effectively with each trigger. (31, 32, 33)

31. Assist the client in identifying relapse triggers and in developing strategies for handling each effectively (or assign the exercise "Keeping Straight" from the *Brief Adolescent Therapy Homework Planner* by Jongsma, Peterson, and McInnis).

32. Direct the client to attend a group or lecture series on substance abuse relapse.

33. Use the story of The Three Little Pigs as a metaphor for recovery by reading the story with the client, then eliciting the key points of the story (e.g., planning, delaying gratification, frustration tolerance, and the message that the big bad wolf is always at the door) and connecting each to recovery and relapse. Assist the client in further identifying what his/her "big bad wolf" is and in always remembering that message.

22. Increase the client's awareness of thinking errors and their connection to relapse. (34, 35, 36)

34. Assign the client to read *It Will Never Happen to Me* (Black) and process five key items from the book with the therapist or group.

35. Assist the client in identifying "thinking errors" (e.g., "I can use just a little this one time; I can control it now; I deserve a little fun; one drink will help me relax to talk to people more easily.").

36. Assign the client to bring up the topic of "thinking errors" or "stinking thinking" at an AA or NA meeting or in a one-to-one contact with his/her sponsor. Afterward, process the gathered information with the therapist.

23. Develop a written relapse prevention or aftercare plan that supports maintaining sobriety. (37, 38)

37. Help the client design and implement a daily schedule or routine, making sure key elements of regular meal- and bedtimes, medication, work, exercise, and meetings are included. Monitor for implementation and follow-through, redirecting as needed.

38. Assign the client to write a personalized relapse/aftercare plan and process the completed plan with the therapist and sponsor.

24. Family members verbalize an understanding of their role in the disease, including their enabling, and their role in the process of recovery. (39, 40)

39. Assign appropriate readings or attendance in a family education component of a chemical dependency program that will increase each member's knowledge of the disease and recovery process (e.g., *Bradshaw on the Family* by Bradshaw, *Adult Children of Alcoholics* by Woititz, or *It Will Never Happen to Me* by Black).

40. Direct the family to attend Al-Anon, *Nar-Anon,* or Tough Love meetings.

25. Family members develop the skills to implement the techniques involved in "tough love." (40, 41, 42)

40. Direct the family to attend Al-Anon, *Nar-Anon,* or Tough Love meetings.

41. Educate the family on the dynamics of enabling the client to continue substance abuse and the need for "tough love." Therapist will follow up by monitoring the family for enabling behaviors in family sessions,

redirecting them when necessary.

42. Assist the client's family members in implementing and sticking with "tough love" techniques.

26. Each family member develops his/her own relapse plan in writing and shares it with the chemically dependent member. (43, 44)

43. Assist the parents in ridding the house of any substances or connected things that could hinder or threaten the client in establishing and maintaining his/her sobriety.

44. Help the family members develop their own individual relapse plans and facilitate a session where the plans are shared with the chemically dependent member.

27. Parents implement child-rearing techniques that are respectful and reasonable and that encourage personal responsibility and growth. (45)

45. Assess the parents' techniques of parenting in order to eliminate or adjust interventions that bring out revenge and rebellion or reduce self-esteem. Train them in intervening as parents in a responsive, respectful, reasonable, yet firm manner.

__. _____
    _____

__. _____
    _____

__. _____
    _____

__. _____
    _____

__. _____
    _____

__. _____
    _____

DIAGNOSTIC SUGGESTIONS

Axis I:	305.00	Alcohol Abuse
	303.90	Alcohol Dependence
	305.20	Cannabis Abuse
	304.30	Cannabis Dependence
	304.20	Cocaine Dependence
	304.50	Hallucinogen Dependence
	305.30	Hallucinogen Abuse
	313.81	Oppositional Defiant Disorder
	312.81 or 2	Conduct Disorder
	300.4	Dysthymic Disorder
	309.28	Adjustment Disorder With Mixed Anxiety and Depressed Mood
	309.4	Adjustment Disorder With Mixed Disturbance of Emotions and Conduct
	_____	_____
	_____	_____
Axis II:	799.9	Diagnosis Deferred
	V71.09	No Diagnosis
	_____	_____
	_____	_____

CONDUCT DISORDER/DELINQUENCY

BEHAVIORAL DEFINITIONS

1. Persistent refusal to comply with rules or expectations in the home, school, or community.
2. Excessive fighting, intimidation of others, cruelty or violence toward people or animals, and destruction of property.
3. History of stealing at home, at school, or in the community.
4. School adjustment characterized by disrespectful attitude toward authority figures, frequent disruptive behaviors, and detentions or suspensions for misbehavior.
5. Repeated conflict with authority figures at home, at school, or in the community.
6. Impulsivity as manifested by poor judgment, taking inappropriate risks, and failing to stop and think about consequences of actions.
7. Numerous attempts to deceive others through lying, conning, or manipulating.
8. Consistent failure to accept responsibility for misbehavior accompanied by a pattern of blaming others.
9. Little or no remorse for misbehavior.
10. Lack of sensitivity to the thoughts, feelings, and needs of other people.
11. Multiple sexual partners, lack of emotional commitment, and engaging in unsafe sexual practices.
12. Use of mood-altering substances on a regular basis.
13. Participation in gang membership and activities.

—. _____
   _____

—. _____
   _____

—. _____

_____

LONG-TERM GOALS

1. Comply with rules and expectations in the home, school, and community on a consistent basis.
2. Eliminate all illegal and antisocial behavior.
3. Terminate all acts of violence or cruelty toward people or animals and the destruction of property.
4. Demonstrate marked improvement in impulse control.
5. Express anger in a controlled, respectful manner on a consistent basis.
6. Resolve the core conflicts that contribute to the emergence of conduct problems.
7. Parents establish and maintain appropriate parent-child boundaries, setting firm, consistent limits when the client acts out in an aggressive or rebellious manner.
8. Demonstrate empathy, concern, and sensitivity for the thoughts, feelings, and needs of others on a regular basis.

—. _____

_____

—. _____

_____

—. _____

_____

SHORT-TERM OBJECTIVES

1. Complete psychological testing. (1)

THERAPEUTIC INTERVENTIONS

1. Arrange for psychological testing of the client to assess whether emotional factors or Attention-Deficit/ Hyperactivity Disorder (ADHD) are contributing to his/her impulsivity and acting-out behaviors; provide feedback to the client and his/her parents.

2. Complete a substance abuse evaluation and comply with the recommendations offered by the evaluation findings. (2)

3. Cooperate with the requirements mandated by the criminal justice system. (3, 4, 5)

2. Conduct or arrange for a substance abuse evaluation and/or treatment for the client (see Chemical Dependence chapter in this *Planner*).

3. Consult with criminal justice officials about the appropriate consequences for the client's antisocial behaviors (e.g., paying restitution, performing community service, serving probation).

4. Encourage and challenge the parents not to protect the client from the legal consequences of his/her antisocial behaviors.

5. Consult with parents, school officials, and criminal justice officials about the need to place the client in an alternative setting (e.g., foster home, group home, or residential program).

4. Recognize and verbalize how feelings are connected to misbehavior. (6, 7)

6. Actively build the level of trust with the client through consistent eye contact, active listening, unconditional positive regard, and warm acceptance to help increase his/her ability to identify and express feelings instead of acting them out.

7. Assist the client in making a connection between his/her feelings and reactive behaviors.

5. Increase the number of statements that reflect the acceptance of responsibility for misbehavior. (8, 9, 10)

8. Firmly confront the client's antisocial behavior and attitude, pointing out consequences for himself/herself and others.

9. Confront statements in which the client lies and/or blames others for his/her misbehaviors and fails to accept responsibility for his/her actions.

10. Explore and process the factors that contribute to the client's pattern of blaming others (e.g., harsh punishment experiences, family pattern of blaming others).

6. Express anger through appropriate verbalizations and healthy physical outlets. (11, 12, 13)

11. Teach the client mediational and self-control strategies (e.g., relaxation, "stop, look, listen, and think") to help him/her express anger in a controlled, respectful manner.

12. Teach the client effective communication and assertiveness skills to express feelings in a controlled fashion and to meet his/her needs through more constructive actions.

13. Train the client in the use of guided imagery or relaxation techniques to help control his/her anger.

7. Reduce the frequency and severity of aggressive, destructive, and antisocial behaviors. (11, 14)

11. Teach the client mediational and self-control strategies (e.g., relaxation, "stop, look, listen, and think") to help him/her

express anger in a controlled, respectful manner.

14. Assist the client in identifying core issues that contribute to the emergence of angry outbursts or aggressive behaviors (or employ the "Anger Control" exercise in the *Brief Adolescent Therapy Homework Planner* by Jongsma, Peterson, and McInnis).

8. Parents establish appropriate boundaries, develop clear rules, and follow through consistently with consequences for misbehavior. (15, 16)

15. Assist the client's parents in establishing clearly defined rules, boundaries, and consequences for misbehavior; ask the client to repeat the rules to demonstrate an understanding of the expectations.

16. Assist the parents in increasing structure to help the client learn to delay gratification for longer-term goals (e.g., completing homework or chores before playing basketball).

9. The client and parents agree to and follow through with the implementation of a reward system, contingency contract, or token economy. (17, 18)

17. Design a reward system and/or contingency contract for the client to reinforce identified positive behaviors at home and school and deter impulsive or rebellious behaviors.

18. Design and implement a token economy to increase the client's positive social behaviors and deter impulsive, acting-out behaviors.

10. Parents increase the frequency of praise and positive reinforcement to the client. (19, 20)

19. Encourage the parents to provide frequent praise and positive reinforcement for the client's positive social behaviors and good impulse control.

20. Instruct the parents to observe and record positive behaviors by the client between therapy sessions; reinforce and encourage the client to continue to engage in these behaviors in the future.

11. Increase compliance with rules at home and school. (17, 21, 22)

17. Design a reward system and/or contingency contract for the client to reinforce identified positive behaviors at home and school and deter impulsive or rebellious behaviors.

21. Assign the client's parents to read material to help them learn to resolve conflict with adolescents more effectively (e.g., *Negotiating Parent/Adolescent Conflict* by Robin and Foster); process the ideas learned from the reading.

22. Disrupt the pattern of the client challenging and defying authority figures by prescribing the symptom. Direct the client to argue with authority figures at a specific time each day to reduce his/her need to argue other issues.

12. Identify family dynamics or stressors that contribute to the emergence of behavioral problems. (23, 24)

23. Conduct family therapy sessions to explore the dynamics that contribute to the

emergence of the client's behavioral problems.

24. Conduct a family therapy session in which the client's family members are given a task or problem to solve together (e.g., building a craft); observe family interactions to assess dynamics; process the experience with them afterward.

13. Increase the time spent with the uninvolved or detached parent(s) in leisure, school, or household activities. (25)

25. Give a directive to uninvolved or disengaged parent(s) to spend more time with the client in leisure, school, or household activities.

14. Parents verbalize appropriate boundaries for discipline to prevent further occurrences of abuse and to ensure the safety of the client and his/her siblings. (26, 27)

26. Explore the client's family background for a history of neglect and physical or sexual abuse that may contribute to his/her behavioral problems.

27. Confront the client's parents to cease physically abusive or overly punitive methods of discipline; implement the steps necessary to protect the client or siblings from further abuse (e.g., report abuse to the appropriate agencies; remove the client or perpetrator from the home).

15. Identify and verbally express feelings associated with past neglect, abuse, separation, or abandonment. (28, 29)

28. Encourage and support the client in expressing feelings associated with neglect, abuse, separation, or abandonment.

29. Assign the client the task of writing a letter to an absent

parent or use the empty chair technique to assist the client in expressing and working through feelings of anger and sadness about past abandonment.

16. Actively participate in the group therapy process. (30)

30. Arrange for the client to participate in group therapy to improve his/her social judgment and interpersonal skills.

17. Decrease frequency of lying, conning, and manipulating others. (9, 31)

9. Confront statements in which the client lies and/or blames others for his/her misbehaviors and fails to accept responsibility for his/her actions.

31. Teach the client the value of honesty as a basis for building trust and mutual respect in all relationships.

18. Increase verbalizations of empathy and concern for other people. (32, 33, 34)

32. Use role-playing and role-reversal techniques to help the client develop sensitivity to the feelings of others in reaction to his/her antisocial behaviors.

33. Direct the client to engage in three altruistic or benevolent acts (e.g., read to a developmentally disabled student, mow grandmother's lawn) before the next session to increase his/her empathy and sensitivity to the needs of others.

34. Assign homework designed to increase the client's empathy and sensitivity toward the thoughts, feelings, and needs of others

(e.g., "Headed in the Right Direction" from the *Brief Adolescent Therapy Homework Planner* by Jongsma, Peterson, and McInnis).

19. Increase the frequency of responsible and positive social behaviors. (35, 36, 37)

35. Place the client in charge of tasks at home (e.g., preparing and cooking a special dish for a family get-together, building shelves in the garage, changing oil in the car) to demonstrate confidence in his/her ability to act responsibly.

36. Assign the client to read *Teen's Solution Workbook* (Shapiro) to improve his/her impulse control and problem-solving skills; process material that was read.

37. Explore periods of time during which the client demonstrated good impulse control and behaved responsibly; process responses and reinforce positive coping strategies used to exercise self-control and deter impulsive behaviors.

20. Establish and maintain steady employment. (38, 39)

38. Refer the client to vocational training to develop basic job skills and find employment.

39. Encourage and reinforce the client's acceptance of the responsibility of a job, the authority of a supervisor, and the employer's rules.

21. Identify and verbalize the risks involved in sexually promiscuous behavior. (40, 41)

40. Provide the client with sex education and discus the risks involved with sexually promiscuous behaviors.

	41. Explore the client's feelings, irrational beliefs, and unmet needs that contribute to the emergence of sexually promiscuous behaviors.
22. Parents agree to seek treatment. (42)	42. Assess the marital dyad for possible substance abuse, conflict, or triangulation that shifts the focus from marriage issues to the client's acting-out behaviors; refer for appropriate treatment, if needed.
23. Comply with a physician evaluation and take medication as prescribed. (43)	43. Arrange for a medication evaluation of the client to improve his/her impulse control and stabilize moods; monitor him/her for psychotropic medication prescription compliance, side effects, and effectiveness.

__. _____   __. _____
    _____   _____
__. _____   __. _____
    _____   _____
__. _____   __. _____
    _____   _____

DIAGNOSTIC SUGGESTIONS

Axis I:	312.81	Conduct Disorder/Childhood-Onset Type
	312.82	Conduct Disorder/Adolescent-Onset Type
	313.81	Oppositional Defiant Disorder
	312.9	Disruptive Behavior Disorder NOS
	314.01	Attention-Deficit/Hyperactivity Disorder, Predominantly Hyperactive-Impulsive Type
	314.9	Attention-Deficit/Hyperactivity Disorder NOS
	312.34	Intermittent Explosive Disorder

	V71.02	Child Antisocial Behavior
	V61.20	Parent-Child Relational Problem
	_____	_____
Axis II:	799.9	Diagnosis Deferred
	V71.09	No Diagnosis on Axis II
	_____	_____
	_____	_____

DEPRESSION

BEHAVIORAL DEFINITIONS

1. Sad or flat affect.
2. Preoccupation with the subject of death.
3. Suicidal thoughts and/or actions.
4. Moody irritability.
5. Isolation from family and/or peers.
6. Deterioration in academic performance.
7. Lack of interest in previously enjoyed activities.
8. Refusal to communicate openly.
9. Use of street drugs to elevate mood.
10. Low energy.
11. Little or no eye contact.
12. Frequent verbalizations of low self-esteem.
13. Reduced appetite.
14. Increased sleep.
15. Poor concentration and indecision.
16. Feelings of hopelessness, worthlessness, or inappropriate guilt.
17. Unresolved grief issues.

—. _____
   _____
   _____
—. _____
   _____
   _____
—. _____
   _____

LONG-TERM GOALS

1. Elevate the mood and show evidence of the usual energy, activities, and socialization level.
2. Show a renewed typical interest in academic achievement, social involvement, and eating patterns, as well as occasional expressions of joy and zest for life.
3. Reduce irritability and increase normal social interaction with family and friends.
4. Acknowledge the depression verbally and resolve its causes, leading to normalization of the emotional state.

—. _____
   _____
—. _____
   _____
—. _____
   _____

SHORT-TERM OBJECTIVES

1. Complete psychological testing to evaluate the depth of the depression. (1, 2)

2. State the connection between rebellion, self-destructive behaviors, or withdrawal and the underlying depression. (3, 4, 5, 6)

THERAPEUTIC INTERVENTIONS

1. Arrange for the administration of psychological testing to facilitate a more complete assessment of the depth of the client's depression.

2. Give feedback to the client and his/her family regarding psychological testing results.

3. Assess the client's level of self-understanding about self-defeating behaviors linked to the depression.

4. Interpret the client's acting-out behaviors as a reflection of the depression.

5. Confront the client's acting-out behaviors as avoidance of the real conflict involving his/her unmet emotional needs.

6. Teach the client the connection between angry, irritable behaviors and feelings of hurt and sadness (or assign the exercise "Surface Behavior/Inner Feelings" in the *Brief Adolescent Therapy Homework Planner* by Jongsma, Peterson, and McInnis).

3. Specify what is missing from life to cause the unhappiness. (7, 8, 9)

7. Reinforce the client's open expression of underlying feelings of anger, hurt, and disappointment.

8. Explore the client's fears regarding abandonment or the loss of love from others.

9. Ask the client to discuss what is missing from his/her life that contributes to the unhappiness.

4. Specify what in the past or present life contributes to sadness. (10, 11, 12)

10. Assist the client in identifying his/her unmet emotional needs and specifying ways to meet those needs (or assign the exercise "Unmet Emotional Needs—Identification and Satisfaction" from the *Brief Adolescent Therapy Homework Planner* by Jongsma, Peterson, and McInnis).

11. Probe aspects of the client's current life that contribute to the sadness.

5. Express emotional needs to significant others. (13, 14, 15)

12. Explore the emotional pain from the client's past that contributes to the feelings of hopelessness and low self-esteem.

13. Hold a family therapy session to facilitate the client's expression of conflict with family members.

14. Support the client's respectful expression of emotional needs to family members and significant others.

15. Teach the parents to encourage, support, and tolerate the client's respectful expression of his/her thoughts and feelings.

6. Implement positive self-talk to strengthen feelings of self-acceptance, self-confidence, and hope. (16, 17)

16. Assist in identifying the cognitive messages that the client gives to himself/herself that reinforce helplessness and hopelessness.

17. Teach and reinforce positive cognitive messages that facilitate the growth of the client's self-confidence and self-acceptance.

7. Stop the verbalized interest in the subject of death. (17, 18)

17. Teach and reinforce positive cognitive messages that facilitate the growth of the client's self-confidence and self-acceptance.

18. Reinforce statements of hope for the future and of the desire to live.

8. Terminate suicidal behaviors and/or verbalizations of the desire to die. (19, 20)

19. Monitor the potential for self-harm and refer the client to a protective setting if necessary.

9. Initiate and respond actively to social communication with family and peers. (21)

10. Cooperate with an evaluation of the necessity for psychotropic medications. (22, 23)

11. Take the prescribed psychotropic medication as directed by the physician. (24)

12. Improve academic performance as evidenced by better grades and positive teacher reports. (25, 26)

13. Increase involvement in extracurricular activity within the school setting. (27, 28)

14. Eat nutritious meals regularly without strong urging from others. (29)

15. Adjust sleep hours to those typical of the developmental stage. (30)

20. Contract with the client for no self-harm.

21. Encourage the client's participation in social/recreational activities that enrich life.

22. Assess the client's need for psychotropic medications.

23. Arrange for a prescription of antidepressant medications for the client.

24. Monitor the client's psychotropic medication compliance, effectiveness, and side effects.

25. Challenge and encourage the client's academic effort.

26. Arrange for a tutor to increase the client's sense of academic mastery.

27. Ask the client to list school-related extracurricular activities (e.g., music groups, clubs, sports) that he/she might pursue to break the pattern of social withdrawal and introspective preoccupation.

28. Ask the client to take steps necessary to become involved with extracurricular activities; reinforce increased social activity.

29. Monitor and encourage the client's food consumption.

30. Monitor the client's sleep patterns and the restfulness of sleep.

16. Verbalize a feeling of being loved and accepted by family and friends. (31, 32)

31. Encourage and reinforce the parents in giving warm, positive, affirming expressions of love to the client.

32. Assist the parents in establishing a routine of positive, structured activities with the client (e.g., playing table games, going to the movies together, engaging in a sport together).

17. Describe an interest and participation in social and recreational activities. (33, 34)

33. Explore with the client pleasurable interests and activities that could be pursued; assign participation and process the experience.

34. Urge the client to formulate a plan that leads to taking action to meet his/her social and emotional needs.

18. Reduce anger and irritability as evidenced by friendly, pleasant interactions with family and friends. (13, 35)

13. Hold a family therapy session to facilitate the client's expression of conflict with family members.

35. Reinforce pleasant social interactions between the client and friends and/or family members.

19. Express negative feelings through artistic modalities. (36)

36. Use art therapy techniques (e.g., drawing, coloring, painting, collage, sculpture) to help the client express depressive feelings. Use the client's artistic products as a springboard for further elaboration of emotions and their causes.

20. Verbalize the amount and frequency of alcohol and/or drug use. (37, 38)

37. Assess the client for substance abuse as a means of coping with depressive feelings.

38. Refer the client for treatment or treat his/her substance abuse problems (see Chemical Dependence chapter in this Planner).

21. Describe the degree of sexual activity engaged in. (39)

39. Assess the client for sexual promiscuity as a means of trying to overcome depression; confront and treat sexual acting out (see Sexual Acting Out chapter in this Planner).

22. Identify the losses that have been experienced and the feelings associated with those losses. (40)

40. Assess the client for unresolved grief and loss issues; treat grief issues that underlie his/her depression (see Grief/Loss chapter in this Planner).

—. _____

—. _____

—. _____

—. _____

—. _____

—. _____

DIAGNOSTIC SUGGESTIONS

Axis I:	300.4	Dysthymic Disorder
	296.2x	Major Depressive Disorder, Single Episode
	296.3x	Major Depressive Disorder, Recurrent
	296.89	Bipolar II Disorder
	296.xx	Bipolar I Disorder
	301.13	Cyclothymic Disorder
	309.0	Adjustment Disorder With Depressed Mood

	310.1	Personality Change Due to (Axis III Disorder)
	V62.82	Bereavement
	_____	_____
	_____	_____
Axis II:	799.9	Diagnosis Deferred
	V71.09	No Diagnosis on Axis II
	_____	_____
	_____	_____

DIVORCE REACTION

BEHAVIORAL DEFINITIONS

1. Infrequent contact or loss of contact with a parental figure due to separation or divorce.
2. Intense emotional outbursts (e.g., crying, yelling, swearing) and sudden shifts in mood due to significant change in the family system.
3. Excessive use of alcohol and drugs as a maladaptive coping mechanism to ward off painful emotions surrounding separation or divorce.
4. Strong feelings of grief and sadness combined with feelings of low self-worth, lack of confidence, social withdrawal, and loss of interest in activities that normally bring pleasure.
5. Feelings of guilt accompanied by the unreasonable belief of having behaved in some manner to cause the parents' divorce and/or failing to prevent the divorce from occurring.
6. Marked increase in frequency and severity of acting-out, oppositional, and aggressive behaviors since the onset of the parents' marital problems, separation, or divorce.
7. Significant decline in school performance and lack of interest or motivation in school-related activities.
8. Pattern of engaging in sexually promiscuous or seductive behaviors to compensate for the loss of security or support within the family system.
9. Pseudomaturity as manifested by denying or suppressing painful emotions about divorce and often assuming parental roles or responsibilities.
10. Numerous psychosomatic complaints in response to anticipated separations, stress, or frustration.
11. Loss of contact with a positive support network due to a geographic move.

—. _____
    _____
    _____
—. _____
    _____
    _____
—. _____
    _____

LONG-TERM GOALS

1. Accept the parents' separation or divorce with understanding and control of feelings and behavior.
2. Establish and/or maintain secure, trusting relationships with the parents.
3. Eliminate feelings of guilt and statements that reflect self-blame for the parents' divorce.
4. Elevate and stabilize mood.
5. Cease maladaptive pattern of engaging in sexually promiscuous or seductive behaviors to meet needs for affection, affiliation, and acceptance.
6. Refrain from using drugs or alcohol and develop healthy coping mechanisms to effectively deal with changes in the family system.
7. Create a strong, supportive social network outside of the immediate family to offset the loss of affection, approval, or support from within the family.
8. Parents establish and maintain a consistent, yet flexible, visitation arrangement that meets the client's emotional needs.
9. Parents establish and maintain appropriate parent-child boundaries in discipline and assignment of responsibilities.
10. Parents consistently demonstrate mutual respect for one another, especially in front of the children.

—. _____
    _____
—. _____
    _____
—. _____
    _____

SHORT-TERM OBJECTIVES

1. Tell the story of the parents' separation or divorce. (1, 2)

2. Identify and express feelings related to the parents' separation or divorce. (2, 3, 4)

3. Describe how the parents' separation or divorce has impacted personal and family life. (5)

THERAPEUTIC INTERVENTIONS

1. Actively build the level of trust with the client through consistent eye contact, active listening, unconditional positive regard, and warm acceptance to improve his/her ability to identify and express feelings connected to parents' separation or divorce.

2. Explore, encourage, and support the client in verbally expressing and clarifying his/her feelings associated with the separation or divorce.

2. Explore, encourage, and support the client in verbally expressing and clarifying his/her feelings associated with the separation or divorce.

3. Use the empty chair technique to help the client express mixed emotions he/she feels toward both parents about the separation or divorce.

4. Ask the client to keep a journal where he/she records experiences or situations that evoke strong emotions pertaining to the divorce. Review the journal in therapy sessions.

5. Develop a timeline where the client records significant developments that have positively or negatively

impacted his/her personal and family life, both before and after the divorce. Allow the client to verbalize his/her feelings about the divorce and subsequent changes in the family system.

4. Express thoughts and feelings within the family system regarding parental separation or divorce. (6, 7, 8)

6. Assist the client in developing a list of questions about the parents' divorce, then suggest ways he/she could find possible answers for each question (e.g., asking parents directly, writing parents a letter).

7. Hold family therapy sessions to allow the client and siblings to express feelings about separation or divorce in presence of parent.

8. Encourage the parents to provide opportunities (e.g., family meetings) at home to allow the client and siblings to express feelings about separation/divorce and subsequent changes in family system.

5. Recognize and affirm self as not being responsible for the parents' separation or divorce. (9, 10)

9. Explore the factors contributing to the client's feelings of guilt and self-blame about parents' separation or divorce; assist him/her in realizing that his/her negative behaviors did not cause parents' divorce to occur.

10. Assist the client in realizing that he/she does not have the power or control to bring the parents back together.

6. Parents verbalize an acceptance of responsibility for the dissolution of the marriage. (11, 12)

7. Identify positive and negative aspects of the parents' separation or divorce. (13)

8. Identify and verbalize unmet needs to the parents. (14, 15)

9. Reduce the frequency and severity of acting-out, oppositional, and aggressive behaviors. (16, 17)

11. Conduct family therapy sessions where parents affirm the client and siblings as not being responsible for separation or divorce.

12. Challenge and confront statements by parents that place blame or responsibility for separation or divorce on the children.

13. Give a homework assignment in which the client lists both positive and negative aspects of parents' divorce; process the list in the next session and allow him/her to express different emotions.

14. Give the parents the directive of spending 10 to 15 minutes of one-on-one time with the client and siblings on a regular daily basis to identify and meet the children's needs.

15. Assign the client homework in the middle stages of therapy to help him/her list unmet needs and identify steps he/she can take to meet those needs (or assign the "Unmet Emotional Needs—Identification and Satisfaction" exercise from the *Brief Adolescent Therapy Homework Planner* by Jongsma, Peterson, and McInnis).

16. Empower the client by reinforcing his/her ability to cope with the divorce and make healthy adjustments.

10. Express feelings of anger about the parents' separation or divorce through controlled, respectful verbalizations and healthy physical outlets. (18, 19)

17. Assist the client in making a connection between underlying painful emotions about divorce and angry outbursts or aggressive behaviors.

18. Assist the client in identifying appropriate and inappropriate ways for the client to express anger about parents' separation or divorce.

19. Teach relaxation and/or guided imagery techniques to help the client learn to control anger more effectively.

11. Parents verbally recognize how their guilt and failure to follow through with limits contributes to the client's acting-out or aggressive behaviors. (20, 21)

20. Encourage and challenge the parents not to allow guilt feelings about the divorce to interfere with the need to impose consequences for oppositional behaviors.

21. Assist the parents in establishing clearly defined rules, boundaries, and consequences for acting-out, oppositional, or aggressive behaviors (see Anger Management and Oppositional Defiant chapters in this Planner).

12. Complete school and homework assignments on a regular basis. (22, 23)

22. Assist the parents in establishing a new study routine to help the client complete school or homework assignments.

23. Design and implement a reward system and/or contingency contract to reinforce completion of school and

13. Decrease the frequency of somatic complaints. (24)

14. Noncustodial parent verbally recognizes his/her pattern of overindulgence and begins to set limits on money and/or time spent in leisure or recreational activities. (25)

15. Noncustodial parent assigns household responsibilities and/or requires the client to complete homework during visits. (26)

16. Reduce the frequency of immature and irresponsible behaviors. (27, 28)

17. Parents cease making unnecessary, hostile, or overly critical remarks about the other parent in the presence of the children. (29)

homework assignments or good academic performance.

24. Refocus the client's discussion from physical complaints to emotional conflicts and the expression of feelings.

25. Encourage the noncustodial parent to set limits on the client's misbehavior and refrain from overindulging the client during visits.

26. Direct the noncustodial parent to assign a chore or have the client complete school or homework assignments during visits.

27. Teach how enmeshed or overly protective parents reinforce the client's immature or irresponsible behaviors by failing to set necessary limits.

28. Have the client and parents identify age-appropriate ways for the client to meet his/her needs for affiliation, acceptance, and approval. Process the list and encourage the client to engage in age-appropriate behaviors.

29. Confront and challenge the parents to cease making unnecessary hostile or overly critical remarks about the other parent in the presence of the client.

18. Parents recognize and agree to cease the pattern of soliciting information about and/or sending messages to the other parent through the children. (30, 31)

19. Disengaged or uninvolved parent follows through with recommendations to spend greater quality time with the client. (32, 33)

20. Identify and express feelings through artwork and music. (34, 35)

30. Counsel the parents about not placing the client in the middle by soliciting information about the other parent or sending messages about adult matters through the client to the other parent.

31. Challenge and confront the client about playing one parent against the other to meet needs, obtain material goods, or avoid responsibility.

32. Hold individual and/or family therapy session to challenge and encourage the noncustodial parent to maintain regular visitation and involvement in the client's life.

33. Give a directive to the disengaged or distant parent to spend more time or perform a specific task with the client (e.g., go on an outing to the mall, assist the client with homework, work on a project around the home).

34. Direct the client to draw a variety of pictures that reflect his/her feelings about the divorce, family move, or change in schools.

35. Instruct the client to sing a song or play a musical instrument that reflects his/her feelings about separation or divorce, then have the client verbalize times when he/she experienced those feelings.

21. Increase participation in positive peer group, extracurricular, or school-related activities. (36)

22. Attend a support group for children of divorce. (37)

23. Increase contacts with adults and build a support network outside the family. (38)

24. Identify and verbalize the feelings, irrational beliefs, stressors, and needs that contribute to sexually promiscuous or seductive behaviors. (39, 40)

25. Complete a substance abuse evaluation and comply with the recommendations offered by the evaluation findings. (41, 42, 43)

36. Encourage the client to participate in school, extracurricular, or positive peer group activities to offset the loss of time spent with the parents.

37. Refer the client to group therapy to help him/her share and work through feelings with other adolescents whose parents are divorcing.

38. Identify a list of adult individuals (e.g., school counselor, neighbor, uncle or aunt, Big Brother or Big Sister, clergy person) outside the family who the client can turn to for support and guidance to help cope with the divorce.

39. Provide sex education and discuss the risks involved with sexually promiscuous or seductive behaviors.

40. Explore the client's feelings, irrational beliefs, stressors, and unmet needs that contribute to the emergence of sexually promiscuous or seductive behaviors.

41. Arrange for substance abuse evaluation and/or treatment for the client (see the Chemical Dependence chapter in this Planner).

42. Explore the client's underlying feelings of depression, insecurity, and rejection that led him/her to escape into substance abuse.

43. Assist the client in constructing and signing an
agreement to refrain from
using substances.

—. _____   —. _____

   _____   _____

—. _____   —. _____

   _____   _____

—. _____   —. _____

   _____   _____

DIAGNOSTIC SUGGESTIONS

Axis I: 309.0   Adjustment Disorder With Depressed Mood
              309.24   Adjustment Disorder With Anxiety
              309.28   Adjustment Disorder With Mixed Anxiety and
                         Depressed Mood
              309.3   Adjustment Disorder With Disturbance of
                         Conduct
              309.4   Adjustment Disorder With Mixed Disturbance
                         of Emotions and Conduct
              300.4   Dysthymic Disorder
              300.02   Generalized Anxiety Disorder
              309.21   Separation Anxiety Disorder
              313.81   Oppositional Defiant Disorder
              300.81   Undifferentiated Somatoform Disorder

              _____   _____

Axis II: 799.9   Diagnosis Deferred
              V71.09   No Diagnosis on Axis II

              _____   _____

              _____   _____

EATING DISORDER

BEHAVIORAL DEFINITIONS

1. Rapid consumption of large quantities of food in a short time followed by self-induced vomiting and/or the use of laxatives due to the fear of weight gain.
2. Extreme weight loss (and amenorrhea in females) with refusal to maintain a minimal healthy weight due to very limited ingestion of food and high frequency of secretive, self-induced vomiting, inappropriate use of laxatives, and/or excessive strenuous exercise.
3. Preoccupation with body image related to a grossly unrealistic assessment of self as being too fat or a strong denial of seeing self as emaciated.
4. Irrational fear of becoming overweight.
5. Fluid and electrolyte imbalance.
6. Threat to life due to inadequate nutrition, fluid and electrolyte imbalance, and a general weakening of body systems resulting from behavioral eating disorder.

—. _____
_____
_____

—. _____
_____
_____

—. _____
_____

LONG-TERM GOALS

1. Restore normal eating patterns, body weight, balanced fluids and electrolytes, and realistic perception of body size.

2. Terminate the pattern of binge eating and purging behavior with a return to normal eating of enough nutritious foods to maintain a healthy weight.
3. Stabilize the medical condition, resume patterns of food intake that will sustain life, and gain weight to a normal level.
4. Gain an awareness of the interconnectedness of low self-esteem and societal pressures with dieting, binge eating, and purging, in order to eliminate eating disorder behaviors.
5. Change the definition of the self so that it does not focus on weight, size, and shape as the primary criteria for self-acceptance.
6. Restructure the distorted thoughts, beliefs, and values that contribute to eating disorder development.

—. _____
_____
—. _____
_____
—. _____
_____

SHORT-TERM OBJECTIVES

1. Describe behavior patterns related to eating; avoiding eating; or controlling calories through vomiting, laxative misuse, or excessive exercise. (1, 2, 3)

2. Cooperate with a full physical and dental exam. (4, 5)

THERAPEUTIC INTERVENTIONS

1. Explore the client's history of eating disorder behaviors as to type, frequency, and chronicity.

2. Assess the client's attitude regarding eating disorder behaviors as to whether there is open acknowledgment of a serious problem.

3. Confront the client's minimization and denial of the seriousness of the eating disorder behavior.

4. Refer the client to a physician for a thorough physical exam.

3. Cooperate with admission to inpatient treatment if a fragile medical condition necessitates such treatment. (4, 6)

4. Attain and maintain balanced fluids and electrolytes as well as resuming reproductive functions. (7, 8)

5. Eat at regular intervals (three meals a day), consuming at least the minimum daily calories necessary to progressively gain weight. (9, 10, 11)

5. Refer the client to a dentist for an exam.

4. Refer the client to a physician for a thorough physical exam.

6. Refer the client for hospitalization, as necessary, if his/her weight loss becomes severe and physical health is jeopardized.

7. Establish a minimum daily caloric intake for the client as well as soliciting agreement for termination of dysfunctional eating behavior.

8. Reinforce the client's weight gain and acceptance of personal responsibility for normal food intake.

9. Assist the client in meal planning.

10. Assist the client in setting realistic weight goals and monitor his/her weight and give realistic feedback regarding body thinness.

11. Establish healthy weight goals for the client per the Body Mass Index (BMI) [BMI = pounds of body weight × 700/height in inches/height in inches; normal range is 20 to 27 and below 18 is medically critical (Wilson, Fairburn, and Agras)], the Metropolitan Height and Weight Tables, or some other recognized standard.

6. Terminate inappropriate food hoarding, exercise, vomiting, and laxative use. (12, 13)

12. Monitor and confront the client's vomiting, food hoarding, excessive exercise, and laxative usage.

13. Assist the client in setting a goal of gradually reducing the frequency of purging, learning to accept the full feeling that accompanies normal eating.

7. Identify and replace irrational beliefs about eating behavior. (14, 15)

14. Assign the client to keep a journal of food intake, thoughts, and feelings, reviewing the journal information to identify distorted thoughts regarding food and weight (or assign the "Reality: Food Intake, Weight, Thoughts, and Feelings" exercise from the *Brief Adolescent Therapy Homework Planner* by Jongsma, Peterson, and McInnis).

15. Assist the client in the identification of negative cognitive messages (e.g., catastrophizing, exaggerating) that mediate his/her dysfunctional eating behavior, then train the client to establish realistic cognitive messages regarding food intake and body size (or assign the "Fears Beneath the Eating Disorder" exercise from the *Brief Adolescent Therapy Homework Planner* by Jongsma, Peterson, and McInnis).

8. Verbalize the acceptance of full responsibility for choices about eating behavior. (8, 16)

    8. Reinforce the client's weight gain and acceptance of personal responsibility for normal food intake.

    16. Emphasize to the client that he/she has responsibility for all decisions regarding eating and unhealthy means of weight control.

9. Set reasonable limits on physical exercise. (12, 17)

    12. Monitor and confront the client's vomiting, food hoarding, excessive exercise, and laxative usage.

    17. Contract with the client to limit exercise to 20 minutes per day or less, especially if he/she is severely underweight.

10. Attend a support group for eating disorder. (18)

    18. Refer the client to a support group for eating disorder.

11. Verbalize a healthy, realistic appraisal of body image. (19)

    19. Confront the client's perfectionistic and unrealistic assessment of his/her body image and assign exercises (e.g., positive self-talk in the mirror, shopping for clothes that flatter the appearance) that reinforce a healthy, realistic body appraisal, even with normal flaws.

12. Verbalize the feelings of low self-esteem, depression, loneliness, anger, loss of control, need for nurturance, or lack of trust that underlie the eating disorder. (20, 21)

    20. Probe the client's emotional struggles that are camouflaged by the eating disorder.

    21. Process the role of passive-aggressive control in the client's fear of losing control of eating or weight.

13. Disclose to family members feelings of ambivalence regarding control and dependency and state how these feelings have affected eating patterns. (22)

14. Verbalize how fear of sexual identity and development has influenced severe weight loss. (23, 24)

15. Identify the relationship between the fear of failure, the drive for perfectionism, and the roots of low self-esteem. (15, 25, 26)

22. Facilitate family therapy sessions that focus on owning feelings, clarifying messages, identifying control and separation conflicts, and developing age-appropriate boundaries.

23. Explore the client's fear regarding sexual development and control of sexual impulses; and how the fear relates to keeping himself/herself unattractively thin or fat.

24. Encourage and reinforce the client's acceptance of normal sexual thoughts, feelings, and desires.

15. Assist the client in the identification of negative cognitive messages (e.g., catastrophizing, exaggerating) that mediate his/her dysfunctional eating behavior, then train the client to establish realistic cognitive messages regarding food intake and body size (or assign the "Fears Beneath the Eating Disorder" exercise from the *Brief Adolescent Therapy Homework Planner* by Jongsma, Peterson, and McInnis).

25. Discuss the client's fear of failure and the role of perfectionism in the search for control and the avoidance of failure; normalize failure experiences as common and necessary for learning.

16. Acknowledge and resolve separation anxiety related to the emancipation process. (27)

17. Develop assertive behaviors that allow for the healthy expression of needs and emotions. (28)

18. State a basis for positive identity that is not based on weight and appearance but on character, traits, relationships, and intrinsic value. (26, 29, 30, 31)

26. Reinforce the client's positive qualities and successes to reduce the fear of failure and build a positive sense of self.

27. Assist the client in identifying and resolving the causes for his/her fear of independence and emancipation from parent figures.

28. Train the client in assertiveness or refer him/her to an assertiveness training class; reinforce his/her assertiveness behaviors in the session and reports of successful assertiveness between sessions.

26. Reinforce the client's positive qualities and successes to reduce the fear of failure and build a positive sense of self.

29. Assist the client in identifying a basis for self-worth apart from body image by reviewing his/her talents, successes, positive traits, importance to others, and intrinsic spiritual value.

30. Assign the client books on eating disorder and distorted body image: (e.g., *Body Traps* by Rodin and/or *Afraid to Eat* by Berg); process the key ideas regarding obsessing over body image.

31. Assign the client to view the video *Bradshaw on Eating Disorders* (Bradshaw; available from Courage to Change).

19. Verbalize the connection between suppressed emotional expression, difficulty with interpersonal issues, and unhealthy food usage. (32)

20. Clean up and replace food after bingeing and purging episodes. (33, 34)

21. Parents state a detachment from responsibility for the client's eating disorder. (35, 36, 37)

32. Teach the client the possible connection between unexpressed thoughts and feelings and the maladaptive use of food.

33. Confront the client regarding the impact of bingeing and purging behavior on household members and the need for consideration of their feelings and rights.

34. Contract with the client to clean up after self and immediately replace food subsequent to bingeing and/or purging.

35. Teach the parents how to successfully detach from taking responsibility for the client's eating behavior.

36. Assist the parents in developing a behavioral contract with the client in which the client pays a consequence (e.g., added household chores or loss of money, privilege, or curfew time) for bingeing on family food, hoarding food, or failing to clean up after purging.

37. Recommend that the client's parents and friends read material on eating disorders (e.g., *Surviving an Eating Disorder* by Siegel, Brisman, and Weinshel); process the concepts in a family therapy session.

22. Understand and verbalize the connection between too restrictive dieting and binge episodes. (38, 39, 40)

38. Assist the client in understanding the relationship between bingeing and the lack of regular mealtimes or total deprivation from specific foods.

39. Refer the client to a dietitian for education in healthy eating and nutritional concerns.

40. Encourage the client to read books on binge eating (e.g., *Overcoming Binge Eating* by Fairburn) to increase his/her awareness of the components of eating disorders.

__. _____   __. _____
    _____   _____
__. _____   __. _____
    _____   _____
__. _____   __. _____
    _____   _____

DIAGNOSTIC SUGGESTIONS

Axis I:	307.1	Anorexia Nervosa
	307.51	Bulimia Nervosa
	307.50	Eating Disorder NOS
	300.4	Dysthymic Disorder
	_____	_____
Axis II:	799.9	Diagnosis Deferred
	V71.09	No Diagnosis on Axis II
	301.6	Dependent Personality Disorder
	_____	_____
	_____	_____

GRIEF/LOSS UNRESOLVED

BEHAVIORAL DEFINITIONS

1. Loss of contact with a parent due to the parent's death.
2. Loss of contact with a parent figure due to termination of parental rights.
3. Loss of contact with a parent due to the parent's incarceration.
4. Loss of contact with a positive support network due to a geographic move.
5. Loss of meaningful contact with a parent figure due to the parent's emotional abandonment.
6. Strong emotional response experienced when the loss is mentioned.
7. Lack of appetite, nightmares, restlessness, inability to concentrate, irritability, tearfulness, or social withdrawal that began subsequent to a loss.
8. Marked drop in school grades, and an increase in angry outbursts, hyperactivity, or clinginess when separating from parents.
9. Feelings of guilt associated with the unreasonable belief in having done something to cause the loss or not having prevented it.
10. Avoidance of talking at length or in any depth about the loss.

__. _____
   _____
__. _____
   _____
__. _____
   _____

LONG-TERM GOALS

1. Begin a healthy grieving process around the loss.
2. Complete the process of letting go of the lost significant other.
3. Work through the grieving and letting-go process and reach the point of emotionally reinvesting in life.
4. Successfully grieve the loss within a supportive emotional environment.
5. Resolve the loss and begin reinvesting in relationships with others and in age-appropriate activities.
6. Resolve feelings of guilt, depression, or anger associated with loss and return to previous level of functioning.

__. _____
_____
_____

__. _____
_____
_____

__. _____
_____

SHORT-TERM OBJECTIVES

1. Develop a trusting relationship with the therapist as evidenced by the open communication of feelings and thoughts associated with the loss. (1, 2)

2. Verbalize and experience feelings connected with the loss. (3, 4, 5)

THERAPEUTIC INTERVENTIONS

1. Actively build level of trust with the client through consistent eye contact, active listening, unconditional positive regard, and warm acceptance while asking him/her to identify and express feelings associated with the loss.

2. Ask the client to tell the story of the loss through drawing pictures of his/her experience.

3. Ask the client to write a letter to the lost person describing his/her feelings

and read this letter to the therapist.

4. Assign the client to utilize *The Healing Your Grieving Heart Journal for Teens* (Wolfelt) to record his/her thoughts and feelings related to the loss.

5. Ask the client to collect and bring to a session various photos and other memorabilia related to the lost loved one (or assign the "Create a Memory Album" exercise from the *Brief Adolescent Therapy Homework Planner* by Jongsma, Peterson, and McInnis).

3. Verbalize an understanding of the process or journey of grief that is unique for each individual. (6, 7, 8)

6. Have the client read sections or the entirety of the books *Common Threads of Teenage Grief* (Tyson) or *Straight Talk about Death for Teenagers* (Grollman) and select three to five key ideas from the reading to discuss with the therapist.

7. Educate the client and his/her parents about the grieving process and assist the parents in how to answer any of the client's questions.

8. Ask the client to watch *Terms of Endearment, Ordinary People, My Girl,* or a similar film that focuses on loss and grieving, and then discuss how various characters coped with the

loss and expressed their grief.

4. Attend a grief support group. (9)

9. Refer the client to a support group for adolescents grieving death or divorce in the family.

5. Identify those activities that have contributed to the avoidance of feelings connected to the loss. (10, 11)

10. Ask the client to list how he/she has avoided the pain of grieving and how that has negatively impacted his/her life.

11. Explore the client's use of mood-altering substances as a means of grief avoidance (see Chemical Dependence chapter in this Planner).

6. Terminate the use of alcohol and illicit drugs. (12)

12. Make a contract with the client to abstain from all mood-altering substances. Monitor for compliance by checking with the client and parents and make a referral for a substance abuse evaluation if he/she is unable to keep the contract.

7. Keep a daily journal of feelings of grief and their triggers. (4, 13)

4. Assign the client to utilize *The Healing Your Grieving Heart Journal for Teens* (Wolfelt) to record his/her thoughts and feelings related to the loss.

13. Assign the client to keep a daily grief journal of thoughts and feelings associated with the loss and how they were triggered. Review the journal in therapy sessions.

8. Verbalize questions about the loss and work to obtain answers for each. (14, 15, 16)

14. Assist the client in developing a list of questions about a specific loss, then try to direct him/her to resources (e.g., books, clergy, parent, counselor) for possible answers for each question.

15. Expand the client's understanding of death by reading *Lifetimes* (Mellonie and Ingpen) to him/her and discussing all questions that arise from the reading.

16. Assist the client in identifying a peer or an adult who has experienced a loss similar to the client's and has successfully worked his/her way through it. Work with the client to develop a list of questions that he/she would like to ask this person (e.g., "What was the experience like for you? What was the most difficult part? What did you find the most helpful?").

9. Verbalize an increase in understanding the process of grieving and letting go. (17, 18)

17. Assign the client to ask questions about grieving to a peer or adult who has successfully resolved a loss, or arrange a conjoint session to ask the questions. Process the experience.

18. Assign the client to interview a member of the clergy about death and to interview an adult who has experienced and successfully

10. Identify positive things about the deceased loved one and/or the lost relationship and how these things may be remembered. (5, 19)

worked through the death of a loved one.

5. Ask the client to collect and bring to a session various photos and other memorabilia related to the lost loved one (or assign the "Create a Memory Album" exercise from the *Brief Adolescent Therapy Homework Planner* by Jongsma, Peterson, and McInnis).

19. Ask the client to list positive things about the deceased and how he/she plans to remember each one; process the list.

11. Decrease the expression of feelings of guilt and blame for the loss. (20, 21)

20. Explore the client's thoughts and feelings of guilt and blame surrounding the loss, replacing irrational thoughts with realistic thoughts.

21. Help the client lift the self-imposed curse he/she believes to be the cause for the loss by asking the person who is perceived as having imposed the curse to take it back or by role-playing a phone conversation for the client to apologize for the behavior he/she believes is the cause for the curse.

12. Verbalize and resolve feelings of anger or guilt focused on self, God, or the deceased loved one that block the grief process. (22, 23, 24)

22. Suggest an absolution ritual (e.g., dedicate time to a charity that the deceased loved one supported) for the client to implement to relieve the guilt or blame for

the loss. Monitor the results and adjust as necessary.

23. Encourage and support the client in sessions to look angry, then act angry, and finally put words to the anger.

24. Assign the client to complete an exercise related to an apology or forgiveness (e.g., writing a letter asking for forgiveness from the deceased, using the empty chair technique to apologize) and to process it with the therapist.

13. Say good-bye to the lost loved one. (25, 26)

25. Assign the client to write a good-bye letter to the deceased (or assign the "Grief Letter" exercise in the *Brief Adolescent Therapy Homework Planner* by Jongsma, Peterson, and McInnis).

26. Suggest the client visit the grave of the loved one with an adult to communicate feelings and say good-bye, perhaps by leaving the good-bye letter or drawing. Process the experience.

14. List how life will demonstrate that the loss is being resolved. (27)

27. Assist the client in developing a list of indicators that the loss is beginning to be resolved (e.g., sleeping undisturbed, feeling less irritable and tearful, experiencing more happy times, recalling the loss with good memories instead of just heartache, reinvesting in life interests).

15. Parents verbalize an increase in their understanding of how to be supportive during the grief process. (7, 28, 29)

7. Educate the client and his/her parents about the grieving process and assist the parents in how to answer any of the client's questions.

28. Train the parents in specific ways they can provide comfort, consolation, love, companionship, and support to the client in grief (e.g., bring up the loss occasionally for discussion, encourage the client to talk freely of the loss, encourage photographs of the loved one to be displayed, spend one-on-one time with the client in quiet activities that may foster sharing of feelings, spend time with the client in diversion activities).

29. Assign the parents to read a book to help them become familiar with the grieving process (e.g., *The Grieving Teen* by Fitzgerald or *Learning to Say Good-Bye* by LeShan).

16. Parents increase their verbal openness about the loss. (30, 31, 32)

30. Refer the parents to a grief/loss support group.

31. Conduct family sessions where each member of the client's family talks about his/her experience related to the loss.

32. Assign the client and parents to play The Good Mourning Game (Bisenius and Norris), first in a

family session and then later at home by themselves. Follow up the assignment by processing with the family members, focusing on what each learned about themselves and about others in the grieving process.

17. Parents facilitate the client's participation in grief healing rituals. (33, 34)

33. Assist the family in the development of new rituals to fill the void created by the loss.

34. Encourage the parents to allow the client to participate in the rituals and customs of grieving if the client is willing to be involved.

18. Participate in memorial services, funeral services, or other grieving rituals. (34)

34. Encourage the parents to allow the client to participate in the rituals and customs of grieving if the client is willing to be involved.

19. Verbalize an understanding of the grief anniversary reaction and state a plan to cope with it. (35)

35. Educate the client and parents in the area of anniversary dates, focusing on what to expect and ways to handle the feelings (e.g., reminisce about the loss with significant others, visit the grave site, celebrate the good memories with a dinner out).

20. Parents who are losing custody verbally say good-bye to the client. (36)

36. Conduct a session with the parents who are losing custody of the client to prepare them to say good-bye to the client in a healthy, affirmative way.

21. Attend and participate in a formal session to say good-bye to the parents whose parental rights are being terminated. (37)

37. Facilitate a good-bye session with the client and the parents who are losing custody, for the purpose of giving the client permission to move on with his/her life. If the parents who are losing custody or the current parents are not available, ask them to write a letter that can be read at the session, or conduct a role play in which the client says good-bye to each parent.

22. Verbalize positive memories of the past and hopeful statements about the future. (38)

38. Ask the client to make a record of his/her life in a book format, using pictures and other memorabilia, to help visualize his/her past, present, and future life (or assign the "Create a Memory Album" exercise from the *Brief Adolescent Therapy Homework Planner* by Jongsma, Peterson, and McInnis). When it is completed, have the client keep a copy and give another to the current parents.

__. _____

__. _____

__. _____

__. _____

__. _____

__. _____

DIAGNOSTIC SUGGESTIONS

Axis I: 296.2x   Major Depressive Disorder, Single Episode
296.3x   Major Depressive Disorder, Recurrent
V62.82   Bereavement
309.0   Adjustment Disorder With Depressed Mood
309.4   Adjustment Disorder With Mixed Disturbance
of Emotions and Conduct
300.4   Dysthymic Disorder

_____   _____

_____   _____

Axis II: 799.9   Diagnosis Deferred
V71.09   No Diagnosis on Axis II

_____   _____

_____   _____

LOW SELF-ESTEEM

BEHAVIORAL DEFINITIONS

1. Verbalizes self-disparaging remarks, seeing self as unattractive, worthless, stupid, a loser, a burden, unimportant.
2. Takes blame easily.
3. Inability to accept compliments.
4. Refuses to take risks associated with new experiences, as she/he expects failure.
5. Avoids social contact with adults and peers.
6. Seeks excessively to please or receive attention/praise of adults and/or peers.
7. Unable to identify or accept positive traits or talents about self.
8. Fears rejection from others, especially peer group.
9. Acts out in negative, attention-seeking ways.
10. Difficulty saying no to others; fears not being liked by others.

—. _____

_____

—. _____

_____

—. _____

_____

LONG-TERM GOALS

1. Elevate self-esteem.
2. Increase social interaction, assertiveness, confidence in self, and reasonable risk-taking.

3. Build a consistently positive self-image.
4. Demonstrate improved self-esteem by accepting compliments, by identifying positive characteristics about self, by being able to say no to others, and by eliminating self-disparaging remarks.
5. See self as lovable and capable.
6. Increase social skill level.

—. _____
_____
—. _____
_____
—. _____
_____

SHORT-TERM OBJECTIVES

1. Verbalize an increased awareness of self-disparaging statements. (1, 2)

2. Decrease frequency of negative self-statements. (3, 4, 5)

THERAPEUTIC INTERVENTIONS

1. Confront and reframe the client's self-disparaging comments.

2. Assist the client in becoming aware of how he/she expresses or acts out (e.g., by lack of eye contact, social withdrawal, expectation of failure or rejection) negative feelings about self.

3. Refer the client to a group therapy that is focused on ways to build self-esteem.

4. Ask the client to read *Reviving Ophelia* (Pipher) or selected parts and have him/her note 5 to 10 key points to discuss with the therapist.

5. Assign the client to read *Why I'm Afraid to Tell You*

Who I Am (Powell) and choose 5 to 10 key points to discuss with the therapist.

3. Decrease verbalized fear of rejection while increasing statements of self-acceptance. (6, 7, 8)

6. Ask the client to make one positive statement about himself/herself daily and record it on a chart or in a journal.

7. Assist the client in developing positive self-talk as a way of boosting his/her confidence and positive self-image.

8. Probe the parents' interactions with the client in family sessions and redirect or rechannel any patterns of interaction or methods of discipline that are negative or critical of the client.

4. Identify positive traits and talents about self. (9, 10, 11)

9. Reinforce verbally the client's use of positive statements of confidence or identification of positive attributes about himself/herself.

10. Develop with the client a list of positive affirmations about himself/herself and ask that it be read three times daily.

11. Assign a mirror exercise in which the client looks daily into a mirror and then records all that he/she sees there. Repeat the exercise a second week, increasing the daily time to four minutes, and have the client look for and record only

the positive things he/she sees. Have the client process what he/she records and what the experience was like with the therapist.

5. Identify and verbalize feelings. (12, 13, 14)

12. Have the client complete the exercise "Self-Esteem—What Is It—How Do I Get It?" from *Ten Days to Self-Esteem* (Burns) and then process the completed exercise with the therapist.

13. Use a therapeutic game (e.g., The Talking, Feeling, and Doing Game by Gardner, available from Creative Therapeutics; Let's See About Me, available from Childswork/Childsplay; or The Ungame by Zakich, available from The Ungame Company) to promote the client becoming more aware of self and his/her feelings.

14. Educate the client in the basics of identifying and labeling feelings, and assist him/her in the beginning to identify what he/she is feeling.

6. Increase eye contact with others. (15, 16)

15. Focus attention on the client's lack of eye contact; encourage and reinforce increased eye contact within sessions.

16. Ask the client to increase eye contact with teachers, parents, and other adults;

review and process reports of attempts and the feelings associated with them.

7. Identify actions that can be taken to improve self-image. (17, 18, 19)

17. Assign the client to read *Feed Your Head* (Hanson) and to select five key ideas from the reading to process with the therapist.

18. Ask the client to draw representations of the changes he/she desires for himself/herself or his/her life situation; help the client develop a plan of implementation for the changes (or assign either the "Three Wishes Game" or the "Three Ways to Change Yourself" exercise from the *Brief Adolescent Therapy Homework Planner* by Jongsma, Peterson, and McInnis).

19. Utilize a brief solution-focused approach (O'Hanlon and Beadle) such as externalizing the problem by framing the difficulty as a stage or something that the client might grow out of or get over in order to de-pathologize the issue and open up new hopes and possibilities for action that might improve the client's self-esteem.

8. Identify and verbalize needs. (20, 21)

20. Assist the client in identifying and verbalizing his/her emotional needs; brainstorm ways to increase the chances of his/her needs being met.

9. Identify instances of emotional, physical, or sexual abuse that have damaged self-esteem. (22)

10. Identify negative automatic thoughts and replace them with positive self-talk messages to build self-esteem. (23, 24)

11. Take responsibility for daily self-care and household tasks that are developmentally age-appropriate. (25)

12. Positively acknowledge and verbally accept praise or compliments from others. (26, 27)

21. Conduct a family session in which the client expresses his/her needs to family and vice versa.

22. Explore for incidents of abuse (emotional, physical, or sexual) and how they have impacted feelings about self. (See Sexual Abuse Victim and/or Physical/Emotional Abuse Victim chapters in this Planner.)

23. Help the client identify his/her distorted negative beliefs about self and the world.

24. Help the client identify, and reinforce the use of, more realistic, positive messages about self and life events.

25. Help the client find and implement daily self-care and household or academic responsibilities that are age-appropriate. Monitor follow-through and give positive feedback when warranted.

26. Use neurolinguistic programming or reframing techniques in which messages about self are changed to assist the client in accepting compliments from others.

27. Ask the client to obtain three letters of recommendation from adults he/she knows but is not related to. The letters are to be sent

directly to the therapist (the therapist provides three addressed, stamped envelopes) and then opened and read in session.

13. Parents identify specific activities for the client that will facilitate development of positive self-esteem. (28, 29)

28. Provide the parents with or have them purchase the book *Full Esteem Ahead!* (Loomans and Loomans) and have them look over the book and then select two to three ideas to implement. Have the parents process the results with the therapist.

29. Ask the parents to involve the client in esteem-building activities (Scouting, experiential camps, music, sports, youth groups, enrichment programs, etc.).

14. Parents verbalize realistic expectations and discipline methods for the client. (30, 31)

30. Explore parents' expectations of the client. Assist, if necessary, in making them more realistic.

31. Train the parents in the 3 R's (related, respectful, and reasonable) of discipline techniques (see *Raising Self-Reliant Children in a Self-Indulgent World* by Glenn and Nelson) in order to eliminate discipline that results in rebellion, revenge, or reduced self-esteem. Assist in implementation, and coach the parents as they develop and improve their skills using this method.

15. Parents attend a didactic series on positive parenting. (32)

16. Increase the frequency of speaking up with confidence in social situations. (33, 34, 35, 36)

32. Ask the parents to attend a didactic series on positive parenting, afterward processing how they can begin to implement some of these techniques.

33. Encourage the client to use the technique "Pretending to Know How" (see Theiss in *101 Favorite Play Therapy Techniques* by Kaduson and Schaefer) or "The Therapist on the Inside" (see Grigoryev in *101 Favorite Play Therapy Techniques*) on one identified task or problem area in the next week. Follow up by processing the experience and results, and then have the client use the technique again on two new situations or problems, and so on.

34. Ask the client to read *How to Say No and Keep Your Friends* (Scott) and to process with the therapist how saying no can boost self-confidence and self-esteem.

35. Use role playing and behavioral rehearsal to improve the client's assertiveness and social skills.

36. Encourage the client to attend an alternative camp or weekend experience to promote his/her personal growth in the areas of trust, self-confidence, and cooperation and in

developing relationships
with others.

17. Parents verbally reinforce
the client's active attempts
to build positive self-
esteem. (32, 37)

32. Ask the parents to attend a
didactic series on positive
parenting, afterward pro-
cessing how they can begin
to implement some of these
techniques.

37. Encourage the parents to
seek out opportunities to
praise, reinforce, and recognize the client's minor or
major accomplishments.

__. _____   __. _____

_____   _____

__. _____   __. _____

_____   _____

__. _____   __. _____

_____   _____

DIAGNOSTIC SUGGESTIONS

Axis I:	300.4	Dysthymic Disorder
	314.01	Attention-Deficit/Hyperactivity Disorder, Predominantly Hyperactive-Impulsive Type
	300.23	Social Phobia
	296.xx	Major Depressive Disorder
	307.1	Anorexia Nervosa
	309.21	Separation Anxiety Disorder
	300.02	Generalized Anxiety
	995.54	Physical Abuse of Child (Victim)
	995.53	Sexual Abuse of Child, (Victim)
	995.5	Neglect of Child, (Victim)
	303.90	Alcohol Dependence
	304.30	Cannabis Dependence
	_____	_____
	_____	_____

Axis II: 317   Mild Mental Retardation
              V62.89   Borderline Intellectual Functioning
              799.9   Diagnosis Deferred
              V71.09   No Diagnosis on Axis II

              _____   _____

              _____   _____

MANIA/HYPOMANIA

BEHAVIORAL DEFINITIONS

1. Loud, overly friendly social style that oversteps social boundaries and shows poor social judgment (e.g., too trusting and self-disclosing too quickly).
2. Inflated sense of self-esteem and an exaggerated, euphoric belief in capabilities that denies any self-limitations or realistic obstacles but sees others as standing in the way.
3. Flight of ideas and pressured speech.
4. High energy and restlessness.
5. Disorganized impulsivity that does not foresee the consequences of the behavior.
6. A reduced need for sleep and a denial of emotional or physical pain.
7. A positive family history of affective disorder.
8. Verbal and/or physical aggression coupled with tantrum-like behavior (e.g., breaking things explosively) if wishes are blocked, which is in contrast to an earlier pattern of obedience and restraint.
9. Poor attention span and susceptibility to distraction.
10. Lack of follow-through in projects even though the energy level is very high, since the behavior lacks discipline and goal-directedness.
11. Impulsive, self-defeating behaviors that reflect a lack of recognition of dangerous consequences (e.g., shoplifting, alcohol abuse, drug abuse, or sexual promiscuity).
12. Outlandish dress and grooming.

__. _____

_____

—. _____
    _____
    _____

—. _____
    _____

LONG-TERM GOALS

1. Increase control over impulses, reduce energy level, and stabilize mood.
2. Decrease irritability and impulsivity, improve social judgment, and develop sensitivity to the consequences of behavior while having more realistic expectations of self.
3. Acknowledge the underlying depression and cope with feelings of fear of loss.
4. Talk about underlying feelings of low self-esteem or guilt and fears of rejection, dependency, and abandonment by significant others.

—. _____
    _____

—. _____
    _____
    _____

—. _____
    _____

SHORT-TERM OBJECTIVES

1. Describe the nature of symptoms related to the mood disorder. (1, 2)

THERAPEUTIC INTERVENTIONS

1. Conduct a thorough diagnostic interview to assess the client for pressured speech, flight of idea, euphoria, inflated self-esteem, impulsivity, lack of discipline, reduced sleep pattern, low frustration tolerance, and/or poor anger management.

2. Administer or arrange for psychological testing to further assess the client for

2. Parents provide psychoso-cial history data regarding the client and his/her ex-tended family, especially in regard to bipolar illness symptoms. (3)

3. Identify stressors that pre-cipitate manic behavior. (4)

4. Take psychotropic medica-tions as directed. (5, 6)

5. Agree to impatient hospital-ization to stabilize moods and reduce risk of harm to self or others. (7)

6. Parents and family mem-bers verbalize greater un-derstanding about the nature of bipolar disorder. (8, 9)

mania/hypomania; provide feedback to the client and parents.

3. Gather psychosocial history information from the client's parents to assess for patterns of mania in the client and bipolar illness in the client's extended family.

4. Explore the stressors that precipitate the client's manic behavior (e.g., school failure, social rejection, family trauma).

5. Arrange for a psychiatric examination for the client to evaluate the necessity for a prescription for mood-stabilizing medication (e.g., lithium carbonate).

6. Monitor the client's compli-ance with and reaction to the psychotropic medica-tion (i.e., side effects and effectiveness).

7. Arrange for inpatient hospi-talization if the client's un-stable and erratic mood swings reach a point where he/she is dangerous to self and others.

8. Educate parents and family members about the nature, treatment, and prognosis of dipolar disorder.

9. Assign the parents to read *Bipolar Disorders* by Waltz to educate them about the symptoms and treatment of bipolar disorder.

7. Demonstrate trust in the therapeutic relationship by sharing fears about dependency, loss, and abandonment. (10, 11, 12, 13)

10. Pledge to be there consistently to help, listen to, and support the client.

11. Explore the client's fears of abandonment by sources of love and nurturance.

12. Probe real or perceived losses in the client's life.

13. Review ways for the client to replace the losses and put them in perspective.

8. Differentiate between real and imagined losses, rejections, and abandonments. (14)

14. Help the client differentiate between real and imagined, actual and exaggerated losses.

9. Identify the causes for low self-esteem and abandonment fears. (15, 16)

15. Explore the causes for the client's low self-esteem and abandonment fears in the family-of-origin history.

16. Hold family therapy sessions to explore and confront parental rejection or emotional abandonment of the client.

10. Decrease grandiose statements and express self more realistically. (17)

17. Confront the client's grandiosity and demandingness gradually but firmly.

11. Achieve mood stability, becoming slower to react with anger, less expansive, and more socially appropriate and sensitive. (18)

18. Set a goal with the client to attempt to control his/her impulses and to be more sensitive to the social impact of his/her behavior.

12. Identify instances of impulsive behavior that have led to negative consequences. (19, 20, 21, 22)

19. Assist the client in listing instances of impulsive behavior and the negative consequences that resulted from those behaviors.

20. Repeatedly focus on the consequences of behavior to reduce thoughtless impulsivity.

21. Facilitate impulse control by using role playing, behavior rehearsal, and role reversal to increase sensitivity to the consequences of behavior.

22. Assign homework to the client designed to help the client understand that impulsive behavior has costly negative consequences for himself/herself and others (or assign the exercise "Action Minus Thought Equals Painful Consequences" from the *Brief Adolescent Therapy Homework Planner* by Jongsma, Peterson, and McInnis).

13. Parents reinforce positive behaviors while setting firm limits on hostility. (23, 24)

23. Meet with the parents to encourage them and teach them through modeling and role playing to set firm limits on the client's angry rebellion while positively reinforcing the client's prosocial, measured behavior.

24. Assign the parents the task of listing rules and contingencies for the home (or assign the exercise "Clear Rules, Positive Reinforcement, Appropriate Consequences" from the *Brief Adolescent Therapy Homework Planner* by Jongsma, Peterson, and McInnis);

14. Accept the limits set on manipulative and hostile behaviors that attempt to control others. (25, 26)

15. Speak more slowly and calmly while maintaining subject focus. (27, 28)

16. Dress and groom in a less attention-seeking manner. (29)

17. Identify positive traits and behaviors that build genuine self-esteem. (30, 31)

process the completed assignment.

25. Set limits on the client's manipulation or acting out by making rules and establishing clear consequences for breaking them.

26. Reinforce the parents in setting reasonable limits on the client's behavior and in expressing their commitment to love him/her unconditionally.

27. Provide structure and focus for the client's thoughts and actions by regulating the direction of conversation and establishing plans for behavior.

28. Verbally reinforce slower speech and more deliberate thought processes.

29. Encourage and reinforce appropriate dress and grooming.

30. Assist the client in identifying strengths and assets to build self-esteem and confidence.

31. Assign the client homework designed to increase his/her genuine self-esteem through the identification and listing of his/her positive character and personality traits (or assign the exercise "I Am A Good Person" from the *Brief Adolescent Therapy Homework Planner* by Jongsma, Peterson, and McInnis).

18. Verbalize the acceptance of and peace with dependency needs. (32, 33, 34)

32. Interpret the fear and insecurity underlying the client's braggadocio, hostility, and denial of dependency.

33. Hold family therapy sessions where the focus is on the client expressing his/her dependency needs and desire to become more independent in a reasonable manner.

34. Encourage the client to share feelings at a deeper level to facilitate openness, intimacy, and trust in relationships and to counteract denial, fear, and superficiality.

19. Identify and replace negative self-talk that produces fear and low self-esteem. (35, 36)

35. Assist the client in identifying negative cognitive messages that feed a fear of rejection and failure.

36. Assist the client in identifying positive, realistic thoughts that can replace the negative self-talk that nurtures low self-esteem and fear of failure or rejection.

___. _____

___. _____

___. _____

___. _____

___. _____

___. _____

DIAGNOSTIC SUGGESTIONS

Axis I: 296.xx   Bipolar I Disorder
296.89   Bipolar II Disorder
301.13   Cyclothymic Disorder
295.70   Schizoaffective Disorder
296.80   Bipolar Disorder NOS
310.1   Personality Change due to (Axis III Disorder)
314.01   Attention-Deficit/Hyperactivity Disorder,
                Predominantly Hyperactive-Impulsive Type

_____   _____

Axis II: 799.9   Diagnosis Deferred
V71.09   No Diagnosis

_____   _____
_____   _____

MEDICAL CONDITION

BEHAVIORAL DEFINITIONS

1. A diagnosis of a chronic illness that is not life threatening but necessitates changes in living.
2. A diagnosis of an acute, serious illness that is life threatening.
3. A diagnosis of a chronic illness that eventually will lead to an early death.
4. Sad affect, social withdrawal, anxiety, loss of interest in activities, and low energy.
5. Suicidal ideation.
6. Denial of the seriousness of the medical condition.
7. Refusal to cooperate with recommended medical treatments.

__. _____
   _____
   _____
__. _____
   _____
   _____
__. _____
   _____

LONG-TERM GOALS

1. Accept the illness and adapt life to necessary changes.
2. Resolve emotional crisis and face terminal illness's implications.
3. Work through the grieving process and face the reality of own death with peace.
4. Accept emotional support from those who care without pushing them away in anger.
5. Resolve depression and find peace of mind despite the illness.

6. Live life to the fullest extent possible even though time may be limited.
7. Cooperate with the medical treatment regimen without passive-aggressive or active resistance.
8. Become as knowledgeable as possible about the diagnosed condition and about living as normally as possible.
9. Reduce fear, anxiety, and worry associated with the medical condition.

—. _____

_____

—. _____

_____

—. _____

_____

SHORT-TERM OBJECTIVES

1. Describe history, symptoms, and treatment of the medical condition. (1, 2, 3)

2. Family members share with each other feelings that are triggered by the client's medical condition. (4)

THERAPEUTIC INTERVENTIONS

1. Gather a history of the facts regarding the client's medical condition, including symptoms, treatment, and prognosis.

2. With the client's informed consent, contact the treating physician and family members for additional medical information regarding the client's diagnosis, treatment, and prognosis.

3. Assist the client in identifying, sorting through, and verbalizing the various feelings generated by his/her medical condition.

4. Meet with family members to facilitate their clarifying and sharing possible feelings of guilt, anger,

3. Identify and grieve the losses or limitations that have been experienced due to the medical condition. (5, 6, 7, 8)

helplessness, and/or sibling attention jealousy associated with the client's medical condition.

5. Ask the client to list the changes, losses, or limitations that have resulted from the medical condition.

6. Educate the client on the stages of the grieving process and answer any questions.

7. Suggest that the client read a book on grief and loss (e.g., *Good Grief* by Westberg, *How Can It Be All Right When Everything Is All Wrong?* by Smedes, or *When Bad Things Happen to Good People* by Kushner).

8. Assign the client to keep a daily grief journal to be shared in therapy sessions.

4. Decrease time spent focused on the negative aspects of the medical condition. (9, 10)

9. Suggest that the client set aside a specific time-limited period each day to focus on mourning the medical condition. After time period is up, have the client resume regular daily activities with agreement to put off thoughts until next scheduled time. (Mourning times could include putting on dark clothing, listening to sad music, and so forth. Clothing should be changed at the end of allotted time period.)

5. Implement faith-based activities as a source of comfort and hope. (11)

6. Verbalize acceptance of the reality of the medical condition and its consequences while decreasing denial. (12, 13)

7. Verbally express fears about deterioration of physical condition and death. (14, 15, 16)

10. Challenge the client to focus his/her thoughts on the positive aspects of life, rather than on the losses associated with his/her medical condition; reinforce instances of such a positive focus.

11. Encourage the client to rely upon his/her spiritual faith promises, activities (e.g., prayer, meditation, worship, music) and fellowship as sources of support.

12. Gently confront the client's denial of the seriousness of his/her condition and of the need for compliance with medical treatment procedures.

13. Reinforce the client's acceptance of his/her medical condition.

14. Explore and process the client's fears associated with deterioration of physical health, death, and dying.

15. Normalize the client's feelings of grief, sadness, or anxiety associated with his/her medical condition; encourage verbal expression of these emotions.

16. Assess the client for and treat his/her depression and anxiety. (See the Depression and Anxiety chapters in this Planner).

8. Attend a support group of others diagnosed with a similar illness. (17)

9. Parents and family members attend a support group. (18)

10. Comply with the medication regimen and necessary medical procedures, reporting any side effects or problems to physicians or therapists. (2, 19, 20, 21)

17. Refer the client to a support group of others living with a similar medical condition.

18. Refer family members to a community-based support group associated with the client's medical condition.

2. With the client's informed consent, contact the treating physician and family members for additional medical information regarding the client's diagnosis, treatment, and prognosis.

19. Monitor and reinforce the client's compliance with the medical treatment regimen.

20. Explore and address the client's misconceptions, fears, and situational factors that interfere with medical treatment compliance.

21. Confront any manipulation, passive-aggressive, and denial mechanisms that block the client's compliance with the medical treatment regimen.

11. Engage in social, productive, and recreational activities that are possible despite the medical condition. (22, 23)

22. Sort out with the client activities that can still be enjoyed alone and with others.

23. Solicit a commitment from the client to increase his/her activity level by engaging in enjoyable and challenging activities; reinforce such engagement.

12. Implement behavioral stress-reduction skills to terminate exacerbation of medical condition due to tension. (24, 25, 26)

24. Teach the client deep muscle relaxation and deep breathing methods along with positive imagery to induce relaxation.

25. Utilize electromyograph (EMG) biofeedback to monitor, increase, and reinforce the client's depth of relaxation.

26. Develop and encourage a routine of physical exercise for the client.

13. Identify and replace negative self-talk and catastrophizing that is associated with the medical condition. (27, 28)

27. Assist the client in identifying the cognitive distortions and negative automatic thoughts that contribute to his/her negative attitude and hopeless feelings associated with the medical condition.

28. Generate with the client a list of positive, realistic self-talk that can replace cognitive distortions and catastrophizing regarding his/her medical condition and its treatment.

14. Implement positive imagery as a means of triggering peace of mind and reducing tension. (29, 30)

29. Teach the client the use of positive, relaxing, healing imagery to reduce stress and promote peace of mind.

30. Encourage the client to rely on faith-based promises of God's love, presence, caring, and support to bring peace of mind.

15. Verbalize increased factual understanding of the medical condition. (31, 32)

31. Provide the client with accurate information regarding symptoms, causes,

treatment, and prognosis for medical condition.

32. Refer the client and parents to reading material and reliable Internet resources for accurate medical information.

16. Identify the sources of emotional support that have been beneficial and additional sources that could be tapped. (33, 34)

33. Probe and evaluate the parents' resources of emotional support.

34. Encourage the parents to reach out for support from church leaders, extended family, hospital social services, community support groups, and God.

17. Parents verbalize fears regarding the possible death or severely disabled life of their child. (35)

35. Draw out parents' unspoken fears about the client's possible death; empathize with their panic, helpless frustration, and anxiety. Reassure them of God's presence as the giver and supporter of life.

18. Family members share any conflicts that have developed between them as each person reacts to the child's illness in a unique way. (36, 37)

36. Explore how each parent is dealing with the stress related to the client's illness and whether conflicts have developed between the parents because of differing response styles. Can they be supportive and accepting of each other?

37. Facilitate a spirit of tolerance for individual difference in each person's internal resources and response styles in the face of threat.

19. Parents verbalize an understanding of the healing potential of hope, faith, touch,
love, and one's own personal
positive presence with the
sick child. (38)

38. Stress the healing power in
the family's constant presence with the ill child and
emphasize that there is
strong healing potential in
creating a warm, caring,
supportive, positive environment for the child.

__. _____

_____

__. _____

_____

__. _____

_____

__. _____

_____

__. _____

_____

__. _____

_____

DIAGNOSTIC SUGGESTIONS

Axis I:

316	Psychological Symptoms Affecting (Axis II Disorder)
309.0	Adjustment Disorder With Depressed Mood
309.24	Adjustment Disorder With Anxiety
309.28	Adjustment Disorder With Mixed Anxiety and Depressed Mood
309.3	Adjustment Disorder With Disturbance of Conduct
309.4	Adjustment Disorder With Disturbance of Emotions and Conduct
296.xx	Major Depressive Disorder
311	Depressive Disorder NOS
300.02	Generalized Anxiety Disorder
300.00	Anxiety Disorder NOS
_____	_____
_____	_____

Axis II:

799.9	Diagnosis Deferred
V71.09	No Diagnosis on Axis II
_____	_____
_____	_____

MENTAL RETARDATION

BEHAVIORAL DEFINITIONS

1. Significantly subaverage intellectual functioning as demonstrated by an IQ score of approximately 70 or below on an individually administered intelligence test.
2. Significant impairments in academic functioning, communication, self-care, home living, social skills, and leisure activities.
3. Difficulty understanding and following complex directions in home, school, or community settings.
4. Short- and long-term memory impairment.
5. Concrete thinking or impaired abstract reasoning abilities.
6. Impoverished social skills as manifested by frequent use of poor judgment, limited understanding of the antecedents and consequences of social actions, and lack of reciprocity in peer interactions.
7. Lack of insight and repeated failure to learn from experience or past mistakes.
8. Low self-esteem as evidenced by frequent self-derogatory remarks (e.g., "I'm so stupid.").
9. Recurrent pattern of acting out or engaging in disruptive behaviors without considering the consequences of the actions.

___. _____

_____

___. _____

_____

___. _____

_____

LONG-TERM GOALS

1. Achieve all academic goals identified on the client's individualized educational plan (IEP).
2. Function at an appropriate level of independence in home, residential, educational, or community settings.
3. Develop an awareness and acceptance of intellectual and cognitive limitations but consistently verbalize feelings of self-worth.
4. Parents and/or caregivers develop an awareness and acceptance of the client's intellectual and cognitive capabilities so that they place appropriate expectations on his/her functioning.
5. Consistently comply and follow through with simple directions in a daily routine at home, in school, or in a residential setting.
6. Significantly reduce the frequency and severity of socially inappropriate or acting-out behaviors.

—. _____
_____
—. _____
_____
—. _____

SHORT-TERM OBJECTIVES	THERAPEUTIC INTERVENTIONS
1. Complete a comprehensive intellectual and cognitive assessment. (1)	1. Arrange for a comprehensive intellectual and cognitive assessment to determine the presence of mental retardation and gain greater insight into the client's learning strengths and weaknesses; provide feedback to the client, parents, and school officials.
2. Complete psychological testing. (2)	2. Arrange for psychological testing to assess whether emotional factors or Attention-Deficit/ Hyperactivity Disorder

(ADHD) are interfering with the client's intellectual and academic functioning; provide feedback to the client and parents.

3. Complete neuropsychological testing. (3)

3. Arrange for a neurological examination or neuropsychological testing to rule out possible organic factors that may be contributing to the client's intellectual or cognitive deficits.

4. Complete an evaluation by physical and occupational therapists. (4)

4. Refer the client to physical and occupational therapists to assess perceptual or sensory-motor deficits and determine the need for ongoing physical and/or occupational therapy.

5. Complete a speech/language evaluation. (5)

5. Refer the client to a speech/language pathologist to assess deficits and determine the need for appropriate therapy.

6. The client and his/her parents comply with recommendations made by a multidisciplinary evaluation team at school regarding educational interventions. (6, 7)

6. Attend an individualized educational planning committee (IEPC) meeting with the client's parents, teachers, and other appropriate professionals to determine his/her eligibility for special education services, design educational interventions, and establish goals.

7. Consult with the client, his/her parents, teachers, and other appropriate school officials about designing effective learning programs or interventions that build on the client's

7. Move to an appropriate residential setting. (8)

8. Attend a program focused on teaching basic job skills. (9)

9. Parents maintain regular communication with the client's teachers and other appropriate school officials. (10)

10. Parents, teachers, and caregivers implement a token economy in the classroom or placement setting. (11)

11. Parents increase praise and other positive reinforcement toward the client in regard to his/her academic performance or social behaviors. (12, 13)

strengths and compensate for weaknesses.

8. Consult with the client's parents, school officials, or mental health professionals about the client's need for placement in a foster home, group home, or residential program.

9. Refer the client to a sheltered workshop or educational rehabilitation center to develop basic job skills.

10. Encourage the parents to maintain regular communication with the client's teacher or school officials to monitor his/her academic, behavioral, emotional, and social progress.

11. Design a token economy for the classroom or residential program to reinforce on-task behaviors, completion of school assignments, good impulse control, and positive social skills.

12. Encourage the parents to provide frequent praise and other reinforcement for the client's positive social behaviors and academic performance.

13. Design a reward system or contingency contract to reinforce the client's adaptive or prosocial behaviors.

12. Parents and family cease verbalizations of denial about the client's intellectual and cognitive deficits. (14, 15)

14. Educate the parents about the symptoms and characteristics of mental retardation.

15. Confront and challenge the parents' denial surrounding their child's intellectual deficits so they cooperate with recommendations regarding placement and educational interventions.

13. Parents recognize and verbally acknowledge their unrealistic expectations of or excessive pressure on the client. (16, 17)

16. Conduct family therapy sessions to assess whether the parents are placing excessive pressure on the client to function at a level that he/she is not capable of achieving.

17. Confront and challenge the parents about placing excessive pressure on the client.

14. Parents recognize and verbally acknowledge that their pattern of overprotectiveness interferes with the client's intellectual, emotional, and social development. (18, 19)

18. Observe parent-child interactions to assess whether the parents' overprotectiveness or infantilization of the client interferes with his/her intellectual, emotional, or social development.

19. Assist the parents or caregivers in developing realistic expectations of the client's intellectual capabilities and level of adaptive functioning.

15. Increase participation in family activities or outings. (20, 21, 22, 23, 24)

20. Encourage the parents and family members to regularly include the client in outings or activities (e.g., attending sporting events, going ice skating, visiting a children's museum).

21. Instruct family members to observe positive behaviors by the client between therapy sessions. Reinforce positive behaviors and encourage the client to continue to exhibit these behaviors.

22. Assign the client a task in the family (e.g., cooking a simple meal, gardening) that is appropriate for his/her level of functioning and provides him/her with a sense of responsibility or belonging.

23. Place the client in charge of a routine or basic task at home to increase his/her self-esteem and feelings of self-worth in the family.

24. Assign homework designed to promote the client's feelings of acceptance and a sense of belonging in the family system, school setting, or community (or assign the "You Belong Here" exercise from the *Brief Adolescent Therapy Homework Planner* (Jongsma, Peterson, and McInnis).

16. Increase the frequency of responsible behaviors at school or residential program. (25)

17. Parents agree to and implement an allowance program that helps the client learn to manage money more effectively. (26)

18. Take a bath or shower, dress self independently, comb hair, wash hands before meals, and brush teeth on a daily basis. (27)

19. Parents consistently implement behavior management techniques to reduce the frequency and severity of temper outbursts or disruptive and aggressive behaviors. (28, 29)

25. Consult with school officials or residential staff about the client performing a job (e.g., raising the flag, helping to run video equipment) to build self-esteem and provide him/her with a sense of responsibility.

26. Counsel the parents about setting up an allowance plan to increase the client's responsibilities and help him/her learn simple money management skills.

27. Design and implement a reward system to reinforce desired self-care behaviors such as combing hair, washing dishes, or cleaning bedroom (or assign the parents to use the "Activities of Daily Living" program from the *Brief Adolescent Therapy Homework Planner* by Jongsma, Peterson, and McInnis).

28. Teach the parents effective behavior management techniques (e.g., time-outs, removal of privileges) to decrease the frequency and severity of the client's temper outbursts, acting out, and aggressive behaviors.

29. Encourage the parents to utilize natural, logical consequences for the client's inappropriate social or maladaptive behaviors.

20. Decrease frequency of impulsive, disruptive, or aggressive behaviors. (30, 31)

30. Teach the client basic mediational and self-control strategies (e.g., "stop, look, listen, and think") to delay gratification and inhibit impulses.

31. Train the client in the use of guided imagery or relaxation techniques to calm himself/herself down and develop greater control of anger.

21. Recognize and verbally identify appropriate and inappropriate social behaviors. (32)

32. Utilize role playing and modeling in individual sessions to teach the client positive social skills. Reinforce new or emerging prosocial behaviors.

22. Increase the ability to identify and express feelings. (33, 34, 35)

33. Educate the client about how to identify and label different emotions.

34. Tell the client to draw faces of basic emotions, then have him/her share times when he/she experienced the different emotions.

35. Teach the client effective communication skills (i.e., proper listening, good eye contact, "I" statements) to improve his/her ability to express thoughts, feelings, and needs more clearly.

23. Express feelings of sadness, anxiety, and insecurity that are related to cognitive and intellectual limitations. (36, 37)

36. Assist the client in coming to an understanding and acceptance of the limitations surrounding his/her intellectual deficits and adaptive functioning.

37. Explore the client's feelings of depression, anxiety, and insecurity that are related to cognitive or intellectual limitations. Provide encouragement and support for the client.

24. Increase the frequency of positive self-statements. (38, 39)

38. Encourage the client to participate in the Special Olympics to build self-esteem.

39. Explore times when the client achieved success or accomplished a goal; reinforce positive steps that the client took to successfully accomplish goals.

25. Identify when it is appropriate to seek help with a task and when it is not. (40)

40. Assist the client in identifying appropriate and inappropriate times to ask for help; identify a list of acceptable resource people to whom the client can turn for support, help, and supervision when necessary.

26. Recognize and verbally identify appropriate and inappropriate sexual behaviors. (41)

41. Provide sex education to help the client identify and verbally recognize appropriate and inappropriate sexual urges and behaviors.

__. _____
   _____

__. _____
   _____

__. _____
   _____

__. _____
   _____

__. _____
   _____

__. _____
   _____

DIAGNOSTIC SUGGESTIONS

Axis I: 299.00   Autistic Disorder
299.80   Rett's Disorder
299.80   Asperger's Disorder
299.10   Childhood Disintegrative Disorder

———   ——————————————

———   ——————————————

Axis II: 317   Mild Mental Retardation
318.0   Moderate Mental Retardation
318.1   Severe Mental Retardation
318.2   Profound Mental Retardation
319   Mental Retardation, Severity Unspecified
V62.89   Borderline Intellectual Functioning
799.9   Diagnosis Deferred
V71.09   No Diagnosis

———   ——————————————

———   ——————————————

NEGATIVE PEER INFLUENCES

BEHAVIORAL DEFINITIONS

1. Strong susceptibility to negative peer influences that contribute to problems with authority figures at home, at school, and in the community; sexual promiscuity; or substance abuse problems.
2. Recurrent pattern of engaging in disruptive, negative attention-seeking behaviors at school or in the community to elicit attention, approval, or support from peers.
3. Excessive willingness to follow the lead of others in order to win approval or acceptance.
4. Propensity for taking ill-advised risks or engaging in thrill-seeking behavior in peer group settings.
5. Identification with negative peer group as a means to gain acceptance or elevate status and self-esteem.
6. Affiliation with negative peer groups or gangs to protect self from harm, danger, or perceived threats in the environment.
7. Tendency to gravitate toward negative peer groups because of underlying feelings of low self-esteem and insecurity.
8. Verbal report of being ostracized, teased, or mocked by peers at school or in the community.
9. History of rejection experiences within family system or peer group that contribute to the desire to seek out negative peer groups for belonging.
10. Social immaturity and pronounced deficits in the area of social skills.
11. Participation in substance abuse and other acting-out behaviors to gain group acceptance.

—. _____

_____

—· _____
    _____
—· _____
    _____

LONG-TERM GOALS

1. Establish positive self-image and feelings of self-worth separate from affiliating with negative peer groups.
2. Achieve a sense of belonging and acceptance within the family and within positive peer groups by consistently engaging in socially appropriate behaviors.
3. Develop positive social skills necessary to establish and maintain positive, meaningful, and lasting peer friendships.
4. Resist negative peer group influences on a regular, consistent basis.
5. Terminate involvement with negative peer groups or gangs.
6. Eliminate all acting-out behavior and delinquent acts.
7. Resolve the core conflicts that contribute to susceptibility to negative peer group influences.

—· _____
    _____
—· _____
    _____
—· _____
    _____

SHORT-TERM OBJECTIVES

THERAPEUTIC INTERVENTIONS

1. Describe the nature of peer relationships. (1, 2, 3)

1. Explore the client's perception of the nature of his/her peer relationships as well as any areas of conflict; encourage and support him/her in expressing thoughts and feelings about peer relationships.

2. Gather a detailed psychosocial history of the client's development, family environment, and interpersonal relationships to gain insight into the factors contributing to his/her desire to affiliate with negative peer groups.

3. Instruct the client to keep a daily journal where he/she records both positive and negative experiences with peers that evoked strong emotions. Process excerpts from this journal in follow-up sessions to uncover factors that contribute to the desire to affiliate with negative peer groups, as well as to identify strengths that the client can use to build positive peer relationships.

2. Identify and verbalize needs that are met through involvement in negative peer groups. (4)

4. Assist the client in identifying the social-emotional needs that he/she attempts to meet through his/her involvement with negative peer groups (e.g., achieve sense of belonging and acceptance, elevate status, obtain material goods, seek protection).

5. Assist the parents in establishing clearly defined rules and boundaries, as well as providing greater structure, to deter the client from being highly susceptible to negative peer influences.

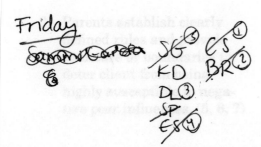

4. Parents and/or teachers implement a reward system to reinforce desired social behaviors. (8)

5. Identify the negative consequences on self and others of participation with negative peer groups. (9, 10)

6. Encourage the parents to maintain regular communication with school officials to monitor the client's relationships with peers; encourage parents and teachers to follow through with firm, consistent limits if the client engages in acting-out, disruptive, or aggressive behavior with peers at school.

7. Establish a contingency contract that identifies specific consequences that the client will receive if he/she engages in disruptive, acting-out, or antisocial behaviors with peers. Have the client repeat terms of contract to demonstrate understanding.

8. Design a reward system for parents and/or teachers to reinforce the client for engaging in specific, positive social behaviors and deter the need to affiliate with negative peer groups (e.g., introduce self to other individuals in positive peer group, display kindness, help another peer with academic or social problems).

9. Have the client list between 5 and 10 negative consequences that his/her participation with negative peer groups has had on himself/herself and others.

10. Firmly confront the client about the impact of his/her involvement with negative peer groups, pointing out consequences for himself/herself and others.

6. Increase the number of statements that reflect acceptance of responsibility for negative social behavior. (11, 12, 13)

11. Challenge and confront statements by the client that minimize the impact that his/her involvement with negative peer groups has on his/her behavior.

12. Confront statements in which the client blames other peers for his/her acting-out, disruptive, or antisocial behaviors and fails to accept responsibility for his/her actions.

13. Challenge the parents to cease blaming the client's misbehavior on his/her peers; instead, encourage parents to focus on the client and set limits for his/her negative social behaviors that occur while affiliating with peers.

7. Implement effective coping strategies to help resist negative peer influences. (14, 15, 16, 17)

14. Teach mediational and self-control techniques (e.g., "Stop, look, listen, and think"; count to 10; walk away) to help the client successfully resist negative peer influences.

15. Utilize role-playing, modeling, or behavioral rehearsal techniques to teach the client more effective ways to resist negative peer influences, meet his/her social

needs, or establish lasting, meaningful friendships (e.g., walk away, change subject, say "no," initiate conversations with positive peers, demonstrate empathy).

16. Assign the client to read *How to Say No and Keep Your Friends* (Scott) to teach him/her effective ways to resist negative peer influences and maintain friendships. Process reading with the client.

17. Explore times when the client was able to successfully resist negative peer influences and not engage in acting-out, disruptive, or antisocial behaviors. Process the experiences and encourage him/her to use similar coping strategies to resist negative peer influences at present or in future.

8. Increase assertive behavior to deal more effectively with negative peer pressure. (18)

18. Teach the client effective communication and assertiveness skills (e.g., "I have to leave now."; "I can't afford to get into any more trouble.") to help him/her successfully resist negative peer pressure.

9. Attend and regularly participate in group therapy sessions that focus on developing positive social skills. (19, 20)

19. Refer the client for group therapy to improve social skills and learn ways to successfully resist negative peer pressure; direct client to self-disclose at least two times in each group therapy session about his/her peer relationships.

20. Refer the client to a behavioral contracting group where he/she and other group members develop contracts each week to increase the frequency of positive peer interactions; review progress with the contracts each week, and praise the client for achieving goals regarding peer interactions.

10. Identify and implement positive social skills that will help to improve peer relationships and establish friendships. (21, 22)

21. Teach positive social skills (e.g., introducing self to others, active listening, verbalizing empathy and concern for others, ignoring teasing) to improve peer relationships and increase chances of developing meaningful friendships [or use Skillstreaming: The Adolescent Kit (McGinnis and Goldstein), available from Childswork/Childsplay, LLC].

22. Give the client a homework assignment of practicing newly learned positive social skills at least once each day between therapy sessions; review implementation, reinforcing success and redirecting for failure.

11. Increase involvement in positive social activities or community organizations. (23, 24)

23. Encourage the client to become involved in positive peer groups or community activities where he/she can gain acceptance and status (e.g., church or synagogue youth groups, YWCA or YMCA functions, school

clubs, Boys Clubs or Girls Clubs).

24. Consult with school officials about ways to increase the client's socialization with positive peer groups at school (e.g., join school choir or newspaper staff, participate in student government, become involved in school fundraiser).

12. Increase frequency of positive interactions with peers. (25, 26, 27, 28)

25. Assign the client the task of initiating one social contact per day with other peers who are identified as being responsible, dependable, friendly, or well liked.

26. Direct the client to initiate three phone contacts per week to different individuals outside of the identified negative peer group.

27. Give the client a directive to invite a peer or friend (outside of negative peer group) for an overnight visit and/or set up an overnight visit at the other peer's or friend's home; process experience in follow-up session.

28. Give the client a homework assignment of engaging in three altruistic or benevolent acts with peers before the next therapy session. Process how others respond to acts of kindness, and encourage the client to engage in similar behavior in the future.

13. Identify and implement positive ways to meet needs other than through participation in negative peer group activities or gang involvement. (29, 30)

29. Brainstorm with the client more adaptive ways for him/her to meet needs for recognition/status, acceptance, material goods, and excitement other than through his/her involvement with negative peer groups or gangs (e.g., attend or participate in sporting events, secure employment, visit amusement park with youth group).

30. Assign the client to view the video entitled *Handling Peer Pressure and Gangs* (part of the Peace Talks series available through Wellness Reproductions & Publishing, LLC) to help the client resist negative peer influences or pressure to join a gang.

14. Identify and list resource people to whom the client can turn for support, comfort, and guidance. (31)

31. Help the client to identify a list of resource people, both peers and adults, at school or in the community to whom he/she can turn for support, comfort, or guidance when he/she is experiencing negative peer pressure and/or feels rejected by peers.

15. Identify and express feelings associated with past rejection experiences. (32, 33)

32. Explore the client's background in peer relationships to assess whether he/she feels rejected, ostracized, or unaccepted by many peers. Assist the client in identifying possible causes of rejection or alienation (e.g., hypersensitivity

to teasing, target of scape-goating, poor social skills).

33. Use the empty chair technique to help the client express his/her feelings of anger, hurt, and sadness toward individuals by whom he/she has felt rejected or alienated in the past.

16. Verbalize recognition of how underlying feelings of low self-esteem and insecurity are related to involvement with negative peer groups. (34, 35, 36, 37)

34. Assist the client in making a connection between underlying feelings of low self-esteem and insecurity and his/her gravitation toward negative peer groups to achieve a sense of belonging and acceptance.

35. Assist the client in identifying more constructive ways to build self-esteem and win approval other than affiliating with negative peer groups that influence him/her to act out and engage in antisocial behavior (e.g., try out for school play, attend a school dance, participate in sporting or recreational activities).

36. Instruct the client to identify 5 to 10 strengths or interests; review the list in follow-up session and encourage the client to utilize his/her strengths to build self-esteem and increase positive peer interactions (or assign the "Show Your Strengths" exercise from the *Brief Adolescent Therapy Homework Planner* by

Jongsma, Peterson, and McInnis).

37. Help the client to identify healthy risks that he/she can take in the near future to improve his/her self-esteem (e.g., try out for sports team, attend new social functions or gathering, initiate conversations with unfamiliar people outside of negative peer group); challenge the client to take three healthy risks before the next therapy session.

17. Overly rigid parents recognize how their strict or harsh enforcement of rules and boundaries contributes to the client's gravitation toward negative peer groups. (38, 39)

38. Explore whether the parents are overly rigid or strict in their establishment of rules and boundaries to the point where the client has little opportunity to socialize with peers and rebels by engaging in acting-out behaviors with negative peer groups.

39. Encourage and challenge the overly rigid parents to loosen rules and boundaries to allow the client increased opportunities to engage in socially appropriate activities or positive peer group activities.

18. Parents recognize how their lack of supervision and failure to follow through with limits contributes to the client's affiliation with negative peer groups. (40)

40. Conduct family therapy session to explore whether the parents' lack of supervision and inability to establish appropriate parent-child boundaries contribute to the client's gravitation toward negative peer group influences.

19. Complete a substance abuse evaluation and comply with the recommendations offered by the evaluation findings. (41)

41. Conduct or arrange for a substance abuse evaluation and/or treatment for the client (see Chemical Dependence chapter in this Planner).

__. _____

_____

__. _____

_____

__. _____

_____

__. _____

_____

__. _____

_____

__. _____

_____

DIAGNOSTIC SUGGESTIONS

Axis I:	313.81	Oppositional Defiant Disorder
	312.82	Conduct Disorder, Adolescent-Onset Type
	312.9	Disruptive Behavior Disorder NOS
	314.01	Attention-Deficit/Hyperactivity Disorder, Predominately Hyperactive-Impulsive Type
	314.9	Attention-Deficit/Hyperactivity Disorder NOS
	V71.02	Adolescent Antisocial Behavior
	V62.81	Relational Problem NOS
	_____	_____
Axis II:	799.9	Diagnosis Deferred
	V71.09	No Diagnosis
	_____	_____
	_____	_____

OPPOSITIONAL DEFIANT

BEHAVIORAL DEFINITIONS

1. Displays a pattern of negativistic, hostile, and defiant behavior toward most adults.
2. Often acts as if parents, teachers, and other authority figures are the "enemy."
3. Erupts in temper tantrums (e.g., screaming, crying, throwing objects, thrashing on ground, or refusing to move) in defiance of direction from an adult caregiver.
4. Consistently argues with adults.
5. Often defies or refuses to comply with reasonable requests and rules.
6. Deliberately annoys people and is easily annoyed by others.
7. Often blames others for own mistakes or misbehavior.
8. Consistently is angry and resentful.
9. Often is spiteful or vindictive.
10. Has experienced significant impairment in social, academic, or occupational functioning.

__. _____
_____

__. _____
_____

__. _____
_____

LONG-TERM GOALS

1. Marked reduction in the intensity and frequency of hostile and defiant behaviors toward adults.
2. Terminate temper tantrums and replace with controlled, respectful compliance with directions from authority figures.
3. Begin to consistently interact with adults in a mutually respectful manner.
4. Bring hostile, defiant behaviors within socially acceptable standards.
5. Replace hostile, defiant behaviors toward adults with respect and cooperation.
6. Resolve the conflict that underlies the anger, hostility, and defiance.
7. Reach a level of reduced tension, increased satisfaction, and improved communication with family and/or other authority figures.

—. _____
   _____
   _____

—. _____
   _____
   _____

—. _____
   _____

SHORT-TERM OBJECTIVES

1. Describe perception of own behavior and feelings toward rules and authority figures. (1, 2)

THERAPEUTIC INTERVENTIONS

1. Actively build the level of trust with the client through consistent eye contact, active listening, unconditional positive regard, and warm acceptance to help increase his/her disclosure of thoughts and feelings.

2. Explore the client's perception of his/her oppositional pattern toward rules and authority figures.

2. Participate in family therapy with a focus on changes that are necessary to produce harmony. (3, 4)

3. Read and process in a family session the story "The Little Crab" from *Stories for the Third Ear* (Wallas). Follow up by using the metaphor of the story as a basis for family/client change, referencing it regularly in future sessions.

4. Facilitate family therapy sessions in which the issues of respect, cooperation, and conflict resolution are addressed and in which possible solutions are reached and implemented.

3. Decrease the frequency and intensity of hostile, negativistic, and defiant interactions with parents/adults. (5, 6)

5. Encourage the client's verbalization of negative, hostile feelings in individual sessions in an open, but respectful, manner.

6. Assist the client in identifying negative, hostile, and defiant behaviors; then offer a paradoxical interpretation or reframing for each (e.g., "You want Mom to set your curfew to an earlier time?").

4. Identify preferred treatment by parents/adults. (7, 8)

7. Establish with the client the basics of treating others respectfully. Teach the principle of reciprocity, asking him/her to agree to treat everyone in a respectful manner for a one-week period to see if others will reciprocate by treating him/her with more respect.

8. Confront the client with the challenges of being in control as his/her parents or other authority figures must be (or assign the exercise "If I Could Run My Family" from the *Brief Adolescent Therapy Homework Planner* by Jongsma, Peterson, and McInnis).

5. Parents use behavior modification principals to intervene on the client's behavior. (9)

9. Assist the parents in identifying and implementing new methods of intervention in the client's behaviors that focus on positive parenting (or assign the parents the exercise "Switching from Defense to Offense" from the *Brief Adolescent Therapy Homework Planner* by Jongsma, Peterson, and McInnis); monitor the parents' follow-through, coaching and giving encouragement as needed.

6. Recognize and verbalize hurt or angry feelings in constructive ways. (5, 10, 11)

5. Encourage the client's verbalization of negative, hostile feelings in individual sessions in an open, but respectful, manner.

10. Assist the client in becoming able to recognize needs and feelings and express them in constructive, respectful ways.

11. Use a therapeutic game [e.g., The Talking, Feeling, and Doing Game (by Gardner; available from Creative Therapeutics), or The Ungame (by Zakich; available from The Ungame

Company)] to expand the client's ability to express feelings respectfully.

7. Verbalize the connection between feelings and behavior. (12, 13)

12. Probe to clarify the client's feelings associated with defiance to help him/her make the connection between feelings and behaviors.

13. Use a set of dominoes and/or Domino Rally to help the client build an awareness of consequences and a sense of internal control. Play dominoes with him/her using an established set of rules. Use Domino Rally by setting it up and allowing the client to start the domino chain reactions. Emphasize the behavioral chain of events that occur, and explain how feelings lead to a chain of behavioral events. (See the chapter by Case in *101 Favorite Play Therapy Techniques* by Kaduson and Schaefer.)

8. Identify and verbalize what is needed from parents and other adults. (10, 14)

10. Assist the client in becoming able to recognize needs and feelings and express them in constructive, respectful ways.

14. Assist the client in reframing complaints into requests for positive change (or assign the exercise "Filing a Complaint" from the *Brief Adolescent Therapy Homework Planner* by Jongsma, Peterson, and McInnis).

9. Increase the frequency of civil, respectful interactions with parents/adults. (7, 15)

10. Identify targets and causes for angry feelings. (16)

11. Demonstrate the ability to play by the rules in a cooperative fashion. (17)

12. Parents clearly state what is acceptable and unacceptable behavior in the family and identify positive and negative consequences of the client's behavior. (18, 19)

7. Establish with the client the basics of treating others respectfully. Teach the principle of reciprocity, asking him/her to agree to treat everyone in a respectful manner for a one-week period to see if others will reciprocate by treating him/her with more respect.

15. Videotape a family session, using appropriate portions to show the family interaction patterns that are destructive; teach family members, using role playing, role reversal, and modeling, to implement more respectful patterns.

16. Ask the client to list all individuals with whom he/she feels angry and the reasons for the anger.

17. Play checkers, first with the client determining the rules (and therapist holding the client to those rules) and then with rules determined by the therapist. Process the experience, and give positive verbal praise to the client for following established rules.

18. Institute with the parents and teachers a system of positive consequences (see Selekman's *Solution-Focused Therapy with Children*) that promote and encourage prosocial and cooperative behaviors (e.g., writing a card to a relative,

mowing a neighbor's lawn, doing a good deed for an elderly neighbor as a consequence for bad behavior).

19. Help the parents to clarify and communicate to the client what constitutes acceptable and unacceptable behavior in the family. Then ask them to implement as a consequence temporary "excommunication" of the child from the family (i.e., denial of interactions and privileges) when unacceptable behavior is exhibited, reinstating the child to good standing (interaction and privileges occurring again naturally) in the presence of acceptable behavior.

13. Parents ignore inappropriate behaviors and reduce unproductive oververbalizing to the client. (20, 21, 22)

20. Conduct family sessions during which the therapist models adolescent interaction techniques for the parents.

21. Instruct the parents to reduce their own unproductive oververbalizations to the client and to ignore nondestructive abusive/negative behaviors.

22. Monitor the parents' use of new techniques, giving feedback and suggesting adjustments as needed.

14. Parents verbalize clear rules, boundaries, and behavioral expectations, and implement time-out and other behavior modification consequences. (23, 24, 25)

23. Assist the parents in defining acceptable and unacceptable behaviors and in developing time-outs (either a set amount of time or until the behavior is under

control) to reinforce these limits.

24. Help the parents to develop and implement a behavior modification contract in which appropriate behaviors would be rewarded with money or special privileges (e.g., attending an event, going on a family outing), while inappropriate behaviors would result in fines (losing money and privileges).

25. Monitor the parents' follow-through in administering the behavior modification contract and/or time-outs. Give feedback, support, and praise as appropriate.

15. Parents acknowledge their own conflicts that influence the client's misbehavior. (26, 27)

26. In family sessions, expose the parental conflict that underlies the client's behavior; refer the parents to conjoint sessions to begin to resolve their issues of conflict.

27. Use a family system approach in individual sessions to assist the client in seeing the family from a different perspective and in moving toward disengaging from dysfunction.

16. Parents implement the Barkley method of oppositional child behavior control. (28)

28. Ask the parents to watch the video *Techniques for Working with Oppositional Defiant Disorder in Children* (Barkley) or read *Your Defiant Child* (Barkley and Benton) to develop an understanding of the condition

and the ways to intervene in the most effective ways; encourage implementation and monitor effectiveness.

17. Identify preferred relational patterns between family members. (29, 30)

29. Facilitate a family session in which the family is sculpted (see *Peoplemaking* by Satir). Process the experience with the family. Then sculpt them as they would like to be.

30. Conduct family sessions during which the family system and its interactions are analyzed. Develop and implement a strategic/ structural/experiential intervention.

18. Parents complete or rule out the emancipation of the child. (31, 32, 33)

31. Explore the options for placement of the client outside the home (e.g., with a relative, in foster care, or respite care, or emancipation) with the parents.

32. Direct the parents to seek legal counsel on the process of emancipation.

33. Support the parents in their decision to emancipate the client, and process the feelings they have regarding their decision.

__. _____

_____

__. _____

_____

__. _____

_____

__. _____

_____

__. _____

_____

__. _____

_____

DIAGNOSTIC SUGGESTIONS

Axis I:

313.81	Oppositional Defiant Disorder	
312.81	Conduct Disorder, Childhood-Onset Type	
312.82	Conduct Disorder, Adolescent-Onset Type	
312.9	Disruptive Behavior Disorder NOS	
314.091	Attention-Deficit/Hyperactivity Disorder, Predominantly Hyperactive-Impulsive Type	
314.9	Attention-Deficit/Hyperactivity Disorder NOS	
V62.81	Relational Problem NOS	
_____	_____	
_____	_____	

Axis II:

799.9	Diagnosis Deferred	
V71.09	No Diagnosis on Axis II	
_____	_____	
_____	_____	

PARENTING

BEHAVIORAL DEFINITIONS

1. Express difficulty maintaining meaningful communication with their teenager.
2. Feel growing disconnection from their teen as he/she develops stronger bonds with a peer group.
3. Lack skills in setting age-appropriate and effective limits for their teen.
4. Increasing conflict between spouses over how to parent/discipline their child.
5. One parent is perceived as overindulgent, while the other is seen as too harsh.
6. A pattern of harsh, rigid, and demeaning behavior toward the child.
7. A pattern of physically and emotionally abusive parenting.
8. Frequently struggle to control their emotional reactions to their child's misbehavior.
9. Have been told by others (e.g., school officials, court authorities, and/or friends) that their teen's behavior needs to be addressed.
10. Their adolescent child has become strongly oppositional toward any rules or limit setting.

__. _____
_____
_____

__. _____
_____
_____

__. _____
_____

LONG-TERM GOALS

1. Achieve a level of competent, effective parenting.
2. Terminate ineffective and/or abusive parenting and implement positive, effective techniques.
3. Strengthen parental team by resolving marital conflicts.
4. Achieve a level of greater family connectedness.
5. Establish and maintain a healthy, functioning parental team.
6. Adopt appropriate expectations for their adolescent as well as themselves as parents.
7. Resolve past childhood or adolescent issues that prevent effective parenting.

—. _____

_____

—. _____

_____

—. _____

_____

SHORT-TERM OBJECTIVES	THERAPEUTIC INTERVENTIONS
1. Provide information on the marital relationship, child behavior expectations, and style of parenting. (1)	1. Engage parents through the use of empathy and normalization of their struggles with parenting and obtain information on their marital relationship, child behavior expectations, and parenting style.
2. Identify specific marital conflicts and work toward their resolution. (2, 3)	2. Analyze the data received from parents about their relationship and parenting and establish or rule out the presence of marital conflicts.

3. Conduct or refer the parents to marital/relationship therapy to resolve the conflicts that are preventing them from being effective parents.

3. Complete recommended evaluation instruments and receive the results. (4, 5, 6)

4. Administer or arrange for the parents to complete the Parenting Stress Index (PSI) or Parent-Child Relationship Inventory (PCRI) instrument.

5. Share results of assessment instruments with the parents and identify issues to begin working on to strengthen the parenting team.

6. Use testing results to identify parental strengths and begin to build the confidence and effectiveness level of the parental team.

4. Express feelings of frustration, helplessness, and inadequacy that each parent experiences in the parenting role. (7, 8, 9)

7. Create a compassionate, empathetic environment where the parents become comfortable enough to let their guard down and express the frustrations of parenting.

8. Educate the parents on the full scope of parenting by using humor or normalization.

9. Help the parents reduce their unrealistic expectations of themselves and of their child.

5. Identify unresolved childhood issues that affect parenting and work toward their resolution. (10, 11, 12)

10. Explore each parent's story of their childhood and identify any unresolved issues that are present.

11. Help the parents identify how past unresolved adolescent issues are affecting their ability to parent effectively.

12. Assist the parents in working through their issues from childhood that are unresolved.

6. Decrease parental reactivity to the child's behaviors. (13, 14, 15)

13. Evaluate the level of the parental team's reactivity to the child's behavior and then help the parents to learn to respond in a more modulated, thoughtful, planned manner.

14. Help the parents become aware of the "hot buttons" they have that the child can push to get a quick negative response and how this overreactive response reduces their effectiveness as parents.

15. Role-play reactive situations with the parents to help them learn to thoughtfully respond instead of automatically reacting to their child's demands or negative behaviors.

7. Identify the child's personality/temperament type that causes challenges and develop specific strategies to more effectively deal with that personality/temperament type. (16, 17)

16. Assist the parents in identifying their adolescent's personality/temperament type and then in developing strategies to more effectively parent him/her.

17. Support, encourage, and empower the parents in implementing new strategies for parenting their adolescent, giving feedback and redirection, as needed.

8. Verbalize increased understanding of the unique trials of parenting adolescents. (18, 19)

18. Teach the parents the concept that adolescence is a time of "normal psychosis" (see *Turning Points* by Pittman) in which the parents need to "ride the adolescent rapids" (see *Preparing for Adolescence* by Dobson) until both survive.

19. Work with the parental team on identifying areas of parenting weaknesses; help them improve their skills and boost their confidence and follow-through.

9. Express verbal support of each other in the parenting process. (20, 21)

20. Assist the parents in identifying and implementing specific ways they can support each other in the process of parenting.

21. Teach the parents the many ways children can split parents from cooperating in order to get their way.

10. Decrease outside pressures, demands, and distractions that drain energy and time from the family. (22, 23)

22. Ask the parents to provide a weekly schedule of their entire family's activities and then evaluate the schedule with them, looking for what activities are valuable and what can possibly be eliminated to create a more focused and relaxed time to parent.

11. Develop and implement realistic and age-appropriate expectations for their children. (24, 25, 26)

23. Give the parents permission not to involve their child and themselves in too numerous activities, organizations, or sports.

24. Have the parents read books to help them develop appropriate limits and expectations for their adolescent (e.g., *Between Parent and Teenager* by Ginott, *Get Out of My Life but First Could You Drive Me and Cheryl to the Mall?* by Wolf, and *Grounded for Life* by Tracy).

25. Ask the parents to read *Parents, Teens, and Boundaries* (Bluestein) to increase their understanding of teens and to aid them in establishing a ground of mutual respect and ongoing dialogue.

26. Assist the parents in developing appropriate and realistic behavioral expectations based on their adolescent's age and level of maturity; encourage them to implement these expectations in a nurturing, instructive manner.

12. Parent's terminate perfectionistic expectations of the child. (27, 28)

27. Point out to the parents any unreasonable and perfectionistic expectations of their adolescent they hold and help them to modify these expectations.

28. Teach the parents the connection between their unrealistic and/or perfectionistic expectations and

13. Parents and child report an increase in connectedness between them. (29, 30, 31)

14. Verbalize an awareness and understanding of a teen's peer group and/or "second family." (32, 33, 34, 35)

their adolescent's rebellious and defiant behaviors.

29. Teach the parents to listen more than talk and to use open-ended questions that encourage and invite ongoing dialogue.

30. Encourage the parents to balance the role of limit setting with affirmations of praise, compliments, and appreciation to the teen whenever it is possible and appropriate.

31. Plant the thought with the parents that just "hanging out at home" or being around/available is what quality time is about.

32. Provide the parents a balanced view of peers and their influence on adolescents.

33. Assist the parents in coping with issues of negative peer groups and negative peer influences (see Negative Peer Influences chapter in this Planner).

34. Educate the parents on the "second family" concept (*The Second Family* by Taffel) and how to handle this influence while staying connected to their teen.

35. Assist the parents in reducing their fear of losing their influence to the adolescent's peer group.

15. Increase the gradual letting go of their adolescent in constructive, affirmative ways. (36, 37)

36. Help, encourage, and support the parents in expressing their concerns and fears about "letting go" of their adolescent (include in this their stories of how they separated from their parents).

37. Guide the parents in identifying and implementing constructive, affirmative ways they can allow and support the healthy separation of their adolescent.

16. Decrease negative parenting discipline techniques while replacing them with positive, respectful techniques. (38, 39, 40)

38. Help the parental team identify any negative parenting methods they employ (e.g., overly harsh consequences, demeaning name-calling, physical abuse) and to recognize how this negatively impacts the children; assist them in implementing new positive methods.

39. Ask the parents to read *Positive Parenting from A to Z* (Renshaw-Joslin) to gain new methods of positive parenting to implement.

40. Encourage, reinforce, and redirect the parents in their efforts to implement and maintain positive methods of parenting.

__. _____

_____

__. _____

_____

__. _____

_____

__. _____

_____

__. _____

_____

__. _____

_____

DIAGNOSTIC SUGGESTIONS

Axis I:

309.3	Adjustment Disorder With Disturbance of Conduct
309.4	Adjustment Disorder With Mixed Disturbance of Emotions and Conduct
V61.21	Neglect of Child
995.5	Neglect of Child (Victim)
V61.2	Parent-Child Relational Problem
V61.1	Partner Relational Problem
V61.21	Physical Abuse of Child
995.5	Physical Abuse of Child (Victim)
V61.21	Sexual Abuse of Child
995.5	Sexual Abuse of Child (Victim)
313.81	Oppositional Defiant Disorder
312.9	Disruptive Behavior Disorder NOS
312.8	Conduct Disorder, Adolescent-Onset Type
314.01	Attention-Deficit/Hyperactivity Disorder, Combined Type
_____	_____
_____	_____

Axis II:

301.7	Antisocial Personality Disorder
301.6	Dependent Personality Disorder
301.81	Narcissistic Personality Disorder
301.83	Borderline Personality Disorder
799.9	Diagnosis Deferred
V71.09	No Diagnosis on Axis II
_____	_____
_____	_____

PEER/SIBLING CONFLICT

BEHAVIORAL DEFINITIONS

1. Frequent, overt, intense fighting (verbal and/or physical) with peers and/or siblings.
2. Projects responsibility for conflicts onto others.
3. Believes that he/she is treated unfairly and/or that parents favor sibling(s) over himself/herself.
4. Peer and/or sibling relationships are characterized by bullying, defiance, revenge, taunting, and incessant teasing.
5. Has virtually no friends, or a few who exhibit similar socially disapproved behavior.
6. Exhibits a general pattern of behavior that is impulsive, intimidating, and unmalleable.
7. Behaviors toward peers are aggressive and lack discernible empathy for others.
8. Parents are hostile toward the client, demonstrating a familial pattern of rejection, quarreling, and lack of respect or affection.

__. _____

_____

__. _____

_____

__. _____

_____

LONG-TERM GOALS

1. Form respectful, trusting peer and sibling relationships.
2. Develop healthy mechanisms for handling anxiety, tension, frustration, and anger.

3. Obtain the skills required to build positive peer relationships.
4. Terminate aggressive behavior and replace with assertiveness and empathy.
5. Compete, cooperate, and resolve conflict appropriately with peers and siblings.
6. Parents acquire the necessary parenting skills to model respect, empathy, nurturance, and lack of aggression.

—. _____
   _____
   _____

—. _____
   _____
   _____

—. _____
   _____

SHORT-TERM OBJECTIVES

THERAPEUTIC INTERVENTIONS

1. Describe relationship with siblings and friends. (1, 2)

1. Actively build a level of trust with client through consistent eye contact, active listening, unconditional positive regard, and warm acceptance to help increase the client's ability to identify and express feelings.

2. Explore the client's perception of the nature of his/her relationships with siblings and peers; assess the degree of denial regarding conflict and projection of the responsibility for conflict onto others.

2. Decrease the frequency and intensity of aggressive actions toward peers or siblings. (3, 4)

3. Instruct the parents and teachers in social learning techniques of ignoring the client's aggressive acts, except when there is danger of physical injury, while making a concerted effort to

attend to and praise all nonaggressive, cooperative, and peaceful behavior.

3. Identify verbally and in writing how he/she would like to be treated by others. (5, 6, 7, 8)

4. Use The Anger Control game (Berg) or a similar game to expose the client to new, constructive ways to manage aggressive feelings.

5. Play with the client and/or family The Helping, Sharing, Caring Game (Gardner) to develop and expand feelings of respect for self and others.

6. Play with the client The Social Conflict Game (Berg) to assist him/her in developing behavior skills to decrease interpersonal antisocialism with others.

7. Ask the client to list the problems that he/she has with siblings and to suggest concrete solutions (or assign the client and parents the exercise "Negotiating a Peace Treaty" from the *Brief Adolescent Therapy Homework Planner* by Jongsma, Peterson, and McInnis).

8. Educate the client about feelings, concentrating on how others feel when they are the focus of aggressive actions and then asking how the client would like to be treated by others.

4. Recognize and verbalize the feelings of others as well as her/his own. (8, 9, 10)

8. Educate the client about feelings, concentrating on how others feel when they

are the focus of aggressive actions and then asking how the client would like to be treated by others.

9. Refer the client to a peer therapy group whose objectives are to increase social sensitivity and behavioral flexibility through the use of group exercises (strength bombardment, trusting, walking, expressing negative feelings, etc.).

10. Use The Talking, Feeling, and Doing Game (Gardner; available from Creative Therapeutics) to increase the client's awareness of self and others.

5. Increase socially appropriate behavior with peers and siblings. (6, 11)

6. Play with the client The Social Conflict Game (Berg) to assist him/her in developing behavior skills to decrease interpersonal antisocialism with others.

11. Conduct or refer the client to a behavioral contracting group therapy in which contracts for positive peer interaction are developed each week and reviewed. Positive reinforcers are verbal feedback and small concrete rewards.

6. Participate in peer group activities in a cooperative manner. (12, 13)

12. Direct the parents to involve the client in cooperative activities (e.g., sports, Scouting).

13. Refer the client to an alternative summer camp that

focuses on self-esteem and cooperation with peers.

7. Identify feelings associated with the perception that parent(s) have special feelings of favoritism toward a sibling. (14)

14. Have the parents read *Helping Your Child Make Friends* (Nevick), then assist them in implementing several of the suggestions with the client to build his/her skills in connecting with others.

8. Respond positively to praise and encouragement as evidenced by smiling and expressing gratitude. (15, 16)

15. Use role playing, modeling, and behavior rehearsal to teach the client to become open and responsive to praise and encouragement.

16. Assist the parents in developing their ability to verbalize affection and appropriate praise to the client in family sessions.

9. Family members decrease the frequency of quarreling and messages of rejection. (17, 18, 19)

17. Work with the parents in family sessions to reduce parental aggression, messages of rejection, and quarreling within the family.

18. Assign the parents to read *Between Parent and Teenager* (Ginott), especially the chapters "Jealousy" and "Children in Need of Professional Help." Process the reading, identifying key changes in family structure or personal interactions that will need to occur to decrease the level of rivalry.

19. Assign the parents to read *Siblings Without Rivalry* (Faber and Mazlish) and process key concepts with

10. Verbalize an understanding of the pain that underlies the anger. (20)

11. Implement a brief solution to sibling conflict that has had success in the past. (21, 22)

12. Parents attend a didactic series on positive parenting. (23)

13. Parents implement a behavior modification plan designed to increase the frequency of cooperative social behaviors. (24, 25, 26)

the therapist; ask the parents to choose two suggestions from the reading and implement them with their children.

20. Probe for rejection experiences with family and friends as the causes for the client's anger.

21. Reframe the family members' rivalry as a stage that they will get through with support, or (if appropriate) normalize the issue of the rivalry as something that occurs in all families to varying degrees (see *A Guide to Possibility Land* by O'Hanlon and Beadle).

22. Probe the client and parents to find "time without the problem," "exceptions," or "the ending or stopping pattern" (see *A Guide to Possibility Land* by O'Hanlon and Beadle).

23. Refer the parents to a positive parenting class.

24. Assist the parents in developing and implementing a behavior modification plan in which the client's positive interaction with peers and siblings is reinforced immediately with tokens that can be exchanged for preestablished rewards. Monitor and give feedback as indicated.

25. Conduct weekly contract sessions with the client and the parents in which the past week's behavior modification contract is reviewed and revised for the following week. Give feedback and model positive encouragement when appropriate.

26. Institute with the client's parents and teachers a system of positive consequences (see *Solution-Focused Therapy with Children* by Selekman) for the client's misbehavior in order to promote prosocial behaviors (e.g., writing a card to a relative, mowing a neighbor's lawn, doing two good deeds for elderly neighbors, assisting a parent for a day with household projects).

14. Family members engage in conflict resolution in a respectful manner. (27, 28)

27. Read and process in a family therapy session the fable "Raising Cain" or "Cinderella" from *Friedman's Fables* (Friedman).

28. Confront disrespectful expression of feelings in family sessions and use modeling, role playing, and behavior rehearsal to teach cooperation, respect, and peaceful resolution of conflict.

15. Parents terminate alliances with children that foster sibling conflict. (29, 30, 31)

29. Assist the parents in identifying specific things they could do within their home (e.g., creating separate rooms, eating at the dinner table) or to alter the family procedures (e.g., not putting

one child in charge of the other) to reduce sibling conflict. Help the parents identify and make all changes and monitor their effectiveness after implementation.

30. Ask the parents to read *How to End the Sibling Wars* (Bieniek) and coach them on implementing several of the suggestions; follow up by monitoring, encouraging, and redirecting as needed.

31. Hold family therapy sessions to assess dynamics and alliances that may underlie peer or sibling conflict.

16. Family members verbalize increased cooperation and respect for one another. (32, 33)

32. Refer the family to an experiential or alternative weekend program (i.e., ropes course, cooperative problem solving, or trust activities). Afterward, process the experience with the family members, focusing on two to three specific things gained in terms of cooperation, respect, and trust.

33. Explore with the siblings to find an appropriate common point they would like to change in the family (e.g., amount of allowance, later bedtime/curfew) and then conduct a family session in which the siblings work together to negotiate the issue with the parents. Coach both sides in negotiating and move the parents

17. Verbalize an acceptance of differences between siblings rather than being critical of each person's uniqueness. (34)

to accept this point on a specific condition of decreased conflict between siblings.

34. Hold a family sibling session in which each child lists and verbalizes an appreciation of each sibling's unique traits or abilities (or assign the exercise "Cloning the Perfect Sibling" from the *Brief Adolescent Therapy Homework Planner* by Jongsma, Peterson, and McInnis).

18. Complete the recommended psychiatric or psychological testing/evaluation. (35)

35. Assess and refer the client for a psychiatric or psychological evaluation.

19. Comply with the recommendations of the mental health evaluations. (36)

36. Facilitate and monitor client and the parents in implementing the recommendations of the evaluations.

__. _____

__. _____

__. _____

__. _____

__. _____

__. _____

DIAGNOSTIC SUGGESTIONS

Axis I:

313.81	Oppositional Defiant Disorder
312.81	Conduct Disorder, Childhood-Onset Type
312.82	Conduct Disorder, Adolescent-Onset Type
312.9	Disruptive Behavior Disorder NOS
314.01	Attention-Deficit/Hyperactivity Disorder, Predominantly Hyperactive-Impulsive Type

	314.9	Attention-Deficit/Hyperactivity Disorder NOS
	V62.81	Relational Problem NOS
	V71.02	Child or Adolescent Antisocial Behavior
	315.00	Reading Disorder
	315.9	Learning Disorder NOS
	_____	_____
	_____	_____
Axis II:	799.9	Diagnosis Deferred
	V71.09	No Diagnosis on Axis II
	_____	_____
	_____	_____

PHYSICAL/EMOTIONAL
ABUSE VICTIM

BEHAVIORAL DEFINITIONS

1. Confirmed self-report or account by others of having been assaulted (e.g., hitting, burning, kicking, slapping, or torture) by an older person.
2. Bruises or wounds as evidence of victimization.
3. Self-reports of being injured by a supposed caregiver coupled with feelings of fear and social withdrawal.
4. Significant increase in the frequency and severity of aggressive behaviors toward peers or adults.
5. Recurrent and intrusive distressing recollections of the abuse.
6. Feelings of anger, rage, or fear when in contact with the perpetrator.
7. Frequent and prolonged periods of depression, irritability, anxiety, and/or apathetic withdrawal.
8. Sleep disturbances (e.g., difficulty falling asleep, night terrors, recurrent distressing nightmares).
9. Running away from home to avoid further physical assaults.

—. _____
   _____

—. _____
   _____

—. _____
   _____

LONG-TERM GOALS

1. Terminate the physical abuse.
2. Escape from the environment where the abuse is occurring and move to a safe haven.
3. Rebuild sense of self-worth and overcome the overwhelming sense of fear, shame, and sadness.
4. Resolve feelings of fear and depression while improving communication and the boundaries of respect within the family.
5. Caregivers establish limits on the punishment of the client such that no physical harm can occur and respect for his/her rights is maintained.
6. Client and his/her family eliminate denial, putting the responsibility for the abuse on the perpetrator and allowing the victim to feel supported.
7. Reduce displays of aggression that reflect abuse and keep others at an emotional distance.
8. Build self-esteem and a sense of empowerment as manifested by an increased number of positive self-descriptive statements and greater participation in extracurricular activities.

—. _____
   _____
   _____
—. _____
   _____
   _____
—. _____
   _____

SHORT-TERM OBJECTIVES	THERAPEUTIC INTERVENTIONS
1. Tell the entire account of the most recent abuse. (1, 2, 3)	1. Actively build the level of trust with the client through consistent eye contact, active listening, unconditional positive regard, and warm acceptance to help him/her increase the ability to identify and express facts and feelings about the abuse.

2. Explore, encourage, and support the client in verbally expressing and clarifying the facts associated with the abuse.

3. Assign the client to complete the "Take the First Step" exercise from the *Brief Adolescent Therapy Homework Planner* (Jongsma, Peterson, and McInnis) in which he/she can read a story of a teenager who was abused and shared it with a trusted adult.

2. Identify the nature, frequency, and duration of the abuse. (2, 4, 5)

2. Explore, encourage, and support the client in verbally expressing and clarifying the facts associated with the abuse.

4. Report physical abuse to the appropriate child protection agency, criminal justice officials, or medical professionals.

5. Consult with the family, a physician, criminal justice officials, or child protection case managers to assess the veracity of the physical abuse charges.

3. Agree to actions taken to protect self and provide boundaries against any future abuse or retaliation. (6, 7, 8)

6. Assess whether the perpetrator or the client should be removed from the client's home.

7. Implement the necessary steps (e.g., removal of the client from the home, removal of the perpetrator from the home) to protect

the client and other children in the home from further physical abuse.

8. Reassure the client repeatedly of concern and caring on the part of the therapist and others who will protect him/her from any further abuse.

4. Identify and express the feelings connected to the abuse. (9)

9. Explore, encourage, and support the client in expressing and clarifying his/her feelings toward the perpetrator and himself/herself (or assign the homework exercise "My Thoughts and Feelings" in the *Brief Adolescent Therapy Homework Planner* (Jongsma, Peterson, and McInnis).

5. Terminate verbalizations of denial or making excuses for the perpetrator. (10, 11, 12)

10. Actively confront and challenge denial within the perpetrator and the entire family system.

11. Confront the client about making excuses for the perpetrator's abuse and accepting blame for it.

12. Reassure the client that he/she did not deserve the abuse but that he/she deserves respect and a controlled response even in punishment situations.

6. Perpetrator takes responsibility for the abuse. (13, 14)

13. Reinforce any and all client statements that put responsibility clearly on the perpetrator for the abuse, regardless of any misbehavior by the client.

14. Hold a family therapy session in which the client and/or therapist confront the perpetrator with the abuse.

7. Perpetrator asks for forgiveness and pledges respect for disciplinary boundaries. (15)

15. Conduct a family therapy session in which the perpetrator apologizes to the client and/or other family member(s) for the abuse.

8. Perpetrator agrees to seek treatment. (16, 17, 18)

16. Require the perpetrator to participate in a child abusers' psychotherapy group.

17. Refer the perpetrator for a psychological evaluation and treatment.

18. Evaluate the possibility of substance abuse with the perpetrator or within the family; refer the perpetrator and/or family member(s) for substance abuse treatment, if indicated.

9. Parents and caregivers verbalize the establishment of appropriate disciplinary boundaries to ensure protection of the client. (19, 20)

19. Counsel the client's family about appropriate disciplinary boundaries.

20. Ask the parents/caregivers to list appropriate means of discipline or correction; reinforce reasonable actions and appropriate boundaries that reflect respect for the rights and feelings of the child.

10. Family members identify the stressors or other factors that may trigger violence. (21, 22)

21. Construct a multigenerational family genogram that identifies physical abuse within the extended family to help the perpetrator recognize the cycle of violence.

22. Assess the client's family dynamics and explore for the stress factors or precipitating events that contributed to the emergence of the abuse.

11. Nonabusive parent and other key family members verbalize support and acceptance of the client. (23)

23. Elicit and reinforce support and nurturance of the client from the nonabusive parent and other key family members.

12. Reduce the expressions of rage and aggressiveness that stem from feelings of helplessness related to physical abuse. (24, 25)

24. Assign the client to write a letter expressing feelings of hurt, fear, and anger to the perpetrator; process the letter.

25. Interpret the client's generalized expressions of anger and aggression as triggered by feelings toward the perpetrator.

13. Decrease the statements of being a victim while increasing the statements that reflect personal empowerment. (26, 27)

26. Empower the client by identifying sources of help against abuse (e.g., phone numbers to call, a safe place to run to, asking for temporary alternate protective placement).

27. Assist the client in writing his/her thoughts and feelings regarding the abuse (or assign the exercise "Letter of Empowerment" in the *Brief Adolescent Therapy Homework Planner* by Jongsma, Peterson, and McInnis).

14. Increase the frequency of positive self-descriptive statements. (28, 29)

28. Assist the client in identifying a basis for self-worth by reviewing his/her

talents, importance to others, and intrinsic spiritual value.

29. Reinforce positive statements that the client has made about himself/herself and the future.

15. Express forgiveness of the perpetrator and others connected with the abuse while insisting on respect for own right to safety in the future. (15, 30, 31)

15. Conduct a family therapy session in which the perpetrator apologizes to the client and/or other family member(s) for the abuse.

30. Assign the client to write a forgiveness letter and/or complete a forgiveness exercise in which he/she verbalizes forgiveness to the perpetrator and/or significant family member(s) while asserting the right to safety. Process this letter.

31. Assign the client a letting-go exercise in which a symbol of the abuse is disposed of or destroyed. Process this experience.

16. Increase socialization with peers and family. (32, 33, 34)

32. Encourage the client to make plans for the future that involve interacting with his/her peers and family.

33. Encourage the client to participate in positive peer groups or extracurricular activities.

34. Refer the client to a victim support group with other children to assist him/her in realizing that he/she

is not alone in this experience.

17. Increase the level of trust of others as shown by increased socialization and a greater number of friendships. (35, 36, 37)

35. Facilitate the client expressing loss of trust in adults and relate this loss to the perpetrator's abusive behavior and the lack of protection provided.

36. Assist the client in making discriminating judgments that allow for trust of some people rather than distrust of all.

37. Teach the client the share-check method of building trust, in which a degree of shared information is related to a proven level of trustworthiness.

18. Verbalize how the abuse has affected feelings toward self. (38, 39)

38. Assign the client to draw pictures that represent how he/she feels about himself/herself.

39. Ask the client to draw pictures of his/her own face that represent how he/she felt about himself/herself before, during, and after the abuse occurred.

19. Verbalize instances of aggressive behavior toward peers and/or authority figures. (40)

40. Assess the client for adopting the aggressive manner that he/she has been exposed to in the home (see Anger Management chapter in this Planner).

20. Recognize how aggressive behavior impacts other people's feelings. (41)

41. Use role-playing and role-reversal techniques to sensitize the client to the feelings of the target of his/her anger.

21. Acknowledge the use of alcohol and/or drugs as an escape from the pain and anger resulting from abuse. (42, 43)

42. Assess the client's use and abuse of alcohol or illicit drugs or refer him/her for a substance abuse evaluation and treatment if indicated (see Chemical Dependence chapter in this Planner).

43. Interpret the client's substance abuse as a maladaptive coping behavior for his/her feelings related to abuse.

__. _____   __. _____
   _____   _____
__. _____   __. _____
   _____   _____
__. _____   __. _____
   _____   _____

DIAGNOSTIC SUGGESTIONS

Axis I:	309.81	Posttraumatic Stress Disorder
	308.3	Acute Stress Disorder
	995.54	Physical Abuse of Child (Victim)
	300.4	Dysthymic Disorder
	296.xx	Major Depressive Disorder
	300.02	Generalized Anxiety Disorder
	307.47	Nightmare Disorder
	313.81	Oppositional Defiant Disorder
	312.81	Conduct Disorder/Childhood-Onset Type
	300.6	Depersonalization Disorder
	300.15	Dissociative Disorder NOS
	_____	_____
	_____	_____
Axis II:	799.9	Diagnosis Deferred
	V71.09	No Diagnosis
	_____	_____
	_____	_____

POSTTRAUMATIC STRESS DISORDER (PTSD)

BEHAVIORAL DEFINITIONS

1. Exposure to threats of death or serious injury, or subjection to actual injury, that resulted in an intense emotional response of fear, helplessness, or horror.
2. Intrusive, distressing thoughts or images that recall the traumatic event.
3. Disturbing dreams associated with the traumatic event.
4. A sense that the event is recurring, as in illusions or flashbacks.
5. Intense distress when exposed to reminders of the traumatic event.
6. Physiological reactivity when exposed to internal or external cues that symbolize the traumatic event.
7. Avoidance of thoughts, feelings, or conversations about the traumatic event.
8. Avoidance of activity, places, or people associated with the traumatic event.
9. Inability to recall some important aspect of the traumatic event.
10. Lack of interest and participation in formerly meaningful activities.
11. A sense of detachment from others.
12. Inability to experience the full range of emotions, including love.
13. A pessimistic, fatalistic attitude regarding the future.
14. Sleep disturbance.
15. Irritability or angry outbursts.
16. Lack of concentration.
17. Hypervigilance.
18. Exaggerated startle response.
19. Symptoms have been present for more than one month.

20. Sad or guilty affect and other signs of depression.
21. Verbally and/or physically violent threats or behavior.

___. _____
    _____
    _____

___. _____
    _____
    _____

___. _____
    _____

LONG-TERM GOALS

1. Recall the traumatic event without becoming overwhelmed with negative emotions.
2. Interact normally with friends and family without irrational fears or intrusive thoughts that control behavior.
3. Return to pretrauma level of functioning without avoiding people, places, thoughts, or feelings associated with the traumatic event.
4. Display a full range of emotions without experiencing loss of control.
5. Develop and implement effective coping skills that allow for carrying out normal responsibilities and participating in relationships and social activities.

___. _____
    _____
    _____

___. _____
    _____
    _____

___. _____
    _____

SHORT-TERM OBJECTIVES	THERAPEUTIC INTERVENTIONS
1. Describe the traumatic event in as much detail as possible. (1, 2, 3)	1. Actively build the level of trust with the client through consistent eye contact, active listening,

unconditional positive regard, and warm acceptance to help him/her increase the ability to identify and express feelings.

2. Gently and sensitively explore the client's recollection of the facts of the traumatic event.

3. Explore the client's emotional reaction at the time of the trauma.

2. Describe how PTSD symptoms have affected personal relationships, functioning at school, and social/recreational life. (4, 5)

4. Ask the client to identify how the traumatic event has negatively impacted his/her life, comparing pretrauma functioning to current functioning.

5. Explore the effect that the PTSD symptoms have had on the client's personal relationships, functioning at school, and social/recreational life.

3. Identify instances of uncontrollable anger. (6)

6. Assess the client for instances of poor anger management that have led to threats of or actual violence against property and/or people.

4. Implement anger control techniques. (7)

7. Teach the client anger management techniques (e.g., taking time out, engaging in physical exercise and relaxation, and expressing feelings assertively). (See Anger Management chapter in this Planner.)

5. Practice and implement relaxation and positive imagery as coping mechanisms for tension, panic, stress, anger, and anxiety. (8, 9, 10)

8. Teach the client deep muscle relaxation, deep breathing exercises, and positive imagery to induce relaxation.

9. Use electromyograph (EMG) biofeedback to increase the client's depth of relaxation.

10. Train the client to calm himself/herself using relaxation tapes as preparation for sleep or for use in coping with tension (e.g., the *Ten Minutes to Relax* audiotapes available from Courage to Change).

6. Report increased comfort and the ability to talk and/or think about the traumatic incident without emotional turmoil. (11, 12)

11. Gradually expose the client to the traumatic event through imaginal systematic desensitization and positive guided imagery to reduce emotional reactivity to the traumatic event.

12. Explore in detail the client's feelings surrounding the traumatic incident, allowing for a gradual reduction in the intensity of the emotional response with repeated retelling.

7. Identify and replace negative self-talk and catastrophizing that is associated with past trauma and current stimulus triggers for anxiety. (13, 14)

13. Explore the client's negative self-talk that is associated with the past trauma and predictions of unsuccessful coping or catastrophizing.

14. Assist the client in replacing distorted, negative, self-defeating thoughts with positive, reality-based self-talk.

8. Approach actual stimuli (in vivo) that trigger memories and feelings associated with past trauma, staying calm by using relaxation techniques and positive self-talk. (8, 14, 15)

8. Teach the client deep muscle relaxation, deep breathing exercises, and positive imagery to induce relaxation.

14. Assist the client in replacing distorted, negative, self-defeating thoughts with positive, reality-based self-talk.

15. Encourage the client to gradually approach previously avoided stimuli that trigger thoughts and feelings associated with the past trauma. Urge use of relaxation, deep breathing, and positive self-talk during the client's approach to each stimulus.

9. Sleep without being disturbed by dreams of the trauma. (8, 10, 16)

8. Teach the client deep muscle relaxation, deep breathing exercises, and positive imagery to induce relaxation.

10. Train the client to calm himself/herself using relaxation tapes as preparation for sleep or for use in coping with tension (e.g., the *Ten Minutes to Relax* audiotapes available from Courage to Change).

16. Monitor the client's sleep patterns and encourage the use of relaxation and positive imagery as aids to sleep.

10. Cooperate with eye movement desensitization and reprocessing (EMDR) technique to reduce emotional reaction to the traumatic event. (17)

17. Use EMDR technique to reduce the client's emotional reactivity to the traumatic event.

11. Participate in a group therapy session focused on
PTSD. (18)

18. Refer the client to or conduct
group therapy sessions that
focus on sharing the traumatic event and its effects
with other PTSD survivors.

12. Take medication as prescribed and report on effectiveness and side effects.
(19, 20)

19. Assess the client's need for
medication (e.g., selective
serotonin reuptake in-
hibitors) and arrange for
prescription if appropriate.

20. Monitor and evaluate the
client's medication compliance and its effectiveness on
his/her level of functioning.

13. Parents verbalize understanding of how PTSD de-
velops and how it impacts
survivors. (21, 22)

21. Conduct family therapy sessions to facilitate family
members giving emotional
support to the client.

22. Teach the client and family
members about trauma
and its impact on survivors
and their subsequent ad-
justment.

14. Verbalize an understanding
of PTSD and the steps to recovery. (23)

23. Assign the client to read
books on PTSD and the re-
covery process (e.g., *I Can't
Get Over It* by Matsakis).

__. _____

    _____

__. _____

    _____

__. _____

    _____

__. _____

    _____

__. _____

    _____

__. _____

    _____

DIAGNOSTIC SUGGESTIONS

Axis I:	309.81	Posttraumatic Stress Disorder
	309.xx	Adjustment Disorder
	995.5	Physical Abuse of Child (Victim)
	995.5	Sexual Abuse of Child (Victim)
	308.3	Acute Stress Disorder
	296.xx	Major Depressive Disorder
	_____	_____
	_____	_____
Axis II:	799.9	Diagnosis Deferred
	V71.09	No Diagnosis on Axis II
	_____	_____
	_____	_____

PSYCHOTICISM

BEHAVIORAL DEFINITIONS

1. Bizarre thought content (delusions of grandeur, persecution, reference, influence, control, somatic sensations, or infidelity).
2. Illogical form of thought or speech (loose association of ideas in speech; incoherence; illogical thinking; vague, abstract, or repetitive speech; neologisms; perseverations; clanging).
3. Perception disturbance (hallucinations, primarily auditory but occasionally visual or olfactory).
4. Disturbed affect (blunted, none, flattened, or inappropriate).
5. Lost sense of self (loss of ego boundaries, lack of identity, blatant confusion).
6. Diminished volition (inadequate interest, drive, or ability to follow a course of action to its logical conclusion; pronounced ambivalence or cessation of goal-directed activity).
7. Relationship withdrawal (withdrawal from involvement with the external world and preoccupation with egocentric ideas and fantasies; alienation feelings).
8. Poor social skills (misinterpretation of the actions or motives of others; maintaining emotional distance from others; feeling awkward and threatened in most social situations; embarrassment of others by failure to recognize the impact of own behavior).
9. Inadequate control over sexual, aggressive, or frightening thoughts, feelings, or impulses (blatantly sexual or aggressive fantasies; fears of impending doom; acting out sexual or aggressive impulses in an unpredictable and unusual manner, often directed toward family and friends).
10. Psychomotor abnormalities (a marked decrease in reactivity to the environment; various catatonic patterns such as stupor, rigidity,

excitement, posturing, or negativism; unusual mannerisms or grimacing).

—. _____
    _____

—. _____
    _____

—. _____
    _____

LONG-TERM GOALS

1. Control or eliminate active psychotic symptoms such that supervised functioning is positive and medication is taken consistently.
2. Significantly reduce or eliminate hallucinations and/or delusions.
3. Eliminate acute, reactive psychotic symptoms and return to normal functioning in affect, thinking, and relating.
4. Interact appropriately in social situations and improve the reality-based understanding of and reaction to the behaviors and motives of others.
5. Attain control over disturbing thoughts, feelings, and impulses.

—. _____
    _____

—. _____
    _____

—. _____
    _____

SHORT-TERM OBJECTIVES

1. Describe thoughts about self and others; history, content, nature, and frequency of hallucinations or delusions; fantasies and fears. (1, 2)

THERAPEUTIC INTERVENTIONS

1. Assess the pervasiveness of the client's thought disorder through a clinical interview.

2. Determine if the client's psychosis is of a brief, reactive nature or long-term

2. Establish trust and therapeutic alliance to begin to express feelings and discuss the nature of psychotic symptoms. (3)

3. Cooperate with psychological testing to assess severity and type of psychosis. (4)

4. Family members and client provide psychosocial history of the client and the extended family. (5)

5. Accept and understand that the distressing thought disorder symptoms are due to mental illness. (6)

6. Take antipsychotic medications consistently with or without supervision. (7, 8)

7. Move to appropriate hospital or residential setting. (9)

with prodromal and reactive elements.

3. Provide supportive therapy characterized by genuine warmth, understanding, and acceptance to reduce the client's distrust, alleviate fears, and promote openness.

4. Administer or arrange for psychological testing to assess the client's severity and type of psychosis; provide feedback to the client and parents.

5. Explore the client's personal and family history for serious mental illness and significant traumas or stressors.

6. Explain to the client the nature of the psychotic process, its biochemical component, and the confusing effect on rational thought.

7. Arrange for the administration of appropriate antipsychotic medications to the client.

8. Monitor the client for medication compliance and redirect if he/she is noncompliant.

9. Arrange for an appropriate level of residential or hospital care if the client may be harmful to self or others or unable to care for his/her own basic needs.

8. Verbally identify the stressors that contributed to the reactive psychosis. (10, 11, 12, 13)

10. Probe the external or internal stressors that may account for the client's reactive psychosis.

11. Explore the client's feelings about the stressors that triggered the psychotic episodes.

12. Assist the client in identifying threats in the environment and develop a plan with the family to reduce these stressors.

13. Explore the client's history for significant separations, losses, or traumas.

9. Family members verbalize increased understanding of and knowledge about the client's illness and treatment. (14)

14. Arrange for family therapy sessions to educate the family regarding the client's illness, treatment, and prognosis.

10. Family members increase positive support of the client to reduce the chances of acute exacerbation of the psychotic episode. (15, 16)

15. Encourage the parents to involve the client in here-and-now-based social and recreational activities (e.g., intramural sports, after-school enrichment programs, YMCA structured programs).

16. Encourage the parents to look for opportunities to praise and reinforce the client for engaging in responsible, adaptive, and prosocial behaviors.

11. Parents increase frequency of communicating to the client with direct eye contact, clear language, and complete thoughts. (17, 18)

17. Assist the family in avoiding double-bind messages that are inconsistent and contradictory, resulting in increased anxiety,

confusion, and psychotic symptoms in the client.

12. Parents terminate hostile, critical responses to the client and increase their statements of praise, optimism, and affirmation. (19, 20)

18. Confront the parents in family therapy when their communication is indirect and disjointed, leaving the client confused and anxious.

19. Hold family therapy sessions to reduce the atmosphere of criticism and hostility toward the client and promote an understanding of the client and his/her illness.

20. Support the parents in setting firm limits without hostility on the client's inappropriate aggressive or sexual behavior.

13. Family members share their feelings of guilt, frustration, and fear associated with the client's mental illness. (21)

21. Encourage the family members to share their feelings of frustration, guilt, fear, or depression surrounding the client's mental illness and behavior patterns.

14. Stay current with school work, completing assignments and interacting appropriately with peers and teachers. (22, 23)

22. Arrange for and/or encourage ongoing academic training while the client is receiving psychological treatment.

23. Contact school personnel (having obtained the necessary confidentiality releases) to educate them regarding the client's unusual behavior and his/her need for an accepting, supportive environment.

15. Verbalize an understanding of the underlying needs, conflicts, and emotions that support the irrational beliefs. (24)

24. Probe the client's underlying needs and feelings (e.g., inadequacy, rejection, anxiety, guilt) that contribute to internal conflict and irrational beliefs.

16. Think more clearly as demonstrated by logical, coherent speech. (25, 26)

25. Gently confront the client's illogical thoughts and speech to refocus disordered thinking.

26. Assist in restructuring the client's irrational beliefs by reviewing reality-based evidence and misinterpretation.

17. Report a diminishing or absence of hallucinations and/or delusions. (27, 28, 29)

27. Encourage the client to focus on the reality of the external world as opposed to distorted fantasy.

28. Differentiate for the client between the sources of stimuli from self-generated messages and the reality of the external world.

29. Interpret the client's inaccurate perceptions or bizarre associations as reflective of unspoken fears of rejection or losing control.

18. Demonstrate control over inappropriate thoughts, feelings, and impulses by verbalizing a reduced frequency of occurrence. (28, 30, 31)

28. Differentiate for the client between the sources of stimuli from self-generated messages and the reality of the external world.

30. Set firm limits on the client's inappropriate aggressive or sexual behavior that emanates from a lack of impulse control or a misperception of reality.

31. Monitor the client's daily level of functioning (i.e., reality orientation, personal hygiene, social interactions, affect appropriateness) and give feedback that either redirects or reinforces the behavior.

19. Begin to show limited social functioning by responding appropriately to friendly encounters. (32, 33)

32. Use role playing and behavioral rehearsal of social situations to explore and teach the client alternative positive social interactions with family and friends.

33. Reinforce socially and emotionally appropriate responses to others.

20. Family members accept a referral to a support group. (34)

34. Refer family members to a community-based support group designed for the families of psychotic clients.

—. _____

_____

—. _____

_____

—. _____

_____

—. _____

_____

—. _____

_____

—. _____

_____

DIAGNOSTIC SUGGESTIONS

Axis I: 297.1   Delusional Disorder
298.8   Brief Psychotic Disorder
295.xx   Schizophrenia
295.30   Schizophrenia, Paranoid Type
295.70   Schizoaffective Disorder
295.40   Schizophreniform Disorder
296.xx   Bipolar I Disorder
296.89   Bipolar II Disorder

	296.24	Major Depressive Disorder, Single Episode With Psychotic Features
	296.34	Major Depressive Disorder, Recurrent With Psychotic Features
	310.1	Personality Change Due to (Axis III Disorder)
	_____	_____
	_____	_____
Axis II:	799.9	Diagnosis Deferred
	V71.09	No Diagnosis
	_____	_____
	_____	_____

RUNAWAY

BEHAVIORAL DEFINITIONS

1. Running away from home for a day or more without parental permission.
2. Pattern of running to the noncustodial parent, relative, or friend when conflicts arise with the custodial parent or guardian.
3. Running away from home and crossing state lines.
4. Running away from home overnight at least twice.
5. Running away at least one time without returning within 48 hours.
6. Poor self-image and feelings of worthlessness and inadequacy.
7. Chaotic, violent, or abusive home environment.
8. Severe conflict with parents.
9. Victim of physical, sexual, or emotional abuse.

—. _____
_____
_____
—. _____
_____
_____
—. _____
_____

LONG-TERM GOALS

1. Develop a closer, more caring relationship with the parents.
2. Reduce the level, frequency, and degree of family conflicts.
3. Attain the necessary skills to cope with family stress without resorting to the flight response.
4. Caregivers terminate any abuse of the client and establish a nurturing family environment with appropriate boundaries.

5. Eliminate the runaway behavior.
6. Begin the process of healthy separation from the family.
7. Parents demonstrate acceptance and respect for the client.

—. _____

_____

—. _____

_____

—. _____

_____

SHORT-TERM OBJECTIVES

1. Verbalize the emotions causing a need to escape from the home environment. (1, 2)

2. Identify and implement alternative reactions to conflictual situations. (3, 4)

THERAPEUTIC INTERVENTIONS

1. Actively build the level of trust with the client in individual sessions through consistent eye contact, active listening, unconditional positive regard, and warm acceptance to help him/her increase the ability to identify and express feelings.

2. Facilitate the client's expression of emotions that prompt the runaway behavior.

3. Ask the client to list all possible constructive ways of handling conflictual situations and process the list with the therapist.

4. Train the client in alternative ways of handling conflictual situations (e.g., being assertive with his/her wishes or plans, staying out of conflicts that are parents' issues) and assist him/her in implementing them into his/her daily life.

3. Increase communication with and the expressed level of understanding of the parents. (5, 6)

5. Conduct family therapy sessions with the client and his/her parents to facilitate healthy, positive communications.

6. Assign the client to attend a problem-solving psychoeducation group.

4. Parents and client express acceptance of and responsibility for their share of the conflict between them. (7)

7. Assist the parents and the client in each accepting responsibility for their share of the conflicts in the home.

5. Parents terminate physical and/or sexual abuse of the client. (8, 9)

8. Explore for the occurrence of physical or sexual abuse to the client with the client and his/her family.

9. Arrange for the client to be placed in respite care or in another secure setting, if necessary, while the family works in family therapy to resolve conflicts that have led to abuse or neglect of the client.

6. Parents acknowledge chemical dependence problem and accept referral for treatment. (10)

10. Evaluate the parents for chemical dependence and its effect on the client; refer parents for treatment if necessary.

7. Parents identify unresolved issues with their parents and begin to move toward resolving each issue. (11, 12)

11. Hold a family session in which a detailed genogram is developed with a particular emphasis on unresolved issues between the client's parents and their own parents. Then assist the client's parents in coming to see the importance of resolving these issues before change can possibly occur in their own family system.

12. Facilitate sessions with the client's parents to assist in working through past unresolved issues with their own parents.

8. Parents decrease messages of rejection. (13)

13. Help the client's parents identify and alter parenting techniques, interactions, or other messages that communicate rejection to the client.

9. Parents attend a didactic group focused on teaching positive parenting skills. (14)

14. Refer the parents to a class teaching positive and effective parenting skills.

10. Parents identify and implement ways they can make the client feel valued and cherished within the family. (14, 15, 16)

14. Refer the parents to a class that teaches positive and effective parenting skills.

15. Assign the parents to read books on parenting [e.g., *Parent Effectiveness Training (P.E.T.)* by Gordon or *Raising Self-Reliant Children in a Self-Indulgent World* by Glenn and Nelsen]; process what they have learned from reading the material assigned.

16. Assist the parents in identifying ways to make the client feel more valued (e.g., work out age-appropriate privileges with the client, give the client specific responsibilities in the family, or ask for client's input on family decisions) as an individual and as part of the family; elicit a commitment from the parents for implementation of client-affirming behaviors.

11. Identify own needs in the family that are unsatisfied. (17)

12. Identify ways that unmet needs might be satisfied by means outside the family. (18)

13. Verbalize hurt and angry feelings connected to the family and how it functions. (19, 20, 21)

17. Ask the client to make a list of his/her needs in the family that are not met. Process the list in an individual session and at appropriate later time in a family therapy session.

18. Assist the client in identifying how he/she might meet his/her own unmet needs (e.g., obtain a Big Brother or Big Sister, find a job, develop a close friendship). Encourage the client to begin to meet those unmet needs that would be age-appropriate to pursue.

19. Assign the client to write a description of how he/she perceives his/her family dynamics and then to keep a daily journal of incidents that support or refute his/her perception (or assign the exercise "Home by Another Name" or "Undercover Assignment" from the *Brief Adolescent Treatment Planner* by Jongsma, Peterson, and McInnis).

20. Assist the client in identifying specific issues of conflict he/she has with the family (or assign the "Airing Your Grievance" exercise from the *Brief Adolescent Treatment Planner* by Jongsma, Peterson, and McInnis).

21. Support and encourage the client when he/she begins to appropriately verbalize

14. Identify and implement constructive ways to interact with the parents. (22)

15. Verbalize fears associated with becoming more independent. (23)

16. Parents identify and implement ways to promote the client's maturity and independence. (24)

17. Verbalize an understanding of various emotions and express them appropriately. (25)

18. Identify specifically how own acting-out behavior rescues the parents from facing their own problems. (26, 27)

anger or other negative feelings.

22. Help the client identify and implement specific constructive ways (e.g., avoiding involvement or siding on issues between parents, stating his/her own feelings directly to the parents on issues involving him/her) to interact with the parents. Confront the client when he/she is not taking responsibility for himself/herself in family conflicts.

23. Explore the client's fears surrounding becoming more independent and responsible for himself/herself.

24. Help the parents find ways to assist in the advancement of the client's maturity and independence (e.g., give the client age-appropriate privileges, encourage activities outside of home, require the client to be responsible for specific jobs or tasks in the home).

25. Educate the client (e.g., using a printed list of feeling adjectives) in how to identify and label feelings and in the value of expressing them in appropriate ways.

26. Assist the client in becoming more aware of her/his role in the family and how it impacts the parents.

19. Family members verbally agree to and then implement the structural or strategic recommendations of the therapist for the family. (28, 29)

27. Facilitate family therapy sessions with the objective of revealing underlying conflicts in order to release the client from being a symptom bearer.

28. Conduct family therapy sessions in which a structural intervention (e.g., parents will not allow the children to get involved in their discussions or disagreements, while assuring the children that the parents can work things out themselves) is developed, assigned, and then implemented by the family. Monitor the implementation and adjust intervention as required.

29. Develop a strategic intervention (parents will be responsible for holding a weekly family meeting and the client will be responsible for raising one personal issue in that forum for them to work out together) and have the family implement it. Monitor the implementation and adjust intervention as needed.

20. Complete psychiatric or other recommended evaluations. (30)

30. Evaluate the client or refer him/her for evaluation for substance abuse, Attention-Deficit/Hyperactivity Disorder (ADHD), affective disorder, or psychotic processes.

21. Comply with all recommendations of the psychiatric or other evaluations. (31)

31. Monitor the client's and the family's compliance with the evaluation recommendations.

22. Move to a neutral living environment that meets both own and parents' approval. (9, 32)

9. Arrange for the client to be placed in respite care or in another secure setting, if necessary, while the family works in family therapy to resolve conflicts that have led to abuse or neglect of the client.

32. Help the parents and the client draw up a contract for the client to live in a neutral setting for an agreed-upon length of time. The contract will include basic guidelines for daily structure and for frequency of contact with the parents and the acceptable avenues by which the contact can take place.

___. _____   ___. _____
    _____   _____
___. _____   ___. _____
    _____   _____
___. _____   ___. _____
    _____   _____

DIAGNOSTIC SUGGESTIONS

Axis I:	314.01	Attention-Deficit/Hyperactivity Disorder, Predominately Hyperactive-Impulsive Type
	312.82	Conduct Disorder, Adolescent-Onset Type
	313.81	Oppositional Defiant Disorder
	300.01	Panic Disorder Without Agoraphobia
	300.4	Dysthymic Disorder
	309.24	Adjustment Disorder With Anxiety
	309.4	Adjustment Disorder With Mixed Disturbance of Emotions and Conduct
	312.30	Impulse-Control Disorder NOS

	V61.20	Parent-Child Relational Problem
	995.54	Physical Abuse of Child (Victim)
	995.53	Sexual Abuse of Child (Victim)
	995.52	Neglect of Child (Victim)
	_____	_____
	_____	_____
Axis II:	799.9	Diagnosis Deferred
	V71.09	No Diagnosis
	301.83	Borderline Personality Disorder
	_____	_____
	_____	_____

SCHOOL VIOLENCE

BEHAVIORAL DEFINITIONS

1. Threats of violence have been made against students, teachers, and/or administrators.
2. Feels alienated from most peers within the school.
3. Subjected to bullying or intimidation from peers.
4. Subjected to ridicule, teasing, or rejection from peers.
5. Loss of temper has led to violent or aggressive behavior.
6. Engages in drug or alcohol abuse.
7. Has access to or a fascination with weapons.
8. Has a history of hurting animals.
9. History of conflict with authority figures.
10. Exhibits poor academic performance.
11. Feels disrespected by peers and adults.
12. Lacks close attachment to family members.

___. _____
   _____
___. _____
   _____
___. _____
   _____

LONG-TERM GOALS

1. Express hurt and anger in nonviolent ways.
2. Develop trusting relationships with peers.
3. Terminate substance abuse as a means of coping with pain and alienation.

4. Improve degree of connection and involvement with parents, siblings, and extended family.
5. Increase involvement in academic and social activities within the school environment.

—. _____

—. _____

—. _____

SHORT-TERM OBJECTIVES

1. Identify attitudes and feelings regarding school experience as well as general emotional status. (1, 2, 3)

THERAPEUTIC INTERVENTIONS

1. Explore the client's attitude and feelings regarding his/her school experience (e.g., academic performance, peer relationships, staff relationships).

2. Administer or arrange for psychological testing to assess the client's emotional adjustment, especially depth of depression (e.g., MMPI-A, MACI, Beck Depression Inventory); evaluate results and give feedback to the client and his/her parents.

3. Assess the current risk of the client's becoming violent (e.g., depth of anger, degree of alienation from peers and family, substance abuse, fascination with and/or access to weapons, articulation of a violence plan, threats made directly or indirectly); notify the proper authorities, if

necessary, and take steps to remove the client's access to weapons.

2. Describe social network and degree of support or rejection felt from others. (4, 5)

4. Develop a sociogram with the client that places friends and other peers in concentric circles, with the client at the center and closest friends on the closest circle; ask him/her to disclose his/her impression of each person.

5. Explore the client's painful experiences of social rejection by peers; use active listening and unconditional positive regard to encourage sharing of feelings.

3. Identify issues that precipitate peer conflict. (6)

6. Assist the client in identifying issues that precipitate his/her conflict with peers.

4. Implement problem-solving skills to resolve peer conflict. (7, 8, 9)

7. Teach the client problem-solving skills (e.g., identify the problem, brainstorm solutions, select an option, implement a cause of action, evaluate the outcome) that can be applied to peer conflict issues.

8. Teach the client means of coping with and improving conflicted peer relationships (e.g., social skills training; outside intervention with bullies; conflict resolution training; reaching out to build new friendships; identifying empathetic resource peers or adults in school to whom the client can turn when hurt, lonely, or angry).

5. Increase participation in structured social activities within the school environment. (10, 11)

6. Identify feelings toward family members. (12, 13)

7. Caregivers and client identify common anger-provoking situations that contribute to loss of control and emergence of violent behavior. (14, 15, 16)

9. Use role playing, modeling, and behavioral rehearsal to assist the client in learning the application of social problem-solving skills.

10. Brainstorm with the client possible extracurricular activities he/she might enjoy being involved in; obtain a commitment to pursue one or two of these choices in order to build a positive attitude toward school and peers.

11. Process the client's experience with increased social involvement; reinforce success and redirect for failures.

12. Explore the client's relationships with and feelings toward his/her family members; be especially alert to feelings of alienation, isolation, emotional detachment, resentment, distrust and anger.

13. In a family therapy session, facilitate an exchange of thoughts and feelings that can lead to increased mutual understanding and a reduction in negative feelings.

14. Assist the client in recognizing early signs (e.g., tiredness, muscular tension, hot face, hostile remarks) that he/she is starting to become frustrated or agitated so that he/she can take steps

to remain calm and cope with frustration.

15. Assist the caregivers and school officials in identifying specific situations or events that routinely lead to explosive outbursts or aggressive behaviors. Teach the caregivers and school officials effective coping strategies to help defuse the client's anger and to deter his/her aggressive behavior.

16. Assign the client to read material regarding learning to manage anger more effectively (e.g., *Everything You Need to Know About Anger* by Licata); process the reading with him/her.

8. Identify family issues that contribute to violent behavior. (17)

17. Conduct family therapy sessions to explore the dynamics (e.g., parental modeling of aggressive behavior; sexual, verbal, or physical abuse of family members; substance abuse in the home; neglect) that may contribute to the emergence of the client's violent behavior.

9. Uninvolved or detached parent(s) increase time spent with the client in recreational, school, or work activities. (18, 19)

18. Instruct the caregivers to set aside between 5 and 10 minutes each day to listen to the client's concerns and to provide him/her with the opportunity to express his/her anger in an adaptive manner.

19. Give a directive to uninvolved or disengaged parent(s) to spend more time

10. Increase active involvement in family activities. (20)

11. Caregivers increase the frequency of praise and positive reinforcement of the client for demonstrating good control of anger. (21)

12. Implement anger management techniques to reduce violent outbursts. (22, 23)

13. Write a letter of forgiveness to a perpetrator of hurt. (24)

with the client in leisure, school, or work activities.

20. Assist the family in identifying several activities they could engage in together, assigning the family to engage in at least one structured activity together every week; process the experience.

21. Design a reward system to help the parents reinforce the client's expression of his/her anger in a controlled manner (or employ the "Anger Control" exercise in the *Brief Adolescent Therapy Homework Planner* by Jongsma, Peterson, and McInnis).

22. Teach the client anger management techniques (e.g., take a time-out, journal feelings, talk to a trusted adult, engage in physical exercise); process his/her implementation of these techniques, reinforcing success and redirecting for failure (see the Anger Management chapter in this Planner).

23. Refer the client to an anger management group. Direct him/her to self-disclose at least one time in each group therapy session about his/her responses to anger-provoking situations.

24. Instruct the client to write a letter of forgiveness to a

target of anger in the latter stages of treatment as a step toward letting go of anger; process the letter in a follow-up session, and discuss what to do with the letter.

14. Identify and replace the irrational beliefs or maladaptive thoughts that contribute to the emergence of destructive or assaultive/aggressive behavior. (25)

25. Assist the client in identifying his/her irrational thoughts that contribute to the emergence of violent behavior (e.g., believing that aggression is an acceptable way to deal with teasing or name-calling, justifying acts of violence or aggression as a means to meet his/her needs or to avoid restrictions). Replace these irrational thoughts with more adaptive ways of thinking to help control anger.

15. Complete a substance abuse evaluation, and comply with the recommendations that are offered by the evaluation findings. (26)

26. Arrange for substance abuse evaluation to assess whether substance abuse problems are contributing to the client's violent behavior; refer him/her for treatment if indicated. (See Substance Abuse chapter in this Planner).

16. Identify and list strengths, interests, or positive attributes. (27, 28)

27. Give the client a homework assignment of identifying between 5 and 10 unique strengths, interests, or positive attributes. Review this list with the client in the following therapy session, and encourage him/her to utilize his/her strengths, interests, or positive attributes to build a positive self-image.

28. Assist the client in taking an inventory of his/her strengths, interests, or accomplishments, then ask him/her to bring objects or symbols to the next therapy session that represent those strengths or interests; encourage him/her to use strengths or interests to build self-esteem (or assign the exercise "Symbols of Self-Worth" from the *Brief Adolescent Therapy Homework Planner* by Jongsma, Peterson, and McInnis).

17. Identify and implement effective strategies to improve self-esteem. (29, 30)

29. Assign the client to view the video entitled *10 Ways to Boost Low Self-Esteem* (available from The Guidance Channel) to learn effective strategies to elevate self-esteem and increase confidence in himself/herself.

30. Instruct the client to complete the exercise entitled "Self-Esteem—What Is It? How Do I Get It?" from *Ten Days to Self-Esteem* (Burns) to help increase his/her self-esteem.

18. Increase the frequency of positive self-descriptive statements. (31, 32)

31. Encourage the client to use positive self-talk (e.g., "I am capable," "I can do this," "I am kind," "I can dance well") as a means of increasing his/her confidence and developing a positive self-image.

32. Instruct the client to make three positive statements

about himself/herself daily and record them in a journal; review and reinforce these journal entries in follow-up therapy sessions.

19. Caregivers increase the frequency of praise and positive reinforcement for the client's prosocial or responsible behaviors. (33, 34)

33. Encourage the parents/caregivers and teachers to provide frequent praise and positive reinforcement for the client's prosocial and responsible behavior to help him/her develop a positive self-image.

34. Instruct the parents/caregivers to observe and record between three and five positive responsible behaviors by the client before the next therapy session. Review these behaviors in the next session, and encourage the client to continue engaging in these behaviors to boost his/her self-esteem.

20. Caregivers cease making overly hostile, critical remarks, and increase positive messages to the client. (35, 36)

35. Confront and challenge the parents/caregivers to cease making overly hostile or critical remarks about the client or his/her behavior that only reinforce his/her feelings of low self-esteem. Encourage the caregivers to verbalize the positive, specific behaviors or changes that they would like to see the client make.

36. Teach the client and his/her parents/caregivers effective communication skills (e.g., practicing active listening, using "I" messages, avoiding blaming statements,

21. Verbalize increased feelings of genuine empathy for others. (37, 38, 39)

identifying specific positive changes that other family members can make) to improve the lines of communication, facilitate closer family ties, and resolve conflict more constructively.

37. Attempt to sensitize the client to his/her lack of empathy for others by reviewing and listing the negative consequences of his/her aggression on others (e.g., loss of trust, increased fear, distancing, physical pain).

38. Use role-reversal techniques to get the client to verbalize the impact of his/her aggression on others.

39. Assign the client to address an "empty chair" in giving an apology for pain that he/she has caused the victim.

___. _____
     _____

___. _____
     _____

___. _____
     _____

___. _____
     _____

___. _____
     _____

___. _____
     _____

DIAGNOSTIC SUGGESTIONS

Axis I:	312.23	Intermittent Explosive Disorder
	312.30	Impulse Control Disorder
	312.8	Conduct Disorder
	312.9	Disruptive Behavior Disorder NOS

	314.01	Attention-Deficit/Hyperactivity Disorder, Predominantly Hyperactive-Impulsive Type
	314.9	Attention-Deficit/Hyperactivity Disorder NOS
	V71.02	Adolescent Antisocial Behavior
	V61.20	Parent-Child Relational Problem
	300.4	Dysthymic Disorder
	296.xx	Major Depression
	296.89	Bipolar II Disorder
	296.xx	Bipolar I Disorder
	_____	_____
	_____	_____
Axis II:	V799.9	Diagnosis Deferred
	V71.09	No Diagnosis on Axis II
	_____	_____
	_____	_____

SEXUAL ABUSE PERPETRATOR

BEHAVIORAL DEFINITIONS

1. Arrest and conviction for a sexually related crime, such as exhibitionism, exposure, voyeurism, or criminal sexual conduct (first, second, or third degree).
2. Sexual abuse of a younger, vulnerable victim.
3. Frequent use of language that has an easily noted sexual content.
4. Evident sexualization of most, if not all, relationships.
5. Focus on and preoccupation with anything of a sexual nature.
6. Positive familial history for incest.
7. History of being sexually abused as a child.
8. Interest in pornographic content in books, magazines, videos, and/or on the Internet that is more than mere curiosity.

—. _____
   _____
   _____

—. _____
   _____
   _____

—. _____
   _____

LONG-TERM GOALS

1. Eliminate all inappropriate sexual behaviors.
2. Establish and honor boundaries that reflect a sense of mutual respect in all interpersonal relationships.
3. Form relationships that are not sexualized.
4. Reach the point of genuine self-forgiveness, and make apologies to the violated individual(s), along with an offer of restitution.

5. Acknowledge and take responsibility for all inappropriate sexual behavior.
6. Resolve issues of his/her own sexual abuse.

—. _____
   _____
   _____

—. _____
   _____
   _____

—. _____
   _____
   _____

SHORT-TERM OBJECTIVES

1. Develop a working relationship with the therapist that allows for sharing thoughts and feelings openly. (1, 2)

2. Sign a no-sexual-contact agreement. (3, 4)

THERAPEUTIC INTERVENTIONS

1. Actively build the level of trust with the client in individual sessions through consistent eye contact, active listening, unconditional positive regard, and warm acceptance to help increase his/her ability to identify and express feelings.

2. Use a celebrity interview format in which the client is asked nonthreatening questions (e.g., his/her likes and dislikes, best times, favorite holidays) to initiate self-disclosure.

3. Assist the client and his/her family in developing and implementing a behaviorally specific no-sexual-contact agreement; ask the client to sign the agreement.

4. Monitor the client's no-sexual-contact agreement along with the parents,

making any necessary adjustments and giving constructive praise and redirection as warranted; if the client is unable to keep the contract, facilitate a referral to a more restrictive setting.

3. Verbally acknowledge the abuse, and take full responsibility for perpetrating it. (1, 5, 6)

1. Actively build the level of trust with the client in individual sessions through consistent eye contact, active listening, unconditional positive regard, and warm acceptance to help increase his/her ability to identify and express feelings.

5. Process all the incidents of sexual misconduct and/or abuse, focusing on getting the whole story out and having the client accept responsibility for his/her behavior.

6. Assign an exercise on sexual boundaries from the Safer Society Press Series (Freeman-Longo and Bays) to begin the client's process of education and treatment of his/her offense cycle (or assign the "Getting Started" exercise from the *Brief Adolescent Therapy Homework Planner* by Jongsma, Peterson, and McInnis).

4. Recognize and honor the personal boundaries of others as shown by the termination of inappropriate sexual contact. (6, 7)

6. Assign an exercise on sexual boundaries from the Safer Society Press Series (Freeman-Longo and Bays) to begin the client's process of education and treatment

of his/her offense cycle (or assign the "Getting Started" exercise from the *Brief Adolescent Therapy Homework Planner* by Jongsma, Peterson, and McInnis).

7. Assist the client in becoming aware of personal space and boundaries and how to honor and respect them; role-play situations with him/her to reinforce and model appropriate actions that show respect for personal space.

5. Decrease the frequency of sexual references in daily speech and sexual actions in daily behavior. (8, 9)

8. Point out to the client sexual references and content in his/her speech and behavior; process the feelings and thoughts that underlie these references.

9. Ask the client to gather feedback from teachers, parents, and so on regarding sexual references in his/her speech and behavior; process the feedback with the client and identify nonsexualized alternatives.

6. Provide a complete sexual history. (10)

10. Gather a thorough sexual history of the client from the client and his/her parents.

7. Verbally acknowledge ever being a victim of sexual, physical, or emotional abuse. (11)

11. Gently explore whether the client was sexually, physically, or emotionally abused by asking specific questions regarding others' respect for the client's physical boundaries when he/she was a child.

8. State a connection between being a sexual abuse victim and a sexual abuse perpetrator. (12)

9. Demonstrate the ability to identify and express feelings. (13, 14)

10. Tell the story of being a victim of sexual, physical, or emotional abuse with appropriate affect. (15, 16)

12. Assist the client in identifying the connections between his/her own sexual abuse victimization and the development of his/her attitudes and patterns of sexual abuse perpetration.

13. Assist the client in becoming capable of identifying, labeling, and expressing his/her feelings, using various therapeutic tools to increase and reinforce his/her new skills (e.g., The Talking, Feeling, and Doing Game by Gardner, available from Creative Therapeutics; the Ungame by Zakich, available from the Ungame Company).

14. Give feedback to the client when he/she does not show awareness of his/her own feelings or those of others, and positive verbal reinforcement when he/she shows awareness without direction.

15. Encourage and support the client in telling the story of being a sexual, physical, or emotional abuse victim (see Sexual Abuse Victim or Physical/Emotional Abuse Victim chapters in this Planner).

16. Prepare, assist, and support the client in telling his/her parents of his/her own abuse experiences.

11. Attend a sexual abuse perpetrators' group treatment. (17)

17. Refer the client to group treatment for sexual abuse perpetrators.

12. Identify thinking errors, feelings, and beliefs that give justification for sexual abuse and ways to handle each effectively. (18)

18. Assist the client in identifying thoughts and beliefs that he/she used as justification for the abuse; assist him/her in identifying socially acceptable thoughts that are respectful, not exploitive, of others.

13. Increase the connection between thinking errors, feelings, and beliefs and sexual offending. (18, 19)

18. Assist the client in identifying thoughts and beliefs that he/she used as justification for the abuse; assist him/her in identifying socially acceptable thoughts that are respectful, not exploitive, of others.

19. Assist the client in making connections between thinking errors and his/her sexually abusive behaviors.

14. Complete psychological testing and comply with the recommendations. (20)

20. Arrange or conduct psychological testing for the client to rule out presence of psychopathology or other severe emotional issue, and interpret the test results for the client and family, emphasizing the importance of following through on each recommendation.

15. Complete a psychiatric evaluation for medications. (21)

21. Refer the client for a psychiatric evaluation as to the need for psychotropic medication.

16. Take the prescribed medications to control impulses, decrease aggression, or stabilize mood. (22)

22. Monitor the client's psychotropic medication prescription compliance, effectiveness, and side effects.

17. Develop and utilize anger management techniques. (13, 23, 24)

13. Assist the client in becoming capable of identifying, labeling, and expressing his/her feelings, using various therapeutic tools to increase and reinforce his/her new skills (e.g., *The Talking, Feeling, and Doing Game* by Gardner, available from Creative Therapeutics; *The Ungame* by Zakich, available from the Ungame Company).

23. Assign the client an exercise in *The Anger Workbook* (Blodeau) to learn to recognize anger and ways to effectively handle these feelings (or assign the "Anger Control" exercise in the *Brief Adolescent Therapy Homework Planner* by Jongsma, Peterson, and McInnis).

24. Refer the client to a group focused on teaching anger management techniques.

18. Increase the formation of positive peer relationships. (25, 26, 27)

25. Assist the client in identifying specific ways he/she can become more involved with peers (e.g., join sports, music, art, hobby, or church youth groups; invite peers over to watch a DVD/video); role-play these situations to build the client's skill and confidence level in initiating these actions.

26. Ask the client to attempt one new social or recreational activity each week and/or to engage a peer in

conversation (five minutes) once daily; process the experience and the results.

27. Assign the client to read material to help build his/her awareness of what is appropriate and inappropriate behavior when interacting with the opposite sex (e.g., *Dating for Dummies* by Browne or *The Complete Idiot's Guide to Dating* by Kuriansky).

19. Verbalize reasonable guidelines to follow to avoid unhealthy, abusive relationships. (28)

28. Teach the client the SAFE formula for relationships: Avoid a relationship if there is anything *S*ecret about it, if it is *A*busive to oneself or others, if it is used to avoid *F*eelings, or if it is *E*mpty of caring and commitment. Monitor his/her use and give feedback and redirection as required.

20. Parents verbalize awareness of the patterns, beliefs, and behaviors that support the client's sexual behavior. (29, 30)

29. Conduct a family session in which a genogram is developed that depicts patterns of interaction and identifies family members who are sexual abuse survivors or perpetrators, or who have been involved in other sexual deviancy.

30. Hold family sessions in which sexual patterns, beliefs, and behaviors are explored; assist the family members in identifying what sexual patterns, beliefs, or behaviors need to be changed and how they can begin to change them.

21. Parents verbalize changes they are trying to make to improve their parenting patterns. (31, 32, 33)

31. Conduct family sessions in which structural interventions are developed and implemented by the family (e.g., family members begin closing doors for privacy within their home, remove children from roles as supervisors of siblings, terminate sexual references within family conversation).

32. Recommend that the parents attend a didactic group on parenting teenagers.

33. Suggest that the parents read material to expand their understanding of adolescents and to build parenting skills (e.g., *Between Parent and Teenager* by Ginott; *Parents, Teens, and Boundaries* by Bluestein; *Raising Self-Reliant Children in a Self-Indulgent World* by Glenn and Nelsen; or *The 7 Habits of Highly Effective Families* by Covey).

22. Parents develop and implement new family rituals. (34)

34. Assist the parents and family members in developing rituals of transition, healing, membership, identity, and new beginnings that give structure, meaning, and connection to their family.

23. Report instances of increased awareness of the feelings of others and self. (14, 35)

14. Give feedback to the client when he/she does not show awareness of the his/her own feelings or those of others and positive verbal reinforcement when he/she

shows awareness without direction.

35. Teach the client the importance of expanding his/her awareness of the his/her feelings and those of others (or assign the exercise "Your Feelings and Beyond" or "Surface Behavior/Inner Feelings" from the *Brief Adolescent Therapy Homework Planner* by Jongsma, Peterson, and McInnis).

24. Report an increase in appropriate sexual fantasies. (36, 37)

36. Ask the client to keep a fantasy journal, recording daily what sexual fantasies are experienced; review the fantasies for patterns that are appropriate or inappropriate and process this feedback with the client.

37. Assist the client in creating appropriate sexual fantasies that involve consenting, age-appropriate individuals; reflect feelings for the other party, and reject fantasies that involve receiving or inflicting pain.

25. Verbalize a desire to make an apology to his/her victim(s). (38, 39, 40)

38. Explore the client's attitude regarding apologizing to his/her victim and forgiving himself/herself (or assign the exercise "Opening the Door to Forgiveness" from the *Brief Adolescent Therapy Homework Planner* by Jongsma, Peterson, and McInnis).

39. Ask the client to write a letter of apology to one of his/her victims; assess the

genuineness of the remorse and guilt present, and give the client feedback.

40. Role-play the client's apology to the victim of sexual abuse to determine if he/she is ready for this step or what additional work may need to be done for him/her to reach that point; use role reversal to sensitize the client to the victim's feelings and reactions.

26. Make an apology to the sexual abuse survivor and the family. (41)

41. Conduct a family session with the families of both the perpetrator and the survivors in which the perpetrator apologizes to the survivor and his/her family.

27. Identify relapse triggers for perpetrating sexual abuse and list strategies to cope with them. (42)

42. Help the client to identify his/her potential relapse triggers (e.g., environmental situations, fantasies, sexually explicit material), assisting him/her in developing behavioral and cognitive coping strategies to implement for each trigger (e.g., avoidance or removing himself/herself from high-risk situations, thought-stopping of inappropriate fantasies, avoiding being alone with young children).

28. Develop and implement an aftercare plan that includes the support of the family. (43, 44)

43. Ask the client and his/her family to develop a written aftercare plan (e.g., relapse prevention strategies, periodic checkups with therapist, support group participation, legal obligations); process the plan in

29. Cooperate with a risk assessment for repeating sexual offenses. (45)

30. Comply with any investigations by child protective services or criminal justice officials. (46)

a family session and make adjustments as necessary.

44. Hold checkup sessions in which the aftercare plan is reviewed for effectiveness and follow-through; give feedback and make adjustments as necessary.

45. Refer the client for a sex-offender-specific risk assessment as part of the process of completing treatment.

46. Report to the appropriate authorities any sexual abuse that comes to light. Ask the client to share the results of the resulting investigation, and then process the results in a session that focuses on the client taking full responsibility for his/her inappropriate sexual behavior(s).

__. _____   __. _____
    _____   _____
__. _____   __. _____
    _____   _____
__. _____   __. _____
    _____   _____

DIAGNOSTIC SUGGESTIONS

Axis I:	312.81	Conduct Disorder, Childhood-Onset Type
	312.82	Conduct Disorder, Adolescent-Onset Type
	302.2	Pedophilia
	302.4	Exhibitionism
	302.82	Voyeurism
	V61.8	Sibling Relational Problem

995.53	Sexual Abuse of Child (Victim)
V71.02	Child or Adolescent Antisocial Behavior
_____	_____
_____	_____

Axis II:

799.9	Diagnosis Deferred
V71.09	No Diagnosis
_____	_____
_____	_____

SEXUAL ABUSE VICTIM

BEHAVIORAL DEFINITIONS

1. Self-report of being sexually abused.
2. Physical signs of sexual abuse (e.g., red or swollen genitalia, blood in the underwear, constant rashes, a tear in the vagina or rectum, venereal disease, hickeys on the body).
3. Vague memories of inappropriate childhood sexual contact that can be corroborated by significant others.
4. Strong interest in or curiosity about advanced knowledge of sexuality.
5. Pervasive pattern of promiscuity or the sexualization of relationships.
6. Recurrent and intrusive distressing recollections or nightmares of the abuse.
7. Acting or feeling as if the sexual abuse were reocurring (including delusions, hallucinations, or dissociative flashback experiences).
8. Unexplainable feelings of anger, rage, or fear when coming into contact with the perpetrator or after exposure to sexual topics.
9. Pronounced disturbance of mood and affect (e.g., frequent and prolonged periods of depression, irritability, anxiety, and fearfulness).
10. Marked distrust of others as manifested by social withdrawal and problems with establishing and maintaining close relationships.
11. Feelings of guilt, shame, and low self-esteem.
12. Excessive use of alcohol or drugs as a maladaptive coping mechanism to avoid dealing with painful emotions connected to sexual abuse.
13. Sexualized or seductive behavior with younger or same-aged children, adolescents, or adults (e.g., sexualized kissing, provocative exhibition of genitalia, fondling, mutual masturbation, anal or vaginal penetration).

—. _____
_____
_____

—. _____
_____
_____

—. _____
_____

LONG-TERM GOALS

1. Obtain protection from all further sexual victimization.
2. Work successfully through the issue of sexual abuse with consequent understanding and control of feelings and behavior.
3. Resolve the issues surrounding the sexual abuse, resulting in an ability to establish and maintain close interpersonal relationships.
4. Establish appropriate boundaries and generational lines in the family to greatly minimize the risk of sexual abuse ever occurring in the future.
5. Achieve healing within the family system as evidenced by the verbal expression of forgiveness and a willingness to let go and move on.
6. Eliminate denial in self and the family, placing responsibility for the abuse on the perpetrator and allowing the survivor to feel supported.
7. Eliminate all inappropriate promiscuous or sexual behaviors.
8. Build self-esteem and a sense of empowerment as manifested by an increased number of positive self-descriptive statements and greater participation in extracurricular activities.

—. _____
_____

—. _____
_____

—. _____
_____

SHORT-TERM OBJECTIVES

1. Tell the entire story of the abuse. (1, 2)

2. Identify the nature, frequency, and duration of the abuse. (3, 4, 5)

3. Decrease secrecy in the family by informing key

THERAPEUTIC INTERVENTIONS

1. Actively build the level of trust with the client through consistent eye contact, active listening, unconditional positive regard, and warm acceptance to help increase his/her ability to identify and express feelings connected to the abuse.

2. Explore, encourage, and support the client in verbally expressing the facts and clarifying his/her feelings associated with the abuse (or assign the exercise "My Story" in the *Brief Adolescent Therapy Homework Planner* by Jongsma, Peterson and McInnis).

3. Report the client's sexual abuse to the appropriate child protection agency, criminal justice officials, or medical professionals.

4. Consult with a physician, criminal justice officials, or child protection case managers to assess the veracity of the sexual abuse charges.

5. Consult with the physician, criminal justice officials, or child protection case managers to develop appropriate treatment interventions for the client.

6. Facilitate conjoint sessions to reveal the client's sexual

members about the abuse. (6, 7)

abuse to key family members or caregivers.

7. Actively confront and challenge denial of the client's sexual abuse within the family system.

4. Implement steps to protect the client from further sexual abuse. (8, 9, 10, 11)

8. Assess whether the perpetrator should be removed from the home.

9. Implement the necessary steps to protect the client and other children in the home from future sexual abuse.

10. Assess whether the client is safe to remain in the home or should be removed.

11. Empower the client by reinforcing steps necessary to protect himself/herself.

5. Parents establish and adhere to appropriate intimacy boundaries within the family. (12)

12. Counsel the client's family members about appropriate intimacy and privacy boundaries.

6. Identify family dynamics or stressors that contributed to the emergence of sexual abuse. (13, 14, 15)

13. Assess the family dynamics and identify the stress factors or precipitating events that contributed to the emergence of the client's abuse.

14. Assign the client to draw a diagram of the house where the abuse occurred, indicating where everyone slept, and share the diagram with the therapist.

15. Construct a multigenerational family genogram that identifies sexual abuse within the extended family

to help the client realize that he/she is not the only one abused and to help the perpetrator recognize the cycle of boundary violation.

7. Identify and express feelings connected to the abuse. (16, 17, 18, 19, 20)

16. Instruct the client to write a letter to the perpetrator that describes his/her feelings about the abuse; process the letter.

17. Utilize the empty chair technique to assist the client in expressing and working through his/her myriad of feelings toward the perpetrator and other family members.

18. Direct the client to keep a journal in which he/she records experiences or situations that evoke strong emotions pertaining to sexual abuse, and share the journal in therapy sessions.

19. Employ art therapy (e.g., drawing, painting, sculpting) to help the client identify and express his/her feelings toward the perpetrator.

20. Use guided fantasy and imagery techniques to help the client express suppressed thoughts, feelings, and unmet needs associated with sexual abuse.

8. Decrease expressed feelings of shame and guilt and affirm self as not being responsible for the abuse. (21)

21. Explore and resolve the client's feelings of guilt and shame connected to the sexual abuse (or assign the

9. Verbalize the way sexual abuse has impacted life. (22)

10. Nonabusive parent and other key family members increase support and acceptance of client. (23, 24, 25)

11. Perpetrator takes responsibility for the abuse. (26, 27)

"You Are Not Alone" exercise in the *Brief Adolescent Therapy Homework Planner* by Jongsma, Peterson, and McInnis).

22. Instruct the client to create a drawing or sculpture that reflects how sexual abuse impacted his/her life and feelings about himself/herself.

23. Elicit and reinforce support and nurturance for the client from other key family members.

24. Assign the parents and family members reading material to increase their knowledge of sexually addictive behavior and learn ways to help the client recover from sexual abuse (e.g., *Out of the Shadows* by Carnes or *Allies in Healing* by Davis).

25. Give directive to disengaged, nonabusive parent to spend more time with the client in leisure, school, or household activities.

26. Hold a therapy session in which the client and/or the therapist confronts the perpetrator with the abuse.

27. Hold a session in which the perpetrator takes full responsibility for the sexual abuse and apologizes to the client and/or other family members.

12. Perpetrator agrees to seek treatment. (28)

13. Verbalize a desire to begin the process of forgiveness of the perpetrator and others connected with the abuse. (29, 30)

28. Require the perpetrator to participate in a sexual offenders' group.

29. Assign the client to write a forgiveness letter and/or complete a forgiveness exercise in which he/she verbalizes forgiveness to the perpetrator and/or significant family members (or assign the "Letter of Forgiveness" exercise in the *Brief Adolescent Therapy Homework Planner* by Jongsma, Peterson, and McInnis). Process the letter.

30. Assign the client a letting-go exercise in which a symbol of the abuse is disposed of or destroyed; process this experience.

14. Verbally identify self as a survivor of sexual abuse. (31, 32)

31. Ask the client to identify the positive and negative consequences of being a victim versus being a survivor; compare and process the lists.

32. Introduce the idea in later stages of therapy that the client can survive sexual abuse by asking, "What will you be doing in the future that shows you are happy and have moved on with your life?" Process his/her responses and reinforce any positive steps that he/she can take to work through issues related to victimization.

15. Attend and actively participate in group therapy with other sexual abuse survivors. (33)

16. Increase the level of trust of others as shown by increased socialization and a greater number of friendships. (34, 35, 36, 37)

17. Decrease the frequency of sexualized or seductive behaviors in interactions with others. (38, 39)

33. Refer the client to a survivor group with other adolescents to assist him/her in realizing that he/she is not alone in having experienced sexual abuse.

34. Encourage the client to participate in positive peer groups and extracurricular activities.

35. Teach the client the share-check method of building trust, in which the degree of shared information is related to a proven level of trustworthiness.

36. Identify appropriate and inappropriate forms of touching and affection; encourage the client to accept and initiate appropriate forms of touching with trusted individuals.

37. Develop a list of resource people outside of the family to whom the client can turn for support, guidance, and affirmation.

38. Assist the client in making a connection between underlying painful emotions (e.g., fear, hurt, sadness, anxiety) and sexualized or seductive behaviors; help the client identify more adaptive ways to meet his/her needs other than through seductive or sexually promiscuous behaviors.

18. Complete a substance abuse evaluation and comply with the recommendations offered by the evaluation findings. (40)

19. Complete psychological testing. (41, 42)

20. Parents comply with recommendations regarding psychiatric or substance abuse treatment. (43)

39. Provide sex education and discuss the risks involved with sexually promiscuous or seductive behaviors.

40. Arrange for a substance abuse evaluation and/or treatment for the client (see Chemical Dependence chapter in this Planner).

41. Arrange for psychological testing of the client to rule out the presence of severe psychological disorders.

42. Assess the client's self-esteem by having him/her draw self-portraits during the beginning, middle, and end stages of therapy.

43. Assess the parents for the possibility of having a psychiatric disorder and/or substance abuse problem. Refer the parents for psychiatric or substance abuse evaluation and/or treatment if it is found that the parents have psychiatric disorders or substance abuse problems.

__. _____
   _____

__. _____
   _____

__. _____
   _____

__. _____
   _____

__. _____
   _____

__. _____
   _____

DIAGNOSTIC SUGGESTIONS

Axis I:

309.81	Posttraumatic Stress Disorder
308.3	Acute Stress Disorder
296.xx	Major Depressive Disorder
309.21	Separation Anxiety Disorder
995.53	Sexual Abuse of Child (Victim)
307.47	Nightmare Disorder
300.15	Dissociative Disorder NOS
_____	_____
_____	_____

Axis II:

799.9	Diagnosis Deferred
V71.09	No Diagnosis on Axis II
_____	_____
_____	_____

SEXUAL ACTING OUT

BEHAVIORAL DEFINITIONS

1. Engagement in sexual intercourse with several different partners with little or no emotional attachment.
2. Engagement in sexual intercourse without birth control and without being at a stage of development to take responsibility for a baby.
3. Sexually active with one partner but with no sense of long-term commitment to each other.
4. No utilization of safe sex practices.
5. Routine public engagement in sexually provocative dress, language, and behavior.
6. Talking freely of own sexual activity without regard for consequences to reputation or loss of respect from others.
7. Use of drugs and/or alcohol to alter mood and judgment prior to and during sexual activity.
8. Low self-esteem evidenced by self-disparaging remarks and predictions of future failure.
9. Depression evidenced by irritability, social isolation, low energy, and sad affect.
10. Hypomania evidenced by impulsivity, high energy, lack of follow-through, and pressured speech.
11. Angry, oppositional pattern of behavior that is in conflict with social mores, parental rules, and authority figures.
12. Conflict and instability within the family of origin.

—. _____

_____

—. _____
_____

—. _____
_____

LONG-TERM GOALS

1. Terminate sexual activity that does not reflect commitment, emotional intimacy, and a caring, mature relationship.
2. Implement birth control and safe sex practices.
3. Develop insight into the maladaptive sexual activity as self-defeating and emanating from emotional needs and conflicts not related to sex.
4. Resolve underlying emotional conflicts that energize the maladaptive sexual activity.
5. Terminate substance abuse and understand its interaction with sexual promiscuity.
6. Resolve family-of-origin conflicts.

—. _____
_____

—. _____
_____

—. _____
_____

SHORT-TERM OBJECTIVES

1. Acknowledge history and current practice of sexual activity. (1, 2, 3)

THERAPEUTIC INTERVENTIONS

1. Actively build the level of trust with the client in individual sessions through consistent eye contact, active listening, unconditional positive regard, and warm acceptance to help increase his/her ability to identify and express intimate facts and feelings.

2. Identify any and all known motivations for sexual activity. (4, 5)

3. Disclose any history of sexual abuse that has occurred in childhood or adolescence and its effect on current sexual activity. (6, 7)

4. Verbalize insight into the sources and impact of low self-esteem. (8, 9, 10, 11)

2. Gather a detailed sexual history that includes number of partners, frequency of activity, birth control and/or safe sex practices used, source of sexual information in childhood, first sexual experience, and degree of emotional attachment to partner.

3. Explore the client's thoughts and feelings that surround the facts of the sexual history and current practice.

4. Ask the client to list all possible reasons he/she has chosen to engage in sexual activity at this early stage of life and why specific partners were selected.

5. Process the pros and cons of each reason given for the client's sexual activity.

6. Explore for any history of the client having been sexually abused (see Sexual Abuse Victim chapter in this Planner).

7. Assist the client in making a connection between being treated as a sexual object in childhood by a perpetrator and treating himself/herself and others as impersonal sexual objects currently.

8. Explore the client's feelings of low self-esteem as to his/her awareness, depth of feeling, and means of

expression (see Low Self-Esteem chapter in this Planner).

9. Assist the client in identifying sources of his/her feelings of low self-esteem (e.g., perceived parental criticism or rejection; physical, sexual, or emotional abuse; academic or social failures).

10. Help the client become aware of his/her fear of rejection and its connection with past rejection or abandonment experiences.

11. Assist the client in making a connection between his/her feelings of low self-esteem, fear of rejection, and current sexual activity.

5. Identify positive ways to build self-esteem. (12, 13)

12. Confront the self-defeating nature of trying to build self-esteem or gain acceptance through sexual activity, and assist the client in developing a constructive plan to build self-esteem.

13. Assign the client a homework exercise in which he/she is asked to draw pictures of the desired changes to himself/herself (or assign "Three Ways to Change Yourself" from the *Brief Adolescent Therapy Homework Planner* by Jongsma, Peterson, and McInnis).

6. Describe family interaction patterns that may lead to feelings of rejection. (14, 15, 16)

14. Explore the dynamics of rejection versus affirmation present in the client's family of origin.

15. Hold family therapy sessions that focus on the family members' feelings toward each other and their style of interacting.

16. Interpret the client's sexual activity as a maladaptive means of seeking affirmation and attention that has been missed in the family.

7. Verbalize a value for sexual activity beyond physical pleasure and/or trying to get someone to like you. (17, 18)

17. Teach the value of reserving sexual intimacy for a relationship that has commitment, longevity, and maturity.

18. Teach that sexual activity is most rewarding when it is a mutual expression of giving oneself as an act of love versus being sexual to try to get someone to love you or only to meet your own needs for pleasure or conquest.

8. Verbalize feelings of depression. (19, 20, 21)

19. Assess the client for signs or symptoms of depression (see Depression chapter in this Planner).

20. Administer or arrange for psychological testing to assess for emotional or personality factors that may contribute to the client's sexual behavior.

21. Interpret the client's sexual activity as a means of seeking relief from depression that only ends up deepening his/her depression.

9. Verbalize an understanding of the serious risks involved in not using birth control or

22. Teach the client the value of using birth control and safe sex practices.

safe sex practices and affirm implementation of same. (22, 23)

10. Admit that the use of drugs and/or alcohol before or during sexual activity is done to escape from feelings of shame, guilt, or fear. (24, 25)

11. Terminate the use of mood-altering drugs and alcohol. (26)

12. Describe a pattern of impulsive behaviors that lead to negative consequences. (27, 28)

23. Explore any underlying wishes (e.g., pregnancy, death) that have influenced the client's maladaptive behavior in not using birth control or safe sex practices.

24. Explore for the client's use of mood-altering drugs or alcohol before or during sexual activity.

25. Assist the client in identifying the role of drugs or alcohol as a means of numbing his/her conscience and escaping feelings of shame, fear, and guilt associated with sexual acting out.

26. Ask the client for a commitment to terminate the use of drugs and alcohol (see Chemical Dependence chapter in this Planner).

27. Assess the client for a pattern of impulsivity that may characterize many aspects of his/her behavior and that may be related to Attention-Deficit/Hyperactivity Disorder (ADHD) or mania [see Attention-Deficit/ Hyperactivity Disorder (ADHD) and Mania chapters in this Planner].

28. Assess the client for the need for psychotropic medications to alleviate the factors underlying his/her maladaptive sexual activity (e.g., depression, mania, ADHD).

13. Cooperate with an assessment for psychotropic medication. (28, 29)

28. Assess the client for the need for psychotropic medications to alleviate the factors underlying his/her maladaptive sexual activity (e.g., depression, mania, ADHD).

29. Refer the client to a physician to be evaluated for a prescription for psychotropic medication.

14. Take medications as prescribed and report as to effectiveness and side effects. (29, 30)

29. Refer the client to a physician to be evaluated for a prescription for psychotropic medication.

30. Monitor the client's compliance with medication and assess for effectiveness and side effects.

___. _____
_____

___. _____
_____

___. _____
_____

___. _____
_____

___. _____
_____

___. _____
_____

DIAGNOSTIC SUGGESTIONS

Axis I:	296.xx	Major Depressive Disorder
	300.4	Dysthymic Disorder
	296.89	Bipolar II Disorder
	296.4x	Bipolar I Disorder, Most Recent Episode Manic
	303.90	Alcohol Dependence
	305.00	Alcohol Abuse
	304.30	Cannabis Dependence
	305.20	Cannabis Abuse

314.01   Attention-Deficit/Hyperactivity Disorder,
            Predominately Hyperactive-Impulsive Type

_____   _____

Axis II: 799.9   Diagnosis Deferred
               V71.09   No Diagnosis on Axis II

_____   _____

_____   _____

SEXUAL IDENTIFY
CONFUSION*

BEHAVIORAL DEFINITIONS

1. Uncertainty about sexual orientation.
2. Sexual fantasies and desires about same-sex partners that cause distress.
3. Feelings of guilt, shame, and/or worthlessness.
4. Depressed mood; diminished interest in activities.
5. Concealment of sexual identity from parents.
6. Recent homosexual experimentation that has created questions about sexual orientation.
7. Parents verbalize distress over concern that the client may be homosexual.
8. Recent disclosure of homosexual identity to parents.
9. Parents express feelings of failure because the client is gay/lesbian.

—. _____
   _____
   _____
—. _____
   _____
   _____
—. _____
   _____

---

*Most of the content of this chapter (with only slight revisions) originates from J. M. Evosevich and M. Avriette, *The Gay and Lesbian Treatment Planner* (New York: John Wiley & Sons, 1999). Copyright © 1999 by J. M. Evosovich and Michael Avriette. Reprinted with permission.

LONG-TERM GOALS

1. Clarify own sexual identity and engage in a wide range of relationships that are supportive of same.
2. Reduce overall frequency and intensity of the anxiety associated with sexual identity so that daily functioning is not impaired.
3. Disclose sexual orientation to parents.
4. Return to previous level of emotional, psychological, and social functioning.
5. Parents accept the client's homosexuality.
6. Resolve all symptoms of depression (e.g., depressed mood, guilt, shame, worthlessness).

—. _____

   _____

—. _____

   _____

—. _____

   _____

SHORT-TERM OBJECTIVES	THERAPEUTIC INTERVENTIONS
1. Describe fear, anxiety, and distress related to confusion over sexual identity. (1, 2)	1. Actively build trust with the client and encourage the expression of fear, anxiety, and distress over his/her sexual identity confusion.
	2. Conduct a suicide assessment and refer the client to the appropriate supervised level of care if a danger to self exists.
2. Contract not to harm self. (3)	3. Encourage the client to verbalize and then sign a no-harm contract.
3. Openly discuss history of sexual desires, fantasies, and experiences. (4)	4. Assess the client's current sexual functioning by asking about his/her history of

sexual experiences, fantasies, and desires.

4. Verbalize reasons for questioning own sexual identify. (5, 6)

5. Ask the client why he/she has questions about his/her sexuality, with specific questions about when he/she began to question his/her sexuality and why.

6. Educate the client about the commonality of same-sex experiences in youth and emphasize that these do not necessarily indicate a homosexual identity.

5. Rate sexual attraction to males and females on a scale of 1 to 10. (7)

7. Have the client rate his/her sexual attraction to males and females on a scale of 1 to 10 (with 10 being extremely attracted and 1 being not at all attracted).

6. Write a future biography detailing life as a heterosexual and as a homosexual to assist self in identifying primary orientation. (8)

8. Assign the client the homework of writing a future biography describing his/her life 20 years in the future, both as a heterosexual and as a homosexual; read and process this biography (e.g., ask the client which life was more satisfying, which life had more regrets).

7. Resolve sexual identity confusion by identifying self as homosexual or heterosexual. (9, 10)

9. Allow the client to evaluate all the evidence from his/her experience in a nonjudgmental atmosphere so as to resolve his/her confusion and identify himself/herself as homosexual or heterosexual.

10. Ask the client to list all the factors that led to a decision

8. Identify and verbalize feelings related to identifying self as gay or lesbian. (11, 12)

9. Verbalize an understanding of how religious beliefs have contributed to hiding or denying sexual orientation. (13, 14)

10. Verbalize an understanding of safer sex practices. (15)

11. List myths about homosexuals and replace them with more realistic, positive beliefs. (16)

12. List the advantages and disadvantages of disclosing one's sexual orientation to

---

regarding his/her sexual identity; process the list.

11. Explore the client's feelings regarding seeing himself/herself as homosexual.

12. Explore the client's negative emotions (e.g., shame, guilt, anxiety, loneliness) related to hiding or denying his/her homosexuality.

13. Explore the client's religious convictions and how these may conflict with identifying himself/herself as homosexual and cause feelings of shame or guilt.

14. Refer the client to a member of the clergy who will listen compassionately to the client's religious struggle over his/her homosexual identity.

15. Teach the client the details of safer sex guidelines.

16. Assist the client in identifying myths about homosexuals (e.g., bad parenting causes homosexuality, homosexuals are not ever happy) and assist him/her in replacing them with more realistic, positive beliefs (e.g., there is no evidence that parenting causes homosexuality, gay men and lesbians can be as happy as heterosexuals).

17. Assign the client to list advantages and disadvantages of disclosing his/her sexual

significant people in one's life. (17)

13. Describe social interaction with peers and identify any isolation and/or homophobia experienced because of having a homosexual identity. (18, 19)

14. Attend a support group for gay and lesbian adolescents. (20)

15. Write a plan detailing when, where, and to whom sexual orientation is to be disclosed. (21, 22)

16. Reveal sexual orientation to family members according to the written plan. (23, 24)

orientation to family members and other significant people in his/her life. Process the list.

18. Explore the client's relationships with peers and assist him/her in describing any homophobic experiences and/or isolation as well as the feelings associated with these experiences.

19. Encourage the client to identify other lesbian and gay adolescents to interact with by reviewing people he/she has met in support groups, at school, or on a job, and encourage him/her to initiate social activities.

20. Refer the client to a lesbian and gay adolescent support group (e.g., Gay and Lesbian Community Service Center, Youth Services).

21. Assign the client homework to write a detailed plan to disclose his/her sexual orientation, including where, when, and to whom it will be disclosed, and possible questions and reactions the recipient might have.

22. Have the client role-play the disclosure of his/her sexual orientation to significant others.

23. Encourage the client to disclose his/her sexual orientation to family members according to the previously written plan.

17. Parents attend conjoint sessions that focus on resolving their feelings about the client's disclosure of his/her homosexual orientation. (25, 26)

18. Parents verbalize an increased understanding of homosexuality. (27, 28)

19. Parents attend a support group for families of homosexuals. (29)

24. Probe the client about the reactions of significant others to his/her disclosure of homosexuality; provide encouragement and positive feedback.

25. Arrange conjoint sessions that allow for a free exchange of thoughts and feelings within the family; encourage the client's parents to attend and participate.

26. Explore the emotional reactions of the parents to the client's disclosure of his/her homosexuality.

27. Educate the parents about homosexuality and answer questions they may have in an honest, direct manner (e.g., assure the parents that homosexuality is not caused by faulty parenting, nor is it considered a mental illness).

28. Assign the parents books that offer positive, realistic information about homosexuality and homosexual adolescents (e.g., *Is It a Choice?* by Marcus; *Beyond Acceptance* by Griffin, Wirth, and Wirth).

29. Refer the parents to a support group for families of homosexuals (e.g., Parents and Friends of Lesbians and Gays) and encourage their attendance.

20. Parents identify any religious beliefs that contribute to rejecting the client's homosexuality. (30)

21. Parents verbalize an understanding that many religious leaders are accepting of homosexuals. (31, 32)

30. Probe the parents about the impact of their religious beliefs on accepting their child's homosexuality.

31. Refer the parents to gay/lesbian-positive clergy to discuss their concerns.

32. Assign the parents to read Chapter 4 in *Beyond Acceptance* (Griffin, Wirth, and Wirth) and "The Bible and Homosexuality: The Last Prejudice" in *The Good Book* (Gomes). Process their reactions to the material read.

—. _____
   _____

—. _____
   _____

—. _____
   _____

—. _____
   _____

—. _____
   _____

—. _____
   _____

DIAGNOSTIC SUGGESTIONS

Axis I:	309.0	Adjustment Disorder With Depressed Mood
	309.28	Adjustment Disorder With Mixed Anxiety and Depressed Mood
	300.00	Anxiety Disorder NOS
	309.24	Adjustment Disorder With Anxiety
	300.4	Dysthymic Disorder
	302.85	Gender Identity Disorder in Adolescents or Adults
	300.02	Generalized Anxiety Disorder
	313.82	Identity Problem
	296.2x	Major Depressive Disorder, Single Episode
	296.3x	Major Depressive Disorder, Recurrent
	V62.89	Phase of Life Problem

	V61.20	Parent-Child Relational Problem
	_____	_____
	_____	_____
Axis II:	799.9	Diagnosis Deferred
	V71.09	No Diagnosis on Axis II
	_____	_____
	_____	_____

SOCIAL PHOBIA/SHYNESS

BEHAVIORAL DEFINITIONS

1. Hiding, limited or no eye contact, and refusal or reticence to respond verbally to overtures from others.
2. Excessive shrinking or avoidance of contact with unfamiliar people for an extended period of time (i.e., six months or longer).
3. Social isolation and/or excessive involvement in isolated activities (e.g., reading, listening to music in room, playing video games).
4. Extremely limited or no close friendships outside of the immediate family members.
5. Hypersensitivity to criticism, disapproval, or perceived signs of rejection from others.
6. Excessive need for reassurance of being liked by others before demonstrating a willingness to get involved with them.
7. Marked reluctance to engage in new activities or take personal risks because of the potential for embarrassment or humiliation.
8. Negative self-image as evidenced by frequent self-disparaging remarks, unfavorable comparisons to others, and a perception of himself/herself as being socially unattractive.
9. Lack of assertiveness because of a fear of being met with criticism, disapproval, or rejection.
10. Heightened physiological distress in social settings manifested by increased heart rate, profuse sweating, dry mouth, muscular tension, and trembling.

—. _____
_____
—. _____
_____
—. _____
_____

LONG-TERM GOALS

1. Eliminate anxiety, shyness, and timidity in most social settings.
2. Establish and maintain long-term (i.e., six months) interpersonal or peer friendships outside of the immediate family.
3. Initiate social contacts regularly with unfamiliar people or when placed in new social settings.
4. Interact socially with peers or friends on a regular, consistent basis without excessive fear or anxiety.
5. Achieve a healthy balance between time spent in solitary activity and social interaction with others.
6. Develop the essential social skills that will enhance the quality of interpersonal relationships.
7. Elevate self-esteem and feelings of security in interpersonal relationships.

—. _____
_____
—. _____
_____
—. _____
_____

SHORT-TERM OBJECTIVES

1. Complete psychological testing. (1)

2. Establish therapeutic alliance. (2)

THERAPEUTIC INTERVENTIONS

1. Arrange for psychological testing to assess the severity of the client's anxiety and gain greater insight into the dynamics contributing to the symptoms; provide feedback to the client and parents.

2. Actively build the level of trust with the client in individual sessions through consistent eye contact, active listening, unconditional positive regard, and warm acceptance to

help increase his/her ability to identify and express feelings.

3. Comply with behavioral and cognitive strategies and gradually increase the frequency and duration of social contacts. (3, 4, 5, 6)

3. Design and implement a systematic desensitization program in which the client gradually increases the frequency and duration of social contacts to help decrease his/her social anxiety.

4. Develop a reward system or contingency contract to reinforce the client for initiating social contacts and/or engaging in leisure and recreational activities with peers.

5. Train the client to reduce anxiety utilizing guided imagery in a relaxed state, with the client visualizing himself/herself dealing with various social situations in a confident manner.

6. Utilize behavioral rehearsal, modeling, and role playing in individual sessions to help the client reduce anxiety, develop social skills, and learn to initiate conversation.

4. Increase positive self-statements in social interactions. (7)

7. Assist the client in developing positive self-talk as a means of managing his/her social anxiety or fears.

5. Initiate one social contact per day. (8, 9)

8. Assign the task of initiating one social contact per day.

9. Utilize the "Greeting Peers" exercise from the *Brief*

Adolescent Therapy Homework Planner (Jongsma, Peterson, and McInnis) to reduce social isolation and help the client begin to take steps toward establishing peer friendships.

6. Increase participation in interpersonal or peer group activities. (10, 11, 12)

10. Direct the client to initiate three phone calls per week to different individuals.

11. Praise and reinforce the client for any emerging positive social behaviors.

12. Give the client a directive to invite a friend for an overnight visit and/or set up an overnight visit at a friend's home; process any fears and anxiety that arise.

7. Identify strengths and interests that can be used to initiate social contacts and develop peer friendships. (13, 14, 15, 16)

13. Ask the client to list how he/she is like his/her peers; use this list to encourage contact with peers who share interests and abilities.

14. Instruct the client to identify 5 to 10 strengths or interests; review the list in the following session and encourage the client to utilize his/her strengths or interests to initiate peer contacts and establish friendships (or assign the "Show Your Strengths" exercise from the *Brief Adolescent Therapy Homework Planner* by Jongsma, Peterson, and McInnis).

15. Ask the client to list or keep a journal of both positive

and negative social experiences; process this material.

16. Have the client list his/her positive role models or heroes. Encourage the client to engage in behaviors or activities that help him/her identify with the role model/hero and connect with peers.

8. Parents and teachers reinforce positive social behaviors. (17, 18)

17. Instruct the parents and teachers to observe and record positive social behaviors by the client between therapy sessions. Reinforce the client and encourage him/her to continue to exhibit the positive social behaviors.

18. Consult with school officials about ways to increase the client's socialization (e.g., write for the school newspaper, tutor a more popular peer, pair with a popular peer on classroom assignments).

9. Decrease the frequency of self-disparaging remarks and negative social behaviors in the presence of peers. (19)

19. Provide feedback on any negative social behaviors that interfere with the client's ability to establish and maintain friendships; assist the client in prosocial alternatives.

10. Increase assertive behaviors to deal more effectively and directly with stress, conflict, or intimidating peers. (20, 21)

20. Teach the client assertiveness skills to help him/her communicate thoughts, feelings, and needs more openly and directly.

21. Identify factors that contributed to the client being

11. Verbally identify positive social skills. (22, 23)

less anxious and more out-going in the past. Challenge and encourage the client to use similar strategies and coping mechanisms in the coming weeks to be more outgoing.

22. Use Skillstreaming: The Adolescent Kit (McGinnis and Goldstein; available from Childswork/Childs-play) to teach the client positive social skills.

23. Utilize The Helping, Shar-ing, Caring Game (Gardner) in therapy session to help develop important social skills.

12. Verbalize how current social anxiety and insecurities are associated with past rejec-tion experiences and criti-cism from significant others. (24, 25, 26)

24. Explore the client's back-ground for a history of re-jection experiences, harsh criticism, abandonment, or trauma that have fostered the client's low self-esteem and social anxiety.

25. Encourage and support the client in verbally expressing and clarifying his/her feel-ings associated with past rejection experiences, harsh criticism, abandonment, or trauma.

26. Direct the client to write a letter to individuals whom he/she perceives as having subjected him/her to unfair criticism, ridicule, or ha-rassment; process the letter.

13. Identify family dynamics or stressors that contribute to

27. Conduct a family therapy session to assess the

social anxiety and shyness. (27, 28)

dynamics contributing to the client's feelings of anxiety and insecurity.

28. Have the client create a family kinetic drawing to obtain insight into family dynamics that may contribute to his/her social phobia.

14. Enmeshed or overly protective parents identify how they reinforce social anxiety and overly dependent behaviors. (27, 29)

27. Conduct a family therapy session to assess the dynamics contributing to the client's feelings of anxiety and insecurity.

29. Teach the parents how being overly enmeshed with the client reinforces his/her dependency and social anxiety while also impeding his/her chances to socialize with peers.

15. Parents reinforce the client's positive social behaviors and set limits on overly dependent behaviors. (30, 31, 32)

30. Encourage the parents to reinforce or reward the client's positive social behaviors (e.g., calling a friend, playing sports at school, in a gym, or in a neighborhood park) and set limits on overly dependent behaviors (e.g., immature whining and complaining, shadowing parents in social settings).

31. Instruct the parents to ignore occasional and mild oppositional or aggressive behaviors by the client during the initial stages of treatment (unless they become too intense or

16. Overly critical parents verbally recognize how their negative remarks contribute to the client's social anxiety, timidity, and low self-esteem. (33, 34)

17. Overly rigid parents recognize the need to loosen rules and boundaries to increase opportunities for the client to socialize with his/her peers. (35)

18. Express feelings through art and music. (36, 37)

frequent) so as not to extinguish the client's emerging assertive behaviors.

32. Assist the client and his/her parents in developing insight into the secondary gain received from social anxiety and withdrawal.

33. Explore whether the parents are overly rigid or strict in their establishment of rules and boundaries to the point where the client has little opportunity to socialize with peers.

34. Utilize the empty chair technique to provide the client with an opportunity to express his/her feelings toward the overly critical, rejecting, or absent parent.

35. Encourage and challenge the overly rigid parents to loosen rules and boundaries to allow the client increased opportunities to socialize with peers.

36. Instruct the client to draw a picture that reflects what he/she fears will happen if he/she asserts himself/herself with others or engages in social activities with unfamiliar people.

37. Have the client sing, play an instrument, or bring in a recording of a song that reflects his/her insecurities and social anxiety.

19. Attend and actively partici-
    pate in the group therapy
    process. (38, 39, 40)

38. Arrange for the client to at-
    tend group therapy to im-
    prove his/her social skills.

39. Direct the client to self-
    disclose two times in each
    group therapy session.

40. Refer the client to an art
    therapy group to help
    him/her express his/her
    feelings and reveal aspects
    of himself/herself to others
    through artwork.

20. Take medication as directed
    by the prescribing physi-
    cian. (41)

41. Arrange for a medication
    evaluation of the client.
    Monitor the client for psy-
    chotropic medication pre-
    scription compliance, side
    effects, and effectiveness,
    consulting with the pre-
    scribing physician at regu-
    lar intervals.

__. _____   __. _____
    _____   _____
__. _____   __. _____
    _____   _____
__. _____   __. _____
    _____   _____

DIAGNOSTIC SUGGESTIONS

Axis I: 300.23   Social Phobia
              309.21   Generalized Anxiety Disorder
              300.02   Anxiety Disorder NOS
              300.00   Separation Anxiety
              300.4   Dysthymic Disorder
              296.xx   Major Depressive Disorder
              311   Depressive Disorder NOS

	309.81	Posttraumatic Stress Disorder
	_____	_____
	_____	_____
Axis II:	799.9	Diagnosis Deferred
	V71.09	No Diagnosis on Axis II
	_____	_____
	_____	_____

SPECIFIC PHOBIA

BEHAVIORAL DEFINITIONS

1. Persistent and unreasonable fear of specific object or situation because an encounter with the phobic stimulus provokes an immediate anxiety response.
2. Avoidance or endurance of the phobic stimulus with intense anxiety resulting in interference of normal routines or marked distress.
3. Sleep disturbed by dreams of the feared stimulus.
4. Dramatic fear reaction to even the mention of the phobic stimulus.
5. Parental reinforcement of the phobia by catering to the client's
   fear.

__. _____

_____

_____

__. _____

_____

_____

__. _____

_____

LONG-TERM GOALS

1. Reduce the fear of the specific stimulus object or situation that previously provoked immediate anxiety.
2. Eliminate the interference from normal routines and remove the
   distress over the feared object or situation.
3. Live phobia-free while responding appropriately to life's fears.
4. Resolve the conflict underlying the phobia.

5. Learn to overcome fears of noise, darkness, people, wild animals, and crowds.

—. _____
_____
—. _____
_____
—. _____
_____

SHORT-TERM OBJECTIVES

1. Verbalize the fear and focus on describing the specific stimulus for it. (1, 2)

2. Construct a hierarchy of situations that evoke increasing anxiety. (3)

3. Become proficient in progressive deep muscle relaxation. (4, 5)

4. Identify a nonthreatening, pleasant scene to promote relaxation through guided imagery. (6)

5. Cooperate with systematic desensitization to the anxiety-provoking stimulus object or situation. (7)

THERAPEUTIC INTERVENTIONS

1. Actively build a level of trust with the client that will promote the open showing of thoughts and feelings, especially fearful ones.

2. Discuss and assess the client's fear, its depth, its history of development, and the stimulus for it.

3. Direct and assist the client in the construction of a hierarchy of anxiety-producing situations.

4. Train the client in progressive relaxation methods.

5. Use biofeedback techniques to facilitate the client's relaxation skills.

6. Train the client in the use of relaxing guided imagery for anxiety relief.

7. Direct systematic desensitization (i.e., imagery-based graduated exposure to phobic stimulus while deeply

relaxed) procedures to reduce the client's phobic response.

6. Engage in in vivo desensitization to the anxiety-provoking stimulus object or situation. (8)

8. Assign the client to and/or accompany him/her in in vivo desensitization (graduated live exposure) to the phobic stimulus object or situation (or assign the homework exercise "Gradually Facing a Phobic Fear" from the *Brief Adolescent Therapy Homework Planner* by Jongsma, Peterson, and McInnis).

7. Collect pleasant pictures or stories regarding the phobic stimulus and share them in therapy sessions. (9, 10)

9. Use pleasant pictures, readings, or storytelling about the feared object or situation as a means of desensitizing the client to the fear-producing stimulus.

10. Use humor, jokes, riddles, and stories to enable the client to see his/her situation/fears as not as serious as believed and to help instill hope without disrespecting or minimizing his/her fears.

8. Engage in the feared behavior or encounter the feared situation and freely experience the nondevastating anxiety. (8, 11, 12)

8. Assign the client to and/or accompany him/her in in vivo desensitization (graduated live exposure) to the phobic stimulus object or situation (or assign the homework exercise "Gradually Facing a Phobic Fear" from the *Brief Adolescent Therapy Homework Planner* by Jongsma, Peterson, and McInnis).

11. Use a strategic intervention (see Fisch, Watzlawick, and Weakland) in which enactment of a symptom is prescribed, allowing the client to make an obvious, overt display of the anxiety (e.g., if the symptom is fear of screaming in a public place, direct the client to go there and do so). Process the client's catastrophizing expectations.

12. Play an enjoyable game with the client in the presence of the feared object or situation as a way of desensitizing him/her. (This may mean leaving the office to conduct a session.)

9. Family members demonstrate support for the client as he/she tolerates more exposure to the phobic stimulus. (13, 14, 15)

13. Hold family sessions in which the family is instructed to give support as the client faces the phobic stimulus and to withhold support if the client panics and fails to face the fear (see *Turning Points* by Pittman); offer encouragement, support, and redirection as required.

14. Assist the family in overcoming the tendency to reinforce the client's phobia; as the phobia decreases, teach them constructive ways to reward the client's progress.

15. Assess and confront family members when they model phobic fear responses for the

client in the presence of the feared object or situation.

10. Identify the symbolic significance of the phobic stimulus as a basis for fear. (16)

16. Probe, discuss, and interpret the possible symbolic meaning of the client's phobic stimulus object or situation.

11. Verbalize the separate realities of the irrationally feared object or situation and the emotionally painful experience from the past that is evoked by the phobic stimulus. (17)

17. Clarify and differentiate between the client's current irrational fear and past emotionally painful experiences.

12. Verbalize the feelings associated with a past emotionally painful situation that is connected to the phobia. (18, 19)

18. Encourage the client to share feelings from the past through active listening, unconditional positive regard, and questioning.

19. Reinforce the client's insight into the past emotional pain and its connection to present anxiety.

13. Differentiate real situations that can produce rational fear from distorted imagined situations that can produce irrational fear. (20)

20. Help the client differentiate between real and imagined situations that produce fear. Confront the client when he/she responds to imagined situations as if they are real.

14. Implement specific cognitive and behavioral coping strategies to effectively reduce fear in phobic situations. (21, 22, 23, 24)

21. Teach the client cognitive and behavioral coping strategies (e.g., diversion, deep breathing, positive self-talk, muscle relaxation) to implement when experiencing fear.

22. Assign the client a specific exercise from the *Anxiety and Phobia Workbook* (Bourne) to help expand

his/her skills in coping with panic attacks and/or fears. Process the completed exercises with the therapist and assist the client in implementing new coping skills.

23. Facilitate a role play with the client around one of his/her fears. Process the experience, then repeat the role play using a designed strategy for coping with the identified fear.

24. Read the story "The Green Dragon" from *Stories for the Third Ear* (Wallas) and assist the client in looking at solutions and/or optional ways of dealing with his/her fearful feelings that are present in the story.

15. Implement positive self-talk to terminate fearful response to phobic situations. (25, 26, 27)

25. Identify the distorted schemas and related automatic thoughts that mediate the client's anxiety response.

26. Use cognitive restructuring techniques to train the client in revising distorted core schemes that trigger negative self-talk; assist the client in replacing negative messages with positive, realistic messages that will counteract a fear response.

27. Ask the client to read the section "How to Conquer Anxiety, Fears, and Phobias" from *The Feeling Good Handbook* (Burns) and gather five key concepts to process with the therapist.

16. Implement the strategy of recalling the therapist's reassurances and encouragement at the time of a phobic encounter. (28)

17. Utilize a previously successful coping strategy to reduce current fear. (29)

18. Implement a positive visualization technique to reduce phobic fear. (30)

19. Complete a cost-benefit analysis of the phobic fear. (31)

28. Have the client implement "The Therapist on the Inside" techniques (see Grigoryev in *101 Favorite Play Therapy Techniques* by Kaduson and Schaefer) to help in developing the internal structures necessary for handling fears by evoking the memory of the therapist to act as a coach and consultant in developing ways to work through the particular fear successfully.

29. Employ a brief, solution-focused approach of "Finding What Works" from *A Guide to Possibility Land* (O'Hanlon and Beadle), focusing on what worked for the client in the past, obtaining and expanding the details around what worked, and retrieving what it felt like for the client to have this work. Then encourage him/her to try this approach again.

30. Induce a light trance state in the client and have him/her visualize a movie in which the fear is confronted and successfully handled or neutralized.

31. Assign the client to complete and process with the therapist the "Cost-Benefit Analysis" exercise from *Ten Days to Self-Esteem* (Burns) in which he/she lists the advantages and disadvantages of negative thoughts, fear, or anxiety.

20. Rate the degree of anxiety experienced with each phobic encounter and note its antecedents, coping strategy, and consequences. (32)

21. Complete an evaluation for psychotropic medication and then responsibly take the prescribed medication to alleviate the phobic anxiety. (33, 34)

32. Ask the client to keep a journal of anxiety experiences, their antecedents, and their consequences (or assign the "Panic Attack Rating Form" from the *Brief Adolescent Therapy Homework Planner* by Jongsma, Peterson, and McInnis).

33. Arrange for the prescription of psychotropic medication for the client.

34. Monitor the client for medication compliance and effectiveness.

—. _____
_____
—. _____
_____
—. _____
_____

—. _____
_____
—. _____
_____
—. _____
_____

DIAGNOSTIC SUGGESTIONS

Axis I:
300.00 Anxiety Disorder NOS
300.02 Generalized Anxiety Disorder
300.01 Panic Disorder With Agoraphobia
300.21 Panic Disorder Without Agoraphobia
300.29 Specific Phobia
_____ _____

Axis II:
799.9 Diagnosis Deferred
V71.09 No Diagnosis on Axis II
_____ _____
_____ _____

SUICIDAL IDEATION/ATTEMPT

BEHAVIORAL DEFINITIONS

1. Recurrent thoughts of or a preoccupation with death.
2. Recurrent or ongoing suicidal ideation without any plans.
3. Ongoing suicidal ideation with a specific plan.
4. Recent suicide attempt.
5. History of suicide attempts that required professional or family/ friend intervention on some level (e.g., inpatient, safe house, outpatient, supervision).
6. Positive family history of depression and/or suicide.
7. Expression of a bleak, hopeless attitude regarding life.
8. Recent painful life events (e.g., parental divorce, death of a friend or family member, broken close relationship).
9. Social withdrawal, lethargy, and apathy.
10. Rebellious and self-destructive behavior patterns (e.g., dangerous drug or alcohol abuse, reckless driving, assaultive anger) that indicate a disregard for personal safety and a desperate attempt to escape from emotional distress.

—. _____
   _____

—. _____
   _____

—. _____
   _____

LONG-TERM GOALS

1. Alleviate the suicidal impulses or ideation and return to the highest previous level of daily functioning.
2. Stabilize the suicidal crisis.
3. Place in an appropriate level of care to address the suicidal crisis.
4. Reestablish a sense of hope for future life.
5. Terminate the death wish and renew a zestful interest in social activities and relationships.
6. Cease the perilous lifestyle and resolve the emotional conflicts that underlie the suicidal pattern.

—. _____

_____

—. _____

_____

—. _____

_____

SHORT-TERM OBJECTIVES

1. State the strength of the suicidal feelings, the frequency of the thoughts, and the detail of the plans. (1, 2)

2. Parents, family members, and significant others agree to provide supervision and monitor suicide potential. (3)

3. Cooperate with psychological testing to assess for the

THERAPEUTIC INTERVENTIONS

1. Assess the client's suicidal ideation, taking into account the extent of the ideation, the presence of primary and backup plans, past attempts, and family history.

2. Assess and monitor the client's suicide potential on an ongoing basis.

3. Notify the client's family and significant others of any severe suicidal ideation. Ask them to form a 24-hour suicide watch until the crisis subsides.

4. Arrange for psychological assessment of the client

severity of depression and hopelessness. (4)

(e.g., Minnesota Multiphasic Personality Inventory, Beck Depression Inventory, Reynolds Adolescent Depression Scale) and evaluate the results as to the depth of depression.

4. Cooperate with an evaluation by a physician for antidepressant medication. (5, 6)

5. Assess the client's need for antidepressant medication and arrange for a prescription, if necessary.

6. Monitor the client for medication compliance, effectiveness, and side effects.

5. Cooperate with hospitalization if the suicidal urge becomes uncontrollable. (7)

7. Arrange for hospitalization when the client is judged to be harmful to himself/herself.

6. Verbalize a promise (as part of a suicide prevention contract) to contact the therapist or some other emergency helpline if a serious urge toward self-harm arises. (8, 9, 10, 11)

8. Elicit a promise from the client that he/she will initiate contact with the therapist or a helpline if the suicidal urge becomes strong and before any self-injurious behavior.

9. Provide the client with an emergency helpline telephone number that is available 24 hours a day.

10. Make a written contract with the client, identifying what he/she will and will not do when experiencing suicidal thoughts or impulses (or complete the "No Self-Harm Contract" exercise from the *Brief Adolescent Therapy Homework Planner* by Jongsma, Peterson, and McInnis).

7. Parents increase the safety of the home by removing firearms or other lethal weapons from the client's easy access. (12)

8. Increase communication with the parents, resulting in feeling attended to and understood. (13)

9. Identify feelings of sadness, anger, and hopelessness related to a conflicted relationship with the parents. (14, 15)

10. Verbalize an understanding of the motives for self-destructive behavior patterns. (16, 17, 18)

11. Offer to be available to the client through telephone contact if a life-threatening urge develops.

12. Encourage the parents to remove firearms or other lethal weapons from the client's easy access.

13. Meet with the parents to assess their understanding of the causes for the client's distress and to explain the client's perspective and need for empathy.

14. Probe the client's feelings of despair related to his/her family relationships.

15. Hold family therapy sessions to promote communication of the client's feelings of sadness, hurt, and anger.

16. Explore the sources of emotional pain underlying the client's suicidal ideation and the depth of his/her hopelessness.

17. Interpret the client's sadness, wish for death, or dangerous rebellion as an expression of hopelessness and helplessness (a cry for help).

18. Encourage the client to express his/her feelings related to the suicidal behavior in order to clarify them and increase insight into the causes and motives for the behavior.

11. Verbally report and demonstrate an increased sense of hope for self. (19, 20, 21, 22)

19. Teach the client the benefit of sharing emotional pain instead of internalizing it and brooding over it (or assign the client to read the short story "Renewed Hope" from the *Brief Adolescent Therapy Homework Planner* by Jongsma, Peterson, and McInnis).

20. Assist the client in finding positive, hopeful things in his/her life at the present time.

21. Reinforce all of the client's statements that reflect hope and resolution of the suicidal urge.

22. Ask the client to bring to session symbols of achievement and personal meaning and reinforce their importance (or assign the exercise "Symbols of Self-Worth" from the *Brief Adolescent Therapy Homework Planner* by Jongsma, Peterson, and McInnis).

12. Implement more positive cognitive processing patterns that maintain a realistic and hopeful perspective. (23, 24, 25)

23. Assist the client in developing coping strategies for suicidal ideation (e.g., more physical exercise, less internal focus, increased social involvement, more expression of feelings).

24. Assist the client in developing an awareness of the cognitive messages that reinforce hopelessness and helplessness.

25. Identify and confront catastrophizing, fortune-telling, and mind-reading tendencies in the client's cognitive processing, teaching more realistic self-talk of hope in the face of pain.

13. Identify how previous attempts to solve interpersonal problems have failed, resulting in helplessness. (26)

26. Review with the client previous problem-solving attempts and discuss new alternatives that are available (e.g., assertiveness, brainstorming with a friend, sharing with a mentor, compromise, acceptance).

14. Develop and implement a penitence ritual of expressing grief for victims and absolving self of responsibility for surviving an incident fatal to others. (27)

27. Develop a penitence ritual for the client who is a survivor of an incident fatal to others and implement it with him/her.

15. Strengthen the social support network with friends by initiating social contact and participating in social activities with peers. (28, 29, 30)

28. Encourage the client to reach out to friends and participate in enriching social activities by assigning involvement in at least one social activity with his/her peers per week. Monitor and process the experience.

29. Use behavioral rehearsal, modeling, and role playing to build the client's social skills with his/her peers.

30. Encourage the client to broaden his/her social network by initiating one new social contact per week versus desperately clinging to one or two friends.

16. Reestablish a consistent
eating and sleeping pattern.
(31)

31. Encourage normal eating
and sleeping patterns and
monitor the client's compliance.

__. _____   __. _____
    _____   _____

__. _____   __. _____
    _____   _____

__. _____   __. _____
    _____   _____

DIAGNOSTIC SUGGESTIONS

Axis I: 296.2x   Major Depressive Disorder, Single Episode
               296.3x   Major Depressive Disorder, Recurrent
               300.4   Dysthymic Disorder
               296.xx   Bipolar I Disorder
               296.89   Bipolar II Disorder, Most Recent Episode
                         Depressed
               311   Depressive Disorder NOS
               309.81   Posttraumatic Stress Disorder

               _____   _____

Axis II: 301.83   Borderline Personality Disorder
               799.9   Diagnosis Deferred
               V71.09   No Diagnosis on Axis II

               _____   _____
               _____   _____

Appendix A

SAMPLE CHAPTER WITH QUANTIFIED LANGUAGE

ANGER MANAGEMENT

BEHAVIORAL DEFINITIONS*

1. Angry outbursts that are out of proportion to the precipitating event that occur _____ times per day/week.
2. Screaming, cursing, or using verbally abusive language when frustrated or stressed that occurs _____ times per day/week.
3. Fighting, intimidation of others, and acts of cruelty or violence toward people or animals that occur _____ times per day/week.
4. Verbal threats of harm to parents, adult authority figures, siblings, or peers that occur _____ times per day/week.
5. Pattern of destroying property or throwing objects when angry that occurs _____ times per day/week.
6. Failure to accept responsibility for loss of control, accompanied by repeated pattern of blaming others for his/her anger control problems that occurs _____ times per day/week.

---

*NOTE: For each behavioral definition, look for or include valid reports of differential levels of occurrence (both higher and lower) between certain times of the day; with certain days of the week; with certain friends, siblings, adults, and teacher(s)/parent(s)/guardian(s)/caretaker(s); under certain circumstances; and so on.

7. Engages in passive-aggressive behaviors (e.g., forgetting, pretending not to listen, dawdling, procrastinating, stubborn refusal to comply with reasonable requests or rules) to frustrate or annoy other family members, adults, or peers, that occur _____ times per day/week.
8. Strained interpersonal relationships with peers due to anger control problems and aggressive or destructive behaviors.
9. Underlying feelings of depression, anxiety, or insecurity that contribute to angry outbursts and aggressive behaviors.

__. _____

_____

__. _____

_____

__. _____

_____

LONG-TERM GOALS

1. Express anger through appropriate verbalizations and healthy physical outlets.
2. Significantly reduce the intensity and frequency of angry verbal outbursts.
3. Terminate all acts of violence or cruelty toward people or animals and destruction of property.
4. Interact consistently with adult authority figures in a mutually respectful manner.
5. Markedly reduce the frequency of passive-aggressive behaviors by expressing anger and frustration through controlled, respectful, and direct verbalizations.
6. Resolve the core conflicts that contribute to the emergence of anger control problems.
7. Parents establish and maintain appropriate parent-child boundaries, setting firm, consistent limits when the client reacts in a verbally or physically aggressive or passive-aggressive manner.
8. Demonstrate marked improvement in the ability to listen and respond empathetically to the thoughts, feelings, and needs of others.

__. _____

_____

—. _____
   _____
—. _____
   _____

SHORT-TERM OBJECTIVES

1. By _____ (enter date), the client is to participate in and complete psychological testing. (1)

2. By _____ (enter date), the client is to cooperate with and complete a substance abuse evaluation and comply with the recommendations offered by the evaluation findings. (2)

3. Starting _____ (enter date), the client is to cooperate with the recommendations or requirements mandated by the criminal justice system. (3, 4, 5)

THERAPEUTIC INTERVENTIONS

1. Arrange for psychological testing to assess whether emotional factors or Attention-Deficit/Hyperactivity Disorder (ADHD) are contributing to anger control problems; provide feedback to the client and his/her parents.

2. Arrange for a substance abuse evaluation and/or treatment for the client.

3. Consult with criminal justice officials about the appropriate consequences for the client's destructive or aggressive behaviors (e.g., pay restitution, community service, probation, intensive surveillance).

4. Consult with the parents, school officials, and criminal justice officials about the need to place the client in an alternative setting (e.g., foster home, group home, residential program, or juvenile detention facility).

4. By _____ (enter date), the client's parents are to establish clearly defined rules and appropriate boundaries and follow through with positive and negative consequences for the client's anger control problems _____ (specify target negative anger outburst behaviors, target positive anger control behaviors, the nature of positive and negative consequences, and the schedule of reinforcement). (6, 7, 8)

5. Encourage and challenge the parents not to protect the client from the natural or legal consequences of his/her destructive or aggressive behaviors.

6. Assist the parents in establishing clearly defined rules, boundaries, and consequences for angry outbursts and acts of aggression or destruction.

7. Establish clear rules for the client at home or school; ask him/her to repeat these rules to demonstrate an understanding of the expectations.

8. Assign to the parents readings that teach effective conflict resolution strategies and that help to diffuse the intensity of the client's angry feelings (e.g., *Negotiating Parent/Adolescent Conflict* by Robin and Foster; *Parents, Teens and Boundaries* by Bluestein; *Get Out of My Life but First Could You Drive Me and Cheryl to the Mall?* by Wolf).

5. By _____ (enter date), the client is to increase the number of verbalizations that reflect the acceptance of responsibility: _____ (specify target verbalizations) for angry outbursts and destructive or aggressive behaviors at a level of _____ (enter percentage) of the time. (9, 10)

9. Firmly confront the client about the impact of his/her angry outbursts and destructive or aggressive behaviors, pointing out consequences for himself/herself and others.

10. Confront statements in which the client blames others for his/her anger control problems and fails to accept responsibility for his/her destructive or aggressive behaviors.

6. By _____ (enter date), the client is to express anger through controlled, respectful verbalizations and healthy physical outlets _____ (specify example of respectful verbalizations and physical outlets) at a level of _____ (enter percentage) of the time. (11, 12)

7. By _____ (enter date), the client is to reduce the frequency and intensity of angry verbal outbursts _____ (specify examples of outbursts) when frustrated or stressed to a level of _____ (enter percentage) of the time. (13, 14)

8. By _____ (enter date), the client's parents will agree to and follow through with the implementation of a reward system, contingency contract, or token economy to reinforce the client's positive control of anger: _____ (specify target positive behaviors, types, and schedule of reinforcement). (15, 16, 17)

11. Teach mediational and self-control strategies (e.g., "stop, look, listen, and think"; take deep breaths and count to 10) to help the client express anger through appropriate verbalizations and healthy physical outlets.

12. Train the client in the use of progressive relaxation or guided imagery techniques to help calm himself/herself and decrease intensity of angry feelings.

13. Teach the client effective communication and assertiveness skills to express angry feelings in a controlled manner and meet his/her needs through constructive actions.

14. Inquire into what the client does differently on days when he/she controls anger and does not lash out verbally or physically toward siblings or peers; process his/her responses and reinforce any positive coping mechanisms used to manage anger.

15. Design a reward system and/or contingency contract for the client to reinforce good anger control and deter destructive or aggressive behaviors.

16. Design and implement a token economy to increase the client's positive social behaviors, improve his/her anger control, and deter destructive or aggressive behaviors.

17. Assign a homework exercise designed to help the client learn to express anger in a controlled manner (or assign the "Anger Control" exercise in the *Brief Adolescent Therapy Homework Planner* by Jongsma, Peterson, and McInnis).

9. By _____ (enter date), the client's parents shall increase the frequency of praise and positive reinforcement of the client for his/her demonstration of good control of anger: _____ (specify examples of anger control behaviors and the nature and schedule of reinforcement). (18)

18. Encourage the parents to provide frequent praise and positive reinforcement to the client for displaying good anger control in situations involving conflict or stress.

10. By _____ (enter date), the client is to recognize and verbalize insight regarding how feelings of insecurity or other painful emotions are connected to anger control problems. (19, 20, 21)

19. Assist the client in making a connection between underlying painful emotions (e.g., depression, anxiety, helplessness) and angry outbursts or aggressive behaviors.

20. Help the client to recognize how his/her underlying emotional pain contributes to angry outbursts (or use the "Surface Behavior/Inner Feelings" exercise in the *Brief Adolescent Therapy Homework Planner* by Jongsma, Peterson, and McInnis).

21. Assign the client to read material to help him/her manage anger more effectively (e.g., *S.O.S. Help for*

Emotions by Clark); process this reading with the client.

11. By _____ (enter date), the client is to identify targets or triggers for angry outbursts and aggressive behavior. (22, 23, 24, 25)

22. Direct the client to develop a thorough list of all targets of and causes of anger.

23. Ask the client to keep a daily journal in which he/she documents persons and situations that evoke strong feelings of anger.

24. Assign the client to list significant life experiences that have produced strong feelings of anger, hurt, or disappointment.

25. Utilize the family-sculpting technique, in which the client defines the roles and behaviors of each family member in a scene of his/her choosing, to assess family dynamics that may contribute to the emergence of his/her anger control problems.

12. By _____ (enter date), the client is to identify and verbalize unmet emotional needs directly to significant others: _____ (specify times per week). (26)

26. Assist the client in first identifying unmet needs and then expressing them to significant others.

13. By _____ (enter date), the client is to identify and verbally express feelings associated with past neglect, abuse, separation, or abandonment. (27, 28, 29, 30)

27. Explore the client's family background for a history of physical, sexual, or substance abuse, which may contribute to his/her anger control problems.

28. Encourage and support the client in expressing feelings associated with neglect, abuse, separations, or abandonment.

29. Assign the client the task of writing a letter to the absent or abusive parent. Process the content of the letter to help him/her express and work through feelings of anger, sadness, and helplessness about past abandonment or abuse.

30. Use the empty chair technique to coach the client in expressing angry feelings toward the absent or abusive parent in a constructive manner.

14. Uninvolved or detached parents(s) increase time spent with the client in recreational, school, or work activities: _____ (specify activities and amount of time). (31)

31. Give a directive to uninvolved or disengaged parents to spend more time with the client in leisure, school, or work activities.

15. By _____ (enter date), the client is to express and verbalize forgiveness to the perpetrator or target of anger. (32, 33)

32. Explore and discuss the client's willingness to forgive the perpetrators of emotional or physical pain as a process of letting go of anger.

33. Instruct the client to write a letter of forgiveness to a target of anger as a step toward letting go of his/her anger; process the letter in session, and discuss what to do with the letter.

16. By _____ (enter date), the client is to identify the irrational beliefs or maladaptive thoughts that contribute to the emergence of destructive or aggressive behaviors. (34)

34. Identify and confront irrational thoughts that contribute to the emergence of anger control problems; replace irrational thoughts with more adaptive ways of thinking to help control anger.

17. By _____ (enter date), the client is to participate in an anger control group therapy. (35)

18. By _____ (enter date), the client is to establish and maintain steady employment: _____ (specify number of hours per week) to deter aggressive or destructive behaviors. (36)

19. By _____ (enter date), the client is to increase the frequency of positive interactions with parents, adult authority figures, siblings, and peers: _____ (specify target positive interactions and frequency expected). (37, 38, 39)

20. By _____ (enter date), the client is to express feelings of anger through the medium of art. (40, 41)

35. Refer the client to an anger management group.

36. Instruct the client to seek and secure employment in order to have funds available to make restitution for aggressive or destructive acts, to assume responsibility, and to gain income to meet his/her needs in an adaptive manner.

37. Utilize the Odyssey Islands Game (by Bridge; available from Childswork/Childsplay, LLC) in session to help the client develop positive social skills and improve self-control.

38. Assist the client in identifying more age-appropriate ways of establishing control and/or power than through intimidating or bullying others.

39. Assign the client the task of showing empathy, kindness, or sensitivity to the needs of others (e.g., assisting a younger sibling with homework, performing a cleaning task for an ailing family member).

40. Direct the client to draw pictures of three events or situations that commonly evoke feelings of anger; process his/her thoughts and feelings after he/she completes the drawings.

41. Tell the client to draw an outline of a human body on a large piece of paper or poster board; then ask him/her to fill in the mural with objects, symbols, or pictures that reflect who or what the client is angry about in his/her life. Process the content of the artwork in session.

21. By _____ (enter date), the client is to start taking medication consistently as prescribed by the physician. (42)

42. Refer the client for a medication evaluation to help stabilize his/her moods and improve his/her anger control.

__. _____

_____

__. _____

_____

__. _____

_____

__. _____

_____

__. _____

_____

__. _____

_____

DIAGNOSTIC SUGGESTIONS

Axis I:	313.81	Oppositional Defiant Disorder
	312.34	Intermittent Explosive Disorder
	312.30	Impulse-Control Disorder NOS
	312.8	Conduct Disorder/Adolescent-Onset Type
	312.9	Disruptive Behavior Disorder NOS
	314.01	Attention-Deficit/Hyperactive Disorder, Predominantly Hyperactive-Impulsive Type
	314.9	Attention-Deficit/Hyperactivity Disorder NOS
	V71.02	Adolescent Antisocial Behavior
	V61.20	Parent-Child Relational Problem
	_____	_____
	_____	_____
Axis II:	799.9	Diagnosis Deferred
	V71.09	No Diagnosis on Axis II
	_____	_____
	_____	_____

Appendix B

BIBLIOTHERAPY SUGGESTIONS

General

Many references are made throughout the chapters to a therapeutic homework resource that was developed by the authors as a corollary to the *Child and Adolescent Psychotherapy Treatment Planner* (Jongsma, Peterson, and McInnis). This frequently cited homework resource book is:

Jongsma, A., L. Peterson, and W. McInnis (1999). *Brief Adolescent Therapy Homework Planner.* New York: John Wiley & Sons, Inc.

Academic Underachievement

Martin, M., and C. Greenwood-Waltman, eds. (1995). *Solve Your Child's School-Related Problems.* New York: HarperCollins.
Silverman, S. (1998). *13 Steps to Better Grades.* Plainview, NY: Childswork/ Childsplay, LLC.
Smith, S. (1979). *No Easy Answers.* New York: Bantam Books.

Adoption

Burlingham-Brown, B. (1994). *Why Didn't She Keep Me?* South Bend, IN: Langford.
Covey, S. (1997). *The 7 Habits of Highly Effective Families: Building a Beautiful Family Culture in a Turbulent World.* New York: Golden Books Publishing Co.
Jewett, C. (1982). *Helping Children Cope with Separation and Loss.* Harvard, MA: Harvard Common Press.
Korb-Khalsa, K., S. Azok, and E. Leutenberg (1992). *SEALS & PLUS.* Beachwood, OH: Wellness Reproductions.
Krementz, J. (1996). *How It Feels to Be Adopted.* New York: Alfred Knopf.

Lifton, B. J. (1994). *Journey of the Adopted Self.* New York: Basic Books.

Medina, L. (1984). *Making Sense of Adoption.* New York: Harper & Row.

Schooler, J. (1993). *The Whole Life Adoption Book.* Colorado Springs, CO: Pinon Press.

Schooler, J. (1995). *Searching for a Past.* Colorado Springs, CO: Pinon Press.

Stinson, K. (1998). *I Feel Different.* Los Angeles, CA: Manson Western Co.

Tyson, J. (1997). *Common Threads of Teenage Grief.* Lake Dallas, TX: Helm Seminars.

Anger Management

Bluestein, J. (1993). *Parents, Teens and Boundaries: How to Draw the Line.* Deerfield Beach, FL: Health Communications.

Canter, L., and P. Canter (1988). *Assertive Discipline for Parents.* New York: HarperCollins.

Clark, L. (1998). *S.O.S. Help for Emotions.* Bowling Green, KY: Parents Press.

Katherine, A. (1991). *Boundaries: Where You End and I Begin.* New York: Simon & Schuster.

Potter-Efron, R. (1994). *Angry All the Time.* Oakland, CA: New Harbinger.

Redl, F., and D. Wineman (1951). *Children Who Hate.* New York: Free Press.

Robin, A., and S. Foster (1989). *Negotiating Parent / Adolescent Conflict.* New York: Guilford Press.

Wolf, A. (1992). *Get Out of My Life but First Could You Drive Me and Cheryl to the Mall?: A Parent's Guide to the New Teenager.* New York: Noonday Press.

Anxiety

Benson, J. (1975). *The Relaxation Response.* New York: William Morrow.

Bourne, E. (1995). *Anxiety and Phobia Workbook.* Berkeley, CA: Fine Communications.

Burns, D. (1989). *The Feeling Good Handbook.* New York: William Morrow.

Burns, D. (1993). *Ten Days to Self-Esteem.* New York: William Morrow.

Elkind, D. (1981). *The Hurried Child: Growing Up Too Fast Too Soon.* New York: Addison-Wesley.

Elkind, D. (1984). *All Grown Up and No Place to Go: Teenagers in Crisis.* New York: Addison-Wesley.

Faber, A., and E. Mazlish (1982). *How to Talk So Kids Will Listen and Listen So Kids Will Talk.* New York: Avon Books.

Ginnot, H. (1965). *Between Parent and Child.* New York: Macmillan.

Ginnot, H. (1969). *Between Parent and Teenager.* New York: Macmillan.

McCauley, C. S., and R. Schachter (1988). *When Your Child Is Afraid.* New York: Simon & Schuster.

Moser, A. (1988). *Don't Pop Your Cork on Mondays!* Kansas City, MO: Landmark Editions, Inc.

Attention-Deficit/Hyperactivity Disorder (ADHD)

Alexander-Roberts, C., and P. Elliot (2002). *ADHD and Teens: A Parent's Guide to Making It through the Tough Years.* Cutten, CA: Taylor Publishing.

Barkley, R. (1995). *Taking Charge of ADHD: The Complete, Authoritative Guide for Parents.* New York: Guilford Press.

Crist, J. (1997). *ADHD—A Teenager's Guide.* Plainview, NY: Childswork/ Childsplay.

Dendy-Zeigler, C. (1995). *Teenagers with ADD: A Parent's Guide.* Bethesda, MD: Woodbine House.

Hallowell, E., and J. Rafey (1994). *Driven to Distraction.* New York: Pantheon.

Ingersoll, B. (1988). *Your Hyperactive Child.* New York: Doubleday.

Parker, H. (1992). *The ADD Hyperactivity Handbook for Schools.* Plantation, FL: Impact Publications.

Quinn, P. (1995). *Adolescents and ADD: Gaining the Advantage.* Washington, DC: Magination Press.

Robin, A., and S. Foster (1989). *Negotiating Parent/Adolescent Conflict.* New York: Guilford Press.

Silverman, S. (1998). *13 Steps to Better Grades.* Plainview, NY: Childswork/ Childsplay, LLC.

Autism/Pervasive Developmental Disorder

Brill, M. (1994). *Keys to Parenting the Child with Autism.* Hauppauge, NY: Barrons.

Rimland, B. (1964). *Infantile Autism.* New York: Appleton Century Crofts.

Siegel, B. (1996). *The World of the Autistic Child.* New York: Oxford.

Simons, J., and S. Olsihi (1987). *The Hidden Child.* Bethesda, MD: Woodbine House.

Blended Family

Brown, M. (1947). *Stone Soup.* New York: Simon & Schuster.

Burns, D. (1993). *Ten Days to Self-Esteem.* New York: William Morrow.

Burt, M. (1989). *Stepfamilies Stepping Ahead.* Lincoln, NE: Stepfamily Association.

Covey, S. (1997). *The 7 Habits of Highly Effective Families: Building a Beautiful Family Culture in a Turbulent World.* New York: Golden Books.

Fassler, D., M. Lash, and S. Ives (1988). *Changing Families: An Interactive Guide for Kids and Grownups.* Burlington, VT: Waterfront Books.

Markman, H., S. Stanley, and S. Blumberg (1994). *PREP—Fighting for Your Marriage.* San Francisco: Jossey-Bass.

Newman, M. (1994). *Stepfamily Realities: How to Overcome Difficulties and Have a Happy Family.* Oakland, CA: New Harbinger.

Seuss, Dr. (1961). *The Sneetches and Other Stories.* New York: Random House.

Visher, E., and J. Visher (1982). *How To Win as a Stepfamily.* New York: Brunner/Mazel.

Chemical Dependence

Ackerman, R. (1978). *Children of Alcoholics: A Guide for Educators, Therapists and Parents.* Holmes Beach, FL: Learning Publications.

Alcoholics Anonymous (1976). *Alcoholics Anonymous: The Big Book.* New York: AA World Service.

Anonymous (1982). *Narcotics Anonymous Big Book.* Van Nuys, CA: NA World Service. Independence Press.

Bell, T. (1990). *Preventing Adolescent Relapse.* Independence, MO: Herald House.

Black, C. (1982). *It Will Never Happen to Me.* Denver, CO: MAC Printing and Publishing.

Bradshaw, J. (1988). *Bradshaw on the Family.* Pompano Beach, FL: Health Communications.

Ellis, D. (1986). *Growing Up Stoned.* Pompano Beach, FL: Health Communications.

Fanning, P., and J. O'Neil (1996). *The Addiction Workbook.* San Francisco, CA: New Harbinger.

Ohm, D. (1983). *POT.* Belleville, IL: G. Whiteaker.

Woititz, J. G. (1983). *Adult Children of Alcoholics.* Pompano Beach, FL: Health Communications.

Conduct Disorder/Delinquency

Canter, L., and P. Canter (1988). *Assertive Discipline for Parents.* New York: HarperCollins.

Katherine, A. (1991). *Boundaries: Where You End and I Begin.* New York: Simon & Schuster.

Redl, F., and D. Wineman (1951). *Children Who Hate.* New York: Free Press.

Robin, A., and S. Foster (1989). *Negotiating Parent/Adolescent Conflict.* New York: Guilford Press.

Saxe, S. (1997). "The Angry Tower." In H. Kaduson and C. Schaefer (eds.), *101 Favorite Play Therapy Techniques* (pp. 246–249). Northvale, NJ: Jason Aronson, Inc.

Shapiro, L. E. (1996). *Teens' Solution Workbook.* Plainview, NY: Childswork/Childsplay, LLC.

Shore, H. (1991). *The Angry Monster.* King of Prussia, PA: Center for Applied Psychology.

York, P., D. York, and T. Wachtel (1997). *Toughlove.* New York: Bantam Books.

Depression

Ingersoll, B., and S. Goldstein (1995). *Lonely, Sad and Angry: A Parent's Guide to Depression in Children and Adolescents.* New York: Doubleday.
Kerns, L. (1993). *Helping Your Depressed Child.* Rocklin, CA: Prima.
Moser, A. (1994). *Don't Rant and Rave on Wednesdays!* Kansas City, MO: Landmark Editions, Inc.
Sanford, D. (1993). *It Won't Last Forever.* Sisters, OR: Questar.

Divorce Reaction

Clark, L. (1998). *S.O.S. Help for Emotions.* Bowling Green, KY: Parents Press.
Grollman, E. (1975). *Talking about Divorce.* Boston, MA: Beacon Press.
Krementz, J. (1988). *How It Feels When Parents Divorce.* New York: Alfred A. Knopf.
Swan-Jackson, A., J. Shapiro, S. Klebanoff, and L. Rosenfield (1998). *When Your Parents Split: How to Keep Yourself Together.* Los Angeles, CA: Price Stern Sloan.

Eating Disorder

Berg, F. (1997). *Afraid to Eat.* Hettinger, ND: Healthy Weight Publishing Network.
Fairburn, C. G. (1995). *Overcoming Binge Eating.* New York: Guilford Press.
Metropolitan Height and Weight Tables (1983). New York: Metropolitan Life Insurance Company, Health and Safety Division.
Rodin, J. (1992). *Body Traps.* New York: William Morrow.
Siegel, M., J. Brisman, and M. Weinshel (1988). *Surviving an Eating Disorder: Strategies for Families and Friends.* New York: Harper & Row.
Wilson, G. T., C. G. Fairburn, and W. S. Agras (1997). "Cognitive-Behavioral Therapy for Bulimia Nervosa." In D. M. Garner and P. Garfinkel (eds.), *Handbook of Treatment for Eating Disorders.* New York: Guilford Press.

Grief/Loss Unresolved

Fitzgerald, H. (2000). *The Grieving Teen.* New York: Fireside.
Gof, B. (1969). *Where Is Daddy?* Boston, MA: Beacon Press.
Grollman, E. (1967). *Straight Talk about Death for Teenagers.* Boston, MA: Beacon Press.
Hambrook, D., and E. Eisenberg (1997). *A Mother Loss Workbook.* New York: HarperCollins.
Jewett, C. (1982). *Helping Children Cope with Separation and Loss.* Cambridge, MA: Harvard University Press.

LeShan, E. (1976). *Learning to Say Good-Bye: When a Parent Dies*. New York: Macmillan.

Mellonie, B., and R. Ingpen (1983). *Lifetimes*. New York: Bantam Books.

Nystrom, C. (1990). *Emma Says Goodbye*. Batavia, IL: Lion Publishing Co.

Tyson, J. (1997). *Common Threads of Teenage Grief*. Lake Dallas, TX: Helm Seminars.

Wolfelt, A. (2002). *The Healing Your Grieving Heart Journal for Teens*. Fort Collins, CO: Companion Press.

Low Self-Esteem

Briggs, D. (1970). *Your Child's Self-Esteem*. Garden City, NY: Doubleday.

Burns, D. (1993). *Ten Days to Self-Esteem*. New York: William Morrow.

Dobson, J. (1974). *Hide or Seek: How to Build Self-Esteem in Your Child*. Old Tappan, NJ: F. Revell Co.

Glenn, H., and J. Nelsen (1989). *Raising Self-Reliant Children in a Self-Indulgent World*. Rocklin, CA: Prima.

Hanson, L. (1996). *Feed Your Head: Some Excellent Stuff on Being Yourself*. Center Court, MN: Hazelden.

Harris, C., R. Bean, and A. Clark (1978). *How to Raise Teenagers' Self-Esteem*. Los Angeles, CA: Price Stern Sloan.

Loomans, D., and J. Loomans (1994). *Full Esteem Ahead! 100 Ways to Build Self-Esteem*. Fort Collins, CO: Kramer, Inc.

Moser, A. (1991). *Don't Feed the Monster on Tuesday!* Kansas City, MO: Landmark Editions, Inc.

Pipher, M. (1994). *Reviving Ophelia*. Newburgh, NY: Courage to Change.

Powell, J. (1969). *Why I'm Afraid to Tell You Who I Am*. Allen, TX: Argus Communications.

Sanford, D. (1986). *Don't Look at Me*. Portland, OR: Multnomah Press.

Scott, S. (1997). *How to Say No and Keep Your Friends*. Highland Ranch, CO: HRC Press.

Shapiro, L. (1993). *The Building Blocks of Self-Esteem*. King of Prussia, PA: Center for Applied Psychology.

Mania/Hypomania

DePaulo, R., and K. Ablow (1989). *How to Cope with Depression*. New York: McGraw-Hill.

Dumont, L. (1991). *Surviving Adolescence: Helping Your Child through the Struggle*. New York: Villard Books.

Waltz, M. (2000). *Bipolar Disorders: A Guide to Helping Children and Adolescents*. Sebastopol, CA: Patient-Centered Guides.

Medical Condition

Bluebond-Langner, M. (1996). *In the Shadow of Illness*. Princeton, NJ: Princeton University Press.

Fromer, M. (1998). *Surviving Childhood Cancer: A Guide for Families*. Oakland, CA: New Harbinger.

Kushner, H. (1981). *When Bad Things Happen to Good People*. New York: Schocken Books.

Smedes, L. (1982). *How Can It Be All Right When Everything Is All Wrong?* San Francisco, CA: Harper.

Westberg, G. (1962). *Good Grief*. Philadelphia, PA: Augsburg Fortress Press.

Mental Retardation

Trainer, M. (1991). *Differences in Common*. Rockville, MD: Woodbine House.

Negative Peer Influences

Faber, A., and E. Mazlish (1982). *How to Talk So Kids Will Listen and Listen So Kids Will Talk*. New York: Avon Books.

Scott, S. (1997). *How to Say No and Keep Your Friends*. Highland Ranch, CO: HRC Press.

Oppositional Defiant

Abern, A. (1994). *Everything I Do You Blame on Me*. Plainview, NY: Childswork/Childsplay, LLC.

Barkley, R. and C. Benton (1998). *Your Defiant Child: Eight Steps to Better Behavior*. New York: Guilford.

Bayard, R. T., and J. Bayard (1983). *How to Deal with Your Acting-Up Teenager: Practical Self-Help for Desperate Parents*. New York: M. Evans.

Dobson, J. (1978). *The Strong-Willed Child*. Wheaton, IL: Tyndale House.

Gardner, R. (1990). *The Girls and Boys Book about Good and Bad Behavior*. Cresskill, NJ: Creative Therapeutics.

Ginott, H. (1969). *Between Parent and Teenager*. New York. Macmillan.

Greenspan, S. (1995). *The Challenging Child*. Reading, MA: Perseus Books.

Kaye, K. (1991). *Family Rules: Raising Responsible Children*. New York: St. Martins.

Wenning, K. (1996). *Winning Cooperation from Your Child*. New York: Aronson.

York, P., D. York, and T. Wachtel (1997). *Toughlove*. New York: Bantam Books.

Parenting

Bluestein, J. (1993). *Parents, Teens and Boundaries: How to Draw the Line*. Deerfield Beach, FL: Health Communications.

Dobson, J. (2000). *Preparing for Adolescence: How to Survive the Coming Years of Change*. New York: Regal Press.

Ginott, H. (1969). *Between Parent and Teenager.* New York: Macmillan.

Renshaw-Joslin, K. (1994). *Positive Parenting from A to Z.* New York: Fawcett Books.

Taffel, R. (2001). *The Second Family: How Adolescent Power Is Challenging the American Family.* New York: St. Martin's Press.

Tracy, F. (1994). *Grounded for Life: Stop Blowing Your Fuse and Start Communicating.* Seattle, WA: Parenting Press.

Wolf, A. (1992). *Get Out of My Life but First Could You Drive Me and Cheryl to the Mall?: A Parent's Guide to the New Teenager.* New York: Noonday Press.

Peer/Sibling Conflict

Baruch, D. (1949). *New Ways in Discipline.* New York: Macmillan.

Bieniek, D. (1996). *How to End the Sibling Wars.* King of Prussia, PA: Childswork/Childsplay, LLC.

Faber, A., and E. Mazlish (1982). *How to Talk So Kids Will Listen and Listen So Kids Will Talk.* New York: Avon.

Faber, A., and E. Mazlish (1987). *Siblings Without Rivalry.* New York: Norton.

Ginott, H. (1965). *Between Parent and Child.* New York: Macmillan.

Ginott, H. (1969). *Between Parent and Teenager.* New York: Macmillan.

Nevick, R. (1996). *Helping Your Child Make Friends.* King of Prussia, PA: Childswork/Childsplay, LLC.

Physical/Emotional Abuse Victim

Miller, Alice (1984). *For Your Own Good.* New York: Farrar Straus Group.

Monahon, Cynthia (1983). *Children and Trauma: A Parent's Guide to Helping Children Heal.* New York: Lexington Press.

Posttraumatic Stress Disorder

Flannery Jr., Raymond (1995). *Post-Traumatic Stress Disorder: The Victim's Guide to Healing and Recovery.* New York: Crossroad Publishing.

Matsakis, Aphrodite (1996). *I Can't Get Over It: A Handbook for Trauma Survivors.* Oakland, CA: New Harbinger.

Psychoticism

Dumont, L. (1991). *Surviving Adolescence: Helping Your Child through the Struggle.* New York: Villard.

Torry, M. D., and E. Fuller (1988). *Surviving Schizophrenia: A Family Manual.* New York: Harper & Row.

Runaway

Elkind, D. (1984). *All Grown Up and No Place to Go: Teenagers in Crisis.* New York: Addison-Wesley.

Glenn, H., and J. Nelsen (1989). *Raising Self-Reliant Children in a Self-Indulgent World.* Rocklin, CA: Prima.

Gordon, T. (1970). *Parent Effectiveness Training (P.E.T.).* New York: Wyden Books.

Millman, H., and C. Schaefer (1977). *Therapies for Children: A Handbook of Effective Treatment for Problem Behaviors.* San Francisco, CA: Jossey-Bass.

Wegscheider, S. (1981). *Another Chance: Hope and Health for the Alcoholic Family.* Palo Alto, CA: Science and Behavioral Books.

School Violence

Burns, D. (1993). *Ten Days to Self-Esteem.* New York: William Morrow.

Fried, S., and P. Fried (1998). *Bullies & Victims: Helping Your Child Survive the Schoolyard Battlefield.* New York: M. Evans & Co.

Huml, F. (1998). *Ready-to-Use Violence Prevention Skills Lessons and Activities for Secondary Students.* New York: Jossey-Bass.

Licata, R. (1994). *Everything You Need to Know About Anger.* New York: Rosen Publishing Group.

Shearin-Karres, E. (2000). *Violence Proof Your Kids Now.* Berkely, CA: Conari Press.

Sexual Abuse Perpetrator

Blodeau, L. (1997). *The Anger Workbook.* New York: Fine Communications.

Bluestein, J. (1993). *Parents, Teens and Boundaries: How to Draw the Line.* Deerfield Beach, FL: Health Communications.

Browne, J. (1997). *Dating for Dummies.* Foster City, CA: IDG Books.

Covey, S. (1997). *The 7 Habits of Highly Effective Families: Building a Beautiful Family Culture in a Turbulent World.* New York: Golden Books Publishing Co.

Ginott, H. (1969). *Between Parent and Teenager.* New York: Macmillan.

Glenn, H., and J. Nelsen (1989). *Raising Self-Reliant Children in a Self-Indulgent World.* Rocklin, CA: Prima.

Katherine, A. (1991). *Boundaries: Where You End and I Begin.* New York: Simon & Schuster.

Kuriansky, J. (1999). *The Complete Idiot's Guide to Dating.* New York: Alpha Books.

Sexual Abuse Victim

Carnes, P. (1983). *Out of the Shadows: Understanding Sexual Addictions.* Minneapolis, MN: Comp Care Publications.

Davis, L. (1991). *Allies in Healing.* New York: HarperCollins.

Katherine, A. (1991). *Boundaries: Where You End and I Begin.* New York: Simon & Schuster.

Sexual Acting Out

Scott, S. (1997). *How to Say No and Keep Your Friends.* Highland Ranch, CO: HRC Press.

Pipher, M. (1994). *Reviving Ophelia.* Newburgh, NY: Courage to Change.

Sexual Identity Confusion

Bradley, S., and K. Zucker (1995). *Gender Identity Disorder and Psychosexual Problems in Children and Adolescents.* New York: Guilford Press.

Gomes, P. (1998). *The Good Book: Reading the Bible with Mind and Heart.* New York: Avon Books.

Griffin, C., A. Wirth, and M. Wirth (1996). *Beyond Acceptance: Parents of Lesbians and Gays Talk about Their Experiences.* New York: St. Martin Press.

Grima, T., ed. (1995). *Not the Only One: Lesbian and Gay Fiction for Teens.* Boston, MA: Alyson.

Heron, A., ed. (1995). *Two Teenagers in 20: Writings by Gay and Lesbian Youth.* Boston, MA: Alyson.

Jennings, K., ed. (1994). *Becoming Visible: A Reader in Gay and Lesbian History for High School and College Students.* Los Angeles, CA: Alyson.

Marcus, E. (1999). *Is It a Choice? Answers to 300 of the Most Frequently Asked Questions about Gays and Lesbians.* San Francisco, CA: Harper.

Silber, S. (1981). *The Male.* New York: C. Scribner's Sons.

Social Phobia/Shyness

Martin, M., and C. Greenwood-Waltman, ed. (1995). *Solve Your Child's School-Related Problems.* New York: HarperCollins.

Millman, M., C. Schaefer, and J. Cohen (1980). *Therapies for School Behavioral Problems.* San Francisco, CA: Jossey-Bass.

Zimbardo, P. (1987). *Shyness: What It Is and What to Do About It.* New York: Addison-Wesley.

Specific Phobia

Bourne, E. (1995). *Anxiety and Phobia Workbook*. Berkeley, CA: Fine Communications.

Brown, J. (1995). *No More Monsters in the Closet*. New York: Prince Paperbacks.

Burns, D. (1989). *The Feeling Good Handbook*. New York: William Morrow.

Burns, D. (1993). *Ten Days to Self-Esteem*. New York: William Morrow.

Garber, S., M. Garber, and R. Spitzman (1993). *Monsters under the Bed and Other Childhood Fears*. New York: Villard.

Wilson, R. (1986). *Don't Panic: Taking Charge of Anxiety Attacks*. New York: Harper & Row.

Suicidal Ideation/Attempt

Butler, P. (1991). *Talking to Yourself: Learning the Language of Self-Affirmation*. New York: Perigee.

Dumont, L. (1991). *Surviving Adolescence: Helping Your Child through the Struggle*. New York: Villard Books.

McCoy, K. (1994). *Understanding Your Teenager's Depression*. New York: Perigee.

Appendix C

INDEX OF *DSM-IV-TR*™ CODES ASSOCIATED WITH PRESENTING PROBLEMS

Academic Problem   V62.3
     Academic Underachievement

Acute Stress Disorder   308.3
     Physical/Emotional Abuse Victim
     Posttraumatic Stress Disorder
     Sexual Abuse Victim

Adjustment Disorder   309.xx
     Posttraumatic Stress Disorder

Adjustment Disorder With Anxiety   309.24
     Blended Family
     Divorce Reaction
     Medical Condition
     Runaway
     Sexual Identity Confusion

Adjustment Disorder With Depressed Mood   309.0
     Adoption
     Blended Family
     Depression
     Divorce Reaction
     Grief/Loss Unresolved
     Medical Condition
     Sexual Identity Confusion

Adjustment Disorder With Disturbance of Conduct   309.3
     Blended Family
     Divorce Reaction
     Medical Condition
     Parenting

Adjustment Disorder With Mixed Anxiety and Depressed Mood   309.28
     Chemical Dependence
     Divorce Reaction
     Medical Condition
     Sexual Identity Confusion

Adjustment Disorder With Mixed Disturbance of Emotions and Conduct   309.4
     Adoption
     Chemical Dependence
     Divorce Reaction
     Grief/Loss Unresolved
     Medical Condition
     Parenting
     Runaway

Adolescent Antisocial Behavior   V71.02
     Anger Management
     Negative Peer Influences
     School Violence

Alcohol Abuse   305.00
     Chemical Dependence
     Sexual Acting Out

Alcohol Dependence   303.90
     Adoption
     Chemical Dependence
     Low Self-Esteem
     Sexual Acting Out

Anorexia Nervosa   307.1
  Eating Disorder
  Low Self-Esteem

**Antisocial Personality
Disorder**   301.7
  Parenting

Anxiety Disorder NOS   300.00
  Anxiety
  Medical Condition
  Sexual Identity Confusion
  Social Phobia/Shyness
  Specific Phobia

Asperger's Disorder   299.80
  Autism/Pervasive Developmental
    Disorder
  Mental Retardation

**Attention-Deficit/
Hyperactivity Disorder,
Combined Type**   314.01
  Academic Underachievement
  Adoption
  Anxiety
  Attention-Deficit/Hyperactivity
    Disorder (ADHD)
  Parenting

**Attention-Deficit/Hyperactivity
Disorder NOS**   314.9
  Anger Management
  Attention-Deficit/Hyperactivity
    Disorder (ADHD)
  Conduct Disorder/Delinquency
  Negative Peer Influences
  Oppositional Defiant
  Peer/Sibling Conflict
  School Violence

**Attention-Deficit/Hyperactivity
Disorder, Predominantly
Hyperactive-Impulsive Type** 314.01
  Anger Management
  Attention-Deficit/Hyperactivity
    Disorder (ADHD)
  Conduct Disorder/Delinquency
  Low Self-Esteem
  Mania/Hypomania
  Negative Peer Influences
  Oppositional Defiant

  Peer/Sibling Conflict
  Runaway
  School Violence
  Sexual Acting Out

**Attention-Deficit/Hyperactivity
Disorder, Predominantly
Inattentive Type**   314.00
  Academic Underachievement
  Attention-Deficit/Hyperactivity
    Disorder (ADHD)

Autistic Disorder   299.00
  Autism/Pervasive Developmental
    Disorder
  Mental Retardation

Bereavement   V62.82
  Depression
  Grief/Loss Unresolved

Bipolar Disorder NOS   296.80
  Mania/Hypomania

Bipolar I Disorder   296.xx
  Attention-Deficit/Hyperactivity
    Disorder (ADHD)
  Depression
  Mania/Hypomania
  Psychoticism
  School Violence
  Suicidal Ideation/Attempt

**Bipolar I Disorder, Most
Recent Episode Manic**   296.4x
  Sexual Acting Out

Bipolar II Disorder   296.89
  Depression
  Mania/Hypomania
  Psychoticism
  School Violence
  Sexual Acting Out

**Bipolar II Disorder, Most
Recent Episode Depressed**   296.89
  Suicidal Ideation/Attempt

**Borderline Intellectual
Functioning**   V62.89
  Academic Underachievement
  Low Self-Esteem
  Mental Retardation

**Borderline Personality
Disorder**   301.83
  Parenting
  Runaway
  Suicidal Ideation/Attempt

Brief Psychotic Disorder 298.8
  Psychoticism

Bulimia Nervosa   307.51
  Eating Disorder

Cannabis Abuse   305.20
  Chemical Dependence
  Sexual Acting Out

Cannabis Dependence   304.30
  Chemical Dependence
  Low Self-Esteem
  Sexual Acting Out

**Childhood Disintegrative
Disorder**   299.10
  Autism/Pervasive Developmental
    Disorder
  Mental Retardation

**Child or Adolescent
Antisocial Behavior**   V71.02
  Conduct Disorder/Delinquency
  Peer/Sibling Conflict
  Sexual Abuse Perpetrator

Cocaine Dependence   304.20
  Chemical Dependence

Conduct Disorder   312.8
  Chemical Dependence
  School Violence

**Conduct Disorder/Adolescent-
Onset Type**   312.82
  Adoption
  Anger Management
  Attention-Deficit/Hyperactivity
    Disorder (ADHD)
  Conduct Disorder/Delinquency
  Negative Peer Influences
  Oppositional Defiant
  Parenting
  Peer/Sibling Conflict

  Runaway
  Sexual Abuse Perpetrator

**Conduct Disorder/Childhood-
Onset Type**   312.81
  Adoption
  Attention-Deficit/Hyperactivity
    Disorder (ADHD)
  Conduct Disorder/Delinquency
  Oppositional Defiant
  Peer/Sibling Conflict
  Physical/Emotional Abuse Victim
  Sexual Abuse Perpetrator

Cyclothymic Disorder   301.13
  Depression
  Mania/Hypomania

Delusional Disorder   297.1
  Psychoticism

**Dependent Personality
Disorder**   301.6
  Eating Disorder
  Parenting

Depersonalization Disorder 300.6
  Physical/Emotional Abuse Victim

Depressive Disorder NOS   311
  Medical Condition
  Social Phobia/Shyness
  Suicidal Ideation/Attempt

Diagnosis Deferred   799.9
  Adoption
  Anger Management
  Anxiety
  Attention-Deficit/Hyperactivity
    Disorder (ADHD)
  Autism/Pervasive Developmental
    Disorder
  Blended Family
  Chemical Dependence
  Conduct Disorder/Delinquency
  Depression
  Divorce Reaction
  Eating Disorder
  Grief/Loss Unresolved
  Low Self-Esteem
  Mania/Hypomania

Major Depressive Disorder   296.xx
Low Self-Esteem
Medical Condition
Physical/Emotional Abuse Victim
Posttraumatic Stress Disorder
School Violence
Sexual Abuse Victim
Sexual Acting Out
Social Phobia/Shyness

**Major Depressive Disorder,
Recurrent   296.3x**
Depression
Grief/Loss Unresolved
Sexual Identity Confusion
Suicidal Ideation/Attempt

**Major Depressive Disorder,
Recurrent With Psychotic
Features   296.34**
Psychoticism

**Major Depressive Disorder,
Single Episode   296.2x**
Depression
Grief/Loss Unresolved
Sexual Identity Confusion
Suicidal Ideation/Attempt

**Major Depressive Disorder,
Single Episode With
Psychotic Features   296.24**
Psychoticism

Mathematics Disorder   315.1
Academic Underachievement

**Mental Retardation,
Severity Unspecified   319**
Autism/Pervasive Developmental
    Disorder
Mental Retardation

Mild Mental Retardation   317
Academic Underachievement
Autism/Pervasive Developmental
    Disorder
Low Self-Esteem
Mental Retardation

Moderate Mental Retardation   318.0
Mental Retardation

**Narcissistic Personality
Disorder   301.81**
Parenting

Neglect of Child   V61.21
Low Self-Esteem
Parenting

**Neglect of Child (*if focus
of clinical attention is on
the victim*)   995.5**
Low Self-Esteem
Parenting
Runaway

Nightmare Disorder   307.47
Physical/Emotional Abuse Victim
Sexual Abuse Victim

No Diagnosis or Condition   V71.09
Adoption
Anger Management
Anxiety
Attention-Deficit/Hyperactivity
    Disorder (ADHD)
Autism/Pervasive Developmental
    Disorder
Blended Family
Chemical Dependence
Conduct Disorder/Delinquency
Depression
Divorce Reaction
Eating Disorder
Grief/Loss Unresolved
Low Self-Esteem
Mania/Hypomania
Medical Condition
Mental Retardation
Negative Peer Influences
Oppositional Defiant
Parenting
Peer/Sibling Conflict
Physical/Emotional Abuse Victim
Posttraumatic Stress Disorder
Psychoticism
Runaway
School Violence
Sexual Abuse Perpetrator
Sexual Abuse Victim
Sexual Acting Out
Sexual Identity Confusion
Social Phobia/Shyness

Specific Phobia
Suicidal Ideation/Attempt

**Oppositional Defiant
Disorder**   **313.81**
  Academic Underachievement
  Adoption
  Anger Management
  Attention-Deficit/Hyperactivity
    Disorder (ADHD)
  Chemical Dependence
  Conduct Disorder/Delinquency
  Divorce Reaction
  Negative Peer Influences
  Oppositional Defiant
  Parenting
  Peer/Sibling Conflict
  Physical/Emotional Abuse Victim
  Runaway

**Panic Disorder With
Agoraphobia**   **300.21**
  Specific Phobia

**Panic Disorder Without
Agoraphobia**   **300.01**
  Runaway
  Specific Phobia

**Parent-Child Relational
Problem**   **V61.20**
  Anger Management
  Conduct Disorder/Delinquency
  Parenting
  Runaway
  School Violence
  Sexual Identity Confusion

Partner Relational Problem   **V61.1**
  Parenting

Pedophilia   **302.2**
  Sexual Abuse Perpetrator

**Personality Change Due
to . . . [*Indicate the General
Medical Condition*]**   **310.1**
  Depression
  Mania/Hypomania
  Psychoticism

**Pervasive Developmental
Disorder NOS**   **299.80**
  Autism/Pervasive Developmental
    Disorder

Phase of Life Problem   **V62.89**
  Sexual Identity Confusion

Physical Abuse of Child   **V61.21**
  Parenting

**Physical Abuse of Child (*if
focus of clinical attention
is on victim*)**   **995.54**
  Low Self-Esteem
  Parenting
  Physical/Emotional Abuse Victim
  Posttraumatic Stress Disorder
  Runaway

**Posttraumatic Stress
Disorder**   **309.81**
  Blended Family
  Physical/Emotional Abuse Victim
  Posttraumatic Stress Disorder
  Sexual Abuse Victim
  Social Phobia/Shyness
  Suicidal Ideation/Attempt

Profound Mental Retardation **318.2**
  Mental Retardation

**Psychological Symptoms
Affecting (Axis II Disorder)**   **316**
  Medical Condition

Reading Disorder   **315.00**
  Academic Underachievement
  Peer/Sibling Conflict

Relational Problem NOS   **V62.81**
  Blended Family
  Negative Peer Influences
  Oppositional Defiant
  Peer/Sibling Conflict

Rett's Disorder   **299.80**
  Autism/Pervasive Developmental
    Disorder
  Mental Retardation

Schizoaffective Disorder   295.70
  Mania/Hypomania
  Psychoticism

Schizophrenia   295.xx
  Autism/Pervasive Developmental
    Disorder
  Psychoticism

**Schizophrenia, Paranoid
Type**   295.30
  Psychoticism

Schizophreniform Disorder   295.40
  Psychoticism

**Separation Anxiety
Disorder**   309.21
  Divorce Reaction
  Low Self-Esteem
  Sexual Abuse Victim
  Social Phobia/Shyness

Severe Mental Retardation   318.1
  Mental Retardation

Sexual Abuse of Child   V61.21
  Low Self-Esteem
  Parenting

**Sexual Abuse of Child (*if
focus of clinical attention
is on the victim*)**   995.5
  Low Self-Esteem
  Parenting
  Posttraumatic Stress Disorder
  Runaway
  Sexual Abuse Perpetrator
  Sexual Abuse Victim

Sibling Relational Problem   V61.8
  Sexual Abuse Perpetrator

Social Phobia   300.23
  Low Self-Esteem
  Social Phobia/Shyness

Specific Phobia   300.29
  Specific Phobia

**Stereotypic Movement
Disorder**   307.3
  Autism/Pervasive Developmental
    Disorder

**Undifferentiated Somatoform
Disorder**   300.81
  Divorce Reaction

Voyeurism   302.82
  Sexual Abuse Perpetrator

Appendix D

INDEX OF THERAPEUTIC GAMES, WORKBOOKS, TOOL KITS, VIDEO TAPES, AND AUDIO TAPES

PRODUCT	AUTHOR
The Anger Control Game	Berg
The Anger Workbook	Blodeau
Anxiety and Phobia Workbook	Bourne
Bradshaw on Eating Disorders video	Bradshaw
Defiant Disorder in Children video	Barkley
10 Ways to Boost Low Self-Esteem video	Unknown
The Goodbye Game	Unknown
The Good Mourning Game	Bisenius and Norris
Handling Peer Pressure and Gangs video	Unknown
Heartbeat Audiotapes	Lamb
The Helping, Sharing, Caring Game	Gardner
Let's See About Me game	Unknown
A Mother Loss Workbook	Hambrook
My Home and Places game	Flood
Odyssey Islands Game	Bridge
Refusal Skills video	Bureau for At Risk Youth
The Self-Control Game	Shapiro
Skillsstreaming: The Adolescent Kit	McGinnis and Goldstein
The Social Conflict Game	Berg
The Stress and Anxiety Game	Berg
The Talking, Feeling, and Doing Game	Gardner
Teens Solution Workbook	Shapiro
Techniques for Working with Oppositional Defiant Disorder in Children video	Barkley
Ten Minutes to Relax audiotapes	Shapiro
The Ungame	Zakich

These products can be purchased by contacting the following companies:

A.D.D. Warehouse
300 Northwest 70th Avenue,
Suite 102
Plantation, FL 33317
Phone: 1-800-233-9273
www.addwarehouse.com

Childswork/Childsplay, LLC
P.O. Box 1604
Secaucus, NJ 07096-1604
Phone: 1-800-962-1141
www.childswork.com

Courage to Change
P.O. Box 1268
Newburgh, NY 12551
Phone: 1-800-440-4003

Creative Therapeutics
P.O. Box 522
Cresskill, NJ 67626-0522
Phone: 1-800-544-6162
www.rgardner.com

Wellness Reproductions & Publishing, Inc.
A Guidance Channel Company
135 Dupont Street
P.O. Box 760
Plainview, NY 11803-0760
www.wellness-resources.com

Western Psychological Services
Division of Manson Western
Corporation
12031 Wilshire Boulevard
Los Angeles, CA 90025-1251
Phone: 1-800-648-8857
www.wpspublish.com

Appendix E

BIBLIOGRAPHY

Bertolino, B. (1999). *Therapy with Troubled Teenagers*. New York: John Wiley & Sons.

Brown, S. (1985). *Treating the Alcoholic: A Developmental Model of Recovery*. New York: John Wiley & Sons.

Friedman, E. (1990). *Friedman's Fables*. New York: Guilford Press.

Grigoryev, P. (1997). "The Therapist on the Inside." In H. Kaduson and C. Schaefer (eds.), *101 Favorite Play Therapy Techniques*. Northvale, NJ: Jason Aronson, Inc.

James, B. (1989). *Treating Traumatized Children*. New York: Lexington Books.

Jongsma, A., L. M. Peterson, and W. McInnis (1999). *Brief Adolescent Therapy Homework Planner*. New York: John Wiley & Sons.

Kaduson, H., and C. Schaefer, eds. (1990). *101 Favorite Play Therapy Techniques*. Northvale, NJ: Jason Aronson, Inc.

Millman, H., and C. Schaefer (1977). *Therapies for Children: A Handbook of Effective Treatments for Problem Behaviors*. San Francisco, CA: Jossey-Bass.

Millman, H., C. Schaefer, and J. Cohen (1980). *Therapies for School Behavioral Problems*. San Francisco, CA: Jossey-Bass.

O'Hanlon, B., and S. Beadle (1997). *A Guide to Possibility Land*. New York: W.W. Norton.

Pennington, B. (1991). *Diagnosing Learning Disorders*. New York: Guilford Press.

Pittman, F. (1987). *Turning Points*. New York: W.W. Norton.

Robin, A. L., and S. L. Foster (1989). *Negotiating Parent/Adolescent Conflict*. New York: Guilford Press.

Satir, V. (1991). *Peoplemaking*. Palo Alto, CA: Science and Behavior Books.

Selekman, M. (1997). *Solution-Focused Therapy with Children*. New York: Guilford Press.

Theiss, S. (1997). "Pretending to Know How." In H. Kaduson and C. Schaefer (eds.), *101 Favorite Play Therapy Techniques*. Northvale, NJ: Jason Aronson, Inc.

Wadeson, H. (1980). *Art Psychotherapy*. New York: John Wiley & Sons.

Wadeson, H. (1995). *The Dynamics of Art Psychotherapy*. New York: John Wiley & Sons.

Wallas, L. (1985). *Stories for the Third Ear*. New York: W.W. Norton.

Watson, G. S., and A. M. Gross (1997). Mental Retardation and Developmental Disorders. In R. T. Ammerman and M. H. Herson, eds., *Handbook of Prevention and Treatment with Children and Adolescents* (pp. 495–520). New York: John Wiley & Sons.

Watzlawick, P., J. Weakland, and R. Fisch (1974). *Change*. New York: W.W. Norton.